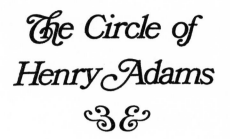

The Circle of
Henry Adams

The Circle of Henry Adams: Art & Artists

by Ernst Scheyer

WAYNE STATE UNIVERSITY

Wayne State University Press

Detroit 1970

Published simultaneously in Canada by
The Copp Clark Publishing Company
517 Wellington Street, West
Toronto 2B, Canada.

LC Catalog Card Number 72-79478
ISBN 0-8143-1418-X

Contents

IV. The Virgin and the Dynamo

Illustrations

Charts

Foreword

*I*n this book Dr. Scheyer has thrown a fresh revealing light upon one of the difficult figures of American intellectual history—What is the place of Henry Adams, and what is the nature and the value of his work as a writer and thinker?

Henry Adams is both difficult to assess and impossible to ignore. It is not merely the problem raised by his captious, quirky "Adams" quality; by his neurotic pose of failure; by the contradictions that earned him the nickname among his friends of "angelic porcupine"; or by the mantle of the gentleman amateur in which he wrapped himself. These are, after all, traits of the surface and the real problem lies deeper. Ours is a departmentalized intellectual life. Henry Adams, sceptical, ironic, elusive, constantly exploring both the entire physical globe of earth on which we live and the inner globe of the mind, fits into no class nor category. He cannot be overlooked either as a professional historian (whose works are little read today) or as a man of letters whose *Education* and *Mont-Saint-Michel and Chartres* left a deep impression on the American mind in our century (although the author was satisfied with neither and considered them unfinished work). Yet the differences of opinion about him are extreme.

Among recent studies, for William H. Jordy (1956) Henry Adams was the most distinguished "scientific" historian America had in the nineteenth century, and a failure. His nine-volume history of the United States in the administrations of Jefferson and Madison is a landmark in "scientific" history that found few readers. His life afterward was anti-climax. He traveled, amused himself, found artists and poets good traveling companions, but his later work is not to be taken seriously. For Robert E. Spiller (1947) Adams was first of all an artist, only secondarily a historian. The works of his old age, the *Education, Mont-Saint-Michel and Chartres,* and his *Letters,* although written for a private audience and published for the general reader after the author's death, make him one of the dozen or so major figures in our literature.

To the elucidation of this fascinating puzzle Dr. Scheyer brings for the first time the training and perspective of the art historian. He is helped also, I suspect, by his continental education, in a culture that produced Schopenhauer, Nietzsche and Spengler, to feel at ease with a writer who defies categories in a search for unifying principles. In the perspective of the art historian, Adams' friendships with artists, his lifelong activity as a collector of art, his studies of world history as recorded in the arts, are not peripheral and unimportant but central. He was not only the aesthetic type of mind, as Kierkegaard defined it; *seeing* was fundamental in his experience, formative in his philosophy. What he learned from art and artists (and his own sense of artistic form) was structural in the search of his final years for the meaning of life and the universe, recorded in the *Education* and *Mont-Saint-Michel and Chartres.* It shaped the search as well as the expression.

The importance of Dr. Scheyer's study, for me, is that many pieces of the puzzle, which formerly did not seem to fit anywhere, fall into place; and Henry Adams, the seeker of unity, is seen as a whole.

By family tradition Adams was part of the American Revolution that separated America from Europe and embodied eighteenth century Enlightenment in the politics of the New World. By professional discipline he was a specialist in the second "Revolution of 1800" whose principals thought of themselves as completing and confirming the first. Yet his activity as an art collector and student of art led him, like his contemporaries Isabella Stewart Gardner and Henry Walters, to revolt against the Enlightenment and turn to the ancient, mystical ages before Greek rationalism came into the world and after it was submerged again in the Middle Ages, to explore the Buddhist East and the world of the living primitives. What he found contributed both reasoned data and intuitive experience in his search for a world view in which art and reason (science), philosophy and history are united.

Dr. Scheyer may be correct in his suggestion that the "ever bleeding wound" of his wife's suicide was the root of Adams' almost pathological sense of defeat and despair. This affected not only his judgment of himself but, an egocentric, he attributed his own sense of failure to his friends. In actual fact, the group of artists among whom we see him move in this book was the most influential, and the closest to the center of national power, of any artists in our history. But that is another story.

What emerges from this fresh perspective is a Henry Adams who was very much a man of his own generation. Like his friend William James, he was one of the Americans who re-knit the intellectual connections between America and Europe, and went far beyond Europe to the world. His generation created the view of the world seen from North America as a whole, ancient and modern, primitive and civilized, East and West, that is the basis for the best in modern American thought.

E. P. Richardson

Philadelphia
February 1970

Preface

The title *The Circle of Henry Adams* refers to Adams' interest in the visual arts, on the basis of which his personal associations with the architect Henry Hobson Richardson, the painter John La Farge, and the sculptor Augustus Saint-Gaudens formed an inner circle. Of course the wider circle of art occasionally overlaps those of literature, music, political history, philosophy, and the natural sciences, but all of these obviously constituted a unity for Henry Adams the esthete, the writer.

The Circle of Henry Adams: Art and Artists has intermittently occupied my interests and thoughts for the last twenty years. A first draft was finished in 1950. Several articles grew from it:

> "Henry Adams as a Collector of Art," *Art Quarterly*, XV (Autumn 1952): 221-233.
>
> "Henry Adams and Henry Hobson Richardson," *Journal of the Society of Architectural Historians*, XII (1953): 7-12.
>
> "Henry Adams' Mont-Saint-Michel and Chartres," Journal of the Society of Architectural Historians, XIII (1954): 3-10.
>
> "The Adams Memorial by Augustus Saint-Gaudens," *Art Quarterly*, XIX (Summer 1956): 178-197.
>
> "The Aesthete Henry Adams," *Criticism*, IV (Fall 1962): 313-327.

During the last twenty years the literature on Henry Adams has grown considerably. Only works mentioned in the notes to the text, however, are enumerated in the references. Ernest Samuels' comprehensive biography of Henry Adams has since been completed and is now available in three volumes (Harvard University Press). I have availed myself of this monumental source work with gratitude.

Still more important to me was the new trend of dealing with Henry Adams as an *artist* in the field of writing and thinking. I feel especially indebted to the work of two Adams scholars, to the delightfully phrased and profound book by Robert A. Hume, *Runaway Star, an Appreciation of Henry Adams* (Cornell University Press), and to the manuscript of my colleague at Wayne State University, Professor Vern Wagner of the English Department, *The Suspension of Henry Adams, a Study of Manner and Matter* (Wayne State University Press). Through this descriptive image of "suspension between opposites," humor and irony are revealed as the core not only of Adams' consummate artistry as a writer that is his unique style, but also as the mainspring of his attitude to life, history, politics, and the arts. All this abetted my *dialectic* approach.

Older sources from which passages have been quoted are:

Adams, *Mont-Saint-Michel and Chartres*
Adams, *The Education of Henry Adams*
Adams, *Letters to a Niece*
Agar, *The Formative Years*
Cater, *Henry Adams and His Friends*
Ford, *Letters of Henry Adams*

These books were published by Houghton Mifflin Company, Boston. Shorter passages were also reprinted from *The Letters of Mrs. Henry Adams*, Little, Brown and Company, Boston. To both these publishing firms, who have granted permission, I should like to express my thanks.

A bibliography of my writings on the visual arts since 1922 precedes the index. It is a gift from friends at the University on the occasion of my seventieth birthday. To the instigators of the idea, Professor and Mrs. Milton Covensky, and to Eugene Schuster, Director of London Arts, who supported it financially, my warmest expression of gratitude is due.

Help in the compilation of the bibliography was extended by F. Warren Peters, Librarian, the Detroit Institute of Arts, and Charles H. Elam. The latter also edited the manuscript, and the book owes much to his painstaking care and patience.

Thanks also go to two of my former students and friends: Gloria Kahn, Instructor of Art History, Wayne State University, for making the index, and to Richard Kinney, Art Director, Wayne State University Press, for designing this book.

An older and even greater indebtedness should be acknowledged to Edgar P. Richardson who, during and since his directorship of the Detroit Institute of Arts, has not only inspired but also aided my interest in Henry Adams. His inspiration was part of my "education as an American."

E. S.

Detroit
January 1970

I
Introduction

1. The Circle and the Century
(Idealism and Realism)

A t the age of seventy-three Henry Brooks Adams
(1838-1918) wrote to the novelist Henry James:

> We all began together and our lives have made more or less of
> a unity, which is, as far as I can see, about the only unity that
> American society in our time had to show. Nearly all are gone.
> Richardson and St. Gaudens, La Farge, Alex Agassiz, Clarence
> King, John Hay, and at the last, your brother, William; and with
> each, a limb of our lives cut off.[1]

Together with Adams these men and a few others (not mentioned in
this particular letter) constituted a circle, or what he called a *unity*
within American society, by which he meant a cultural unity.

The group was by no means homogeneous as far as professions
are concerned. Only the first three were artists: Henry Hobson Richardson (1838-86), architect; Augustus Saint-Gaudens (1848-1907),
sculptor; and John La Farge (1835-1910), painter. Of the others,
Alexander Agassiz (1835-1910), son of the great Harvard naturalist
Louis Agassiz, was a marine zoologist, mine specialist, and an early
collector of the antiquities of Peru. Clarence King (1842-1901) was
a geologist, like Agassiz a mine specialist, and director of the newly
created U.S. Geological Survey. John Milton Hay (1838-1905), probably Henry Adams' most intimate friend, with whom he shared a
house, was a writer and statesman, private secretary to President
Lincoln and co-author of the monumental *History* devoted to Lincoln
(1890), assistant secretary of state (1873), ambassador to Great

Britain (1897), and finally, secretary of state (1898-1905) under Presidents William McKinley and Theodore Roosevelt.

The expatriate Henry James (1843-1916) was a writer of realistic and psychological novels; his brother William (1842-1910) was a psychologist and a philosopher, known in the latter field as a pragmatist, voluntarist, and empiricist.

In his *Education* Henry Adams added to the list of men "who counted as force even in the mental inertia of sixty or eighty million people,"[2] his cousin Phillips Brooks (1835-93), Episcopalian bishop of Massachusetts; (Francis) Brett Harte (1836-1902), humorist and short story writer; two Richardson associates, the architects Charles Follen McKim (1847-1909) and Stanford White (1853-1906); and as senior members of the circle, both born in the twenties, the Hunt brothers—the painter, writer, and lecturer on art, William Morris Hunt (1824-79), a disciple of Thomas Couture and Jean François Millet, and Richard Morris Hunt (1827-95), the first American architect to study at the Ecole des Beaux-Arts in Paris, and the exponent of that nineteenth century eclecticism which triumphed at the Chicago World's Fair of 1893.

It seems at first a motley group which gained its unity chiefly through the personality of Henry Adams, whose many-sidedness it reflected. He was first of all a writer, teacher, and philosopher of history; then a lover and patron of the arts, who gave commissions to H. H. Richardson (the Hay-Adams house in Washington, D.C.) and Augustus Saint-Gaudens (the Adams Monument in Rock Creek Cemetery); a traveler in Europe, and in the Far East and the South Seas with John La Farge, from whom he learned watercolor; a natural scientist, early interested in Darwinism and evolution, geology, paleontology, and prehistory; and finally, an heir to his family's great political tradition and influence as secretary to his father, minister to England during the Civil War, and later behind the political scene as friend and adviser of John Hay, Theodore Roosevelt (1858-1919), and Henry Cabot Lodge the elder (1850-1924).

Henry Adams provided not only the focus for the group but also acted as a center, spiritually through his writings, and practically through the "breakfast table" at his house in Washington, around which the members of the group gathered when they were in the nation's capital. The following letter to the historian William Roscoe Thayer, who had asked Adams' advice for his biography of John Hay, deals with that situation:

> Such ambition as I retain has of late years been directed to creating round my group of friends a certain atmosphere of art and social charm. They were not numerous, but were all superior. John La Farge, Alex Agassiz, Clarence King, St. Gaudens, Hay, and their more-or-less close associates like Bret Harte, John Sargent, Henry James, etc., etc. were distinguished men in any time or country. John Hay alone was a public character, and needs separate treatment. I am glad you have undertaken him.[3]

The letter not only reveals Adams and his house as the social center of the group, but might also imply his own literary treatment of the rest of the group, which he did do in his *Education*.

Among the members of the group Adams was the one most conscious not only of the fact that they formed a circle, but that they also were of a generation and that it was their contemporaneousness that bound them together for good and evil—chiefly for evil. Adams the pessimist thought of his generation as being mortgaged because of its position in a time of transition, the period of the Industrial Revolution. The childhood and adolescence of most of these men fell before the Civil War, largely a pre-industrial or early industrial age in the United States. Their early manhood was spent during the Civil War, their later manhood during the reconstruction period; their old age, insofar as they reached it, during the first decade or so of the twentieth century which ushered in World War I. Then, for most of them there was their common geographical background of New England, their lives spent between Boston, New York, Washington, and the capitals of Europe, and finally, their common educational background. Most of the scholars of the group shared Harvard training; the artists, the cultural institutions of Europe, especially those of Paris.

In some way Adams acted as the jealous guardian and keeper of the circle. He seemed often to believe they lived and created chiefly for each other. Then the circle was turned into a highly walled ring, outside which its members had no real business, no social function, and found no true understanding. We explain that feeling of frustration on Adams' part, which was only occasionally shared by the others, to be a result of his lonely character and his experiences. We do not, however, believe the social isolation of some members of the group, and especially of Adams, is to be explained entirely as a fault of society in the second half of the nineteenth century, but that it was the result of a lack of decision on the part of some of the members, and was an illness many a creative figure suffered during the period.

The problem of aristocratic isolation versus democratic participation, of the individual and the masses, is one of the polarities to which the unity of the latter part of the nineteenth century was hinged. What gave to that half of the century its character, flavor, or style, and what we therefore experience as its unity, was precisely the so often manifested and deplored lack of unity, or as Adams called it, its *multiplicity*. There was the break, the dichotomy, between idealism and materialism, faith and force, freedom and determinism, which constituted that era no less than its desire to overcome it, to dissolve it into unity. All the members of the circle shared it, the scientists and statesmen as well as the philosophers and artists.

The dynamism of the circle was precisely motivated as an attempted balance between idealism and materialism. Its unity of mind, or rather unity of mind in quest of unity, established itself in a dialectic way between the two polarities of the period. It seems to have been characteristic of the time that the circle was so mixed and contained members of the exact sciences, as well as of the free arts and of philosophy, grouped around the unprofessional historian-philosopher-writer Adams. It was likewise characteristic of the search for unity that most of the members transgressed professionalism: scientists like King and Agassiz loved and collected art; an artist like La Farge was interested in the sciences.

The specific and peculiar unity of the circle should perforce make it mandatory to deal with all its members, at least in their relationships to Henry Adams, who was an impartial arbiter between the camps of scientists, politicians, philosophers, and artists. But to do this is beyond our powers and our critical abilities. We must limit the circle to the smaller orbit of the representatives of the visual arts, being aware, however, of the wider sphere of nineteenth century culture and occasionally touching on problems outside the strict sphere of art. Adams' many-sidedness makes that inevitable.

Adams, the many-faceted focus of a circle, was not an isolated figure in his time. One thinks of others like him, more amateur than professional. In the first place there was John Ruskin in England, art critic, though on a much larger scale, art patron, art collector; like Adams, independent and wealthy, and only occasionally assuming the role of college professor; like Adams, active in realms of the mind which lie beyond those of the arts. His championship and patronship of the Pre-Raphaelite group was certainly only a small section of his activities. But he was, more so than Adams, an esthetician, though with a strong activist-moralistic tendency.

When we limit the circle around Adams to its artist members (as we shall from now on), Conrad Fiedler's relation to the painter Hans von Marées and the sculptor Adolf von Hildebrand seems to be the closest parallel. The art patron-philosopher Fiedler, as the brain and the purse of the *Deutsch-Römer*, especially at the time of their common stay in Florence (1873-75), would most nearly correspond to Adams in his relation to La Farge and Saint-Gaudens. But the American circle was never so closely knit, the artists in it never so dependent upon the thinker and patron.

While there were relationships between the Adams circle and the Pre-Raphaelites, there was none between the Adams circle and the German group or contemporary German art in general. In France, to which the artists in the Adams circle had the closest connection, there was nothing comparable to the groups around Adams, Ruskin, and Fiedler. Only to a certain degree might Joris K. Huysmans' relation to Gustave Moreau and Odilon Redon, as an enthusiastic critic and collector of their work, be mentioned as a weaker parallel. Further, Huysmans too, liked Adams, was biased towards the Middle Ages and medieval art. His *Cathédrale* (1898) was published before Adams' *Mont-Saint-Michel and Chartres* (1903) and is the only book comparable to it in character. But we do not want to stretch the Adams-Huysmans parallel unduly. The dissimilarities between their minds, as well as their actions, by far out weigh their similarities.

Among the American, English, German, and French artists just mentioned, there existed, however, a similarity which Edgar P.

Richardson was the first to notice.[4] He grouped them all together in a movement he called *Later Idealism*, and added others, such as Elihu Vedder and William M. Hunt in the United States, George F. Watts and Alfred Stevens in England, Anselm Feuerbach and Arnold Böcklin in Germany, Théodore Chassériau, Pierre Puvis de Chavannes, and Paul Delaroche in France. Richardson was also the first to call upon Adams' *Education* in this connection and to distill as the essence of later idealism a synthesis of the idealistic tradition in art, classicistic as well as romantic, a reaction to the materialistic scientific trends rampant in the second half of the nineteenth century, yet a reaction nevertheless influenced or tainted by certain aspects of realism, the progress of science, and materialism. He cited "the old humanistic imagery of thought . . . dissolved by science."[5] The term *later idealism*, though coined by Richardson for want of a better one and called rather makeshift, suggests in a most welcome way the *too late and too little* character of the movement.

The lateness of the movement, the feeling among so many of the artists of having been born out of their time—either too late or too early—then was partly responsible for that aura of failure, frustration, and melancholia, but also for its aristocratic and esoteric detachment, for that lack of sympathy with the massmind which made them self-styled exiles in their own time and often in their own countries. Not that attempts to come to terms or to grips with the massmind were lacking, but they were all made *from the top down* instead of *from the bottom up*: art organizations, lectures, writings, free courses in art, some of them offered at the new working men's colleges, activity in exhibitions, art schools, and finally, if given a chance, the big bubbles, the mirages, the world's fairs, over-awing as well as befuddling the massmind and masstaste. It is this high-handed action which we mean by too little. Even the murals in churches, schools, and other public buildings, believed by some to be the remedy to heal the breach between art and life, between the artists and the masses, fall under that attitude. They were couched in symbols still largely of Renaissance thought, which many among the so-called educated even failed to experience, partly because classical education was in the process of breaking down, and partly because these symbols were too shopworn, exhausted, and devaluated to register properly.

Even in their use of classical symbols, in which the later idealists seemed to continue the practice of the neoclassicists of around
1800, one is aware of a lack of faith. This turning to the classical
world was not the simple homecoming to the land in which their
grandfathers' thoughts had dwelled, not solid ground, but an isolated
forlorn island, lost in the ocean of ordinary life, desperately looked
for, where the shipwrecked and the exiled might find shelter. Furthermore, the well known classical symbols had lost most of their com-
forting familiarity, even to the later idealists, by giving them the
twist of a new and profound meaning, or by adding to them, or
crossing them with symbols from the Nordic myths (e.g. Walter
Pater's *Marriage of Helena and Faust*), or even from the Eastern
world of Hinduism and Buddhism.

There was a lack of aggressiveness, of doing things simply, so
necessary to build up from the bottom, in order to make up for the
extinction of folk art, and to open up new channels for the latent but
neglected esthetic instincts of the masses. There was a lack of red
corpuscles in the art of the later idealists which made them sus-
pected highbrows to the man in the street, even when they brought
gifts with an overwhelming heart. Although originally protesting
against government schools, regimented academicism, many of the
later idealists were tamed by success—or was it the ardent wish to
function in society?—and made common cause with the old powers.
The American group of later idealists—H. H. Richardson, John La
Farge, Augustus Saint-Gaudens—especially seems to belie the word
failure so often used by their friend and spokesman Henry Adams,
at least in the sense of practical failure. The hydra of futility with her
many heads, variously called the ivory tower, introvertism, or ego-
tism, unleashed by some socially or regionally minded critics of our
time, must be put to shame before the obituaries which praised them
as men of action, public servants of culture, shaping America. The
unpopularity of the artists in Adams' circle, such as La Farge and
Saint-Gaudens, as well as of Adams himself, with these critics is ag-
gravated by their Europeanate character. They seem to have been
compromised, in their eyes, by their friend Henry James, the arch-
priest of the expatriates.

Yet let us see what Henry Adams himself has to say about his
own and his friends' relations to Europe. It seems to us that his at-

titude changed considerably as he grew older. In 1863 when he was still very young, he wrote to his brother Charles Francis of "that young Europe of which I am by tastes and education a part."[6] But in a letter to Henry James written in his old age, he said of himself and the Boston group of his youth, "Improvised Europeans, we were, and —Lord God!—how thin!"[7]

But their love for Europe, their long sojourns there, and their cosmopolitan attitude made them no less American. The impact of their work upon Europeans was very limited. Henry Adams and Henry James wrote for this country, and Richardson, La Farge and Saint-Gaudens created their works for the United States and not for Europe.

What was really behind the so-called anti-American exile attitude of such men as Henry Adams and Henry James? Their hurt love for America and their hurt idealism. They detested America's ugliness and mercantilism, the greed of the American scene, the noisy tempo, the lack of history. Yet there was no fundamental difference between the American fleeing before the barbarism of his country to Europe, and the European escaping from similar conditions to the primitivism of the South Seas. In the case of the Americans it was more than anything else the moral breakdown of the American experiment in which their grandfathers, and even their fathers, could still believe, the failure to change man by it, to curb evil and war by giving man a new start in a new country and so prevent threatening disaster.

It was the awareness of this failure which lurked even behind the success of some of the American later idealists. It was the failure to find conclusive answers to the meaning of life, art, and history, not to speak of the course of their own immediate time and civilization, which frightened them, which made them dissatisfied and restless, as gloomy and cynical as Adams. It often seemed as though, having lost his ideals, Adams enjoyed the decay, the crumbling worlds, the destruction he had foreseen so accurately. Yet if they often fell into the abyss of despair and frustration, they had reached for the highest.

There was no such reaching for the stars in realism, the name given to materialism in the field of the visual arts. Neither the absolute, nor the transcendental, nor balanced form was the realist's aim, but life, the meaning of which was to live fully in all its heights and depths, and through the senses rather than through the mind. Not the Plato of the *Philebus*, having found *beauty absolute* in geometrical shapes, the final goal of the idealistic cubists of our day, but Heraclitus with his universality of change was the philosophical godfather of realism. The old humanistic world of symbols was junked. Gustave Courbet exclaimed brutally: "Show me a goddess and I will paint one. . . . I give you real nature, cruelties, violence and all."[8] But he failed to create an art which became popular with the masses or even largely known to them. His identification of realism with democracy did not lead to democratic art. Instead of the old humanistic symbols, he created new ones, a true allegory (*une allégorie réelle*) in his huge canvas "The Painter in his Studio" (1855), in which the different arts and the virtues and vices were all represented by actual persons of his own circle. To the common man this was no less, probably even more, unintelligible than the old shopworn humanistic symbols, such as Cupid with an arrow. Even the monumental size of Courbet's canvases, his feeling for mass, for which Zola praised him and in which Zola resembled him, failed to impress the dawning century of the masses.

The poet Charles Baudelaire was a most advanced critic not only in the fields of literature (E. A. Poe) and music (Richard Wagner) but also in the visual arts. He was probably the only one to resolve the dialectics of realism and idealism into a synthesis. In 1855, the same year in which Courbet exhibited "The Painter in his Studio" and in which Honoré Daumier's witty lithograph "The Battle of the Schools" was published in *Charivari*, Baudelaire wrote in one of his articles on the *Exposition Universelle* about the common denominator in the art of the antagonists Ingres and Courbet: "But the difference is that the heroic sacrifice offered by M. Ingres in honour of the idea and the tradition of Raphaelesque Beauty is performed by M. Courbet on behalf of external, positive and immediate Nature. . . . their two opposing varieties of fanaticism lead them to the same immolation."[9] Courbet and Ingres, though different in their manner of painting and in their choice of themes, agreed in the belief that painting, in order to be art, must always be transformation, or in Baudelaire's poetic language, *sacrifice* or *immolation* of ocular reality.

It was the poetry of simple life, the magic of real life, which had been discovered anew; Courbet was in love with life in his time and tried to teach this to his contemporaries. While the idealists had treated the world of the mind as though it were real, had *em-bodied* ideas in human figures, landscapes, and painted architecture, the realists dealt with life as though it were sheer magic and spectacle. Maupassant expressed that most adequately for literature as well as painting: "The realist, be he a true artist, will not seek to show us the photographic banality of life, but to give us something more complete, piercing, and honest than reality itself."[10]

It is interesting to note in this statement how at a relatively early date (1853) the existence of photography already burdened the artist's conscience and was looked upon as an antidote to art. It had, however, the true purgative effect of such a medicine. It was, of course, chiefly in the realistic camp that its rivalry was felt as being dangerous, forcing the adherents of the creed to redefine the relations between art and reality, art and life. Courbet was pretty safe from the criticism that the mere duplication of life was more efficiently done by the camera. His brush technique, founded on that of the seventeenth century masters, was loose, broad, patchy, often sketchy, being just the opposite to the exact notations of the early photographer. It is not impossible, however, that the still photography of that early era was reflected in his art by the patient, solemn poses and the frozen gestures of his figures.

In general, Courbet's kind of realism was chiefly one of subject matter, scenes taken from everyday life, but not of technique leading to *trompe-l'oeil*. Courbet's realism could, therefore, blossom into an impressionism in which, by a dynamization of color and brush technique, the painter attempted to catch the fugitive moment and the irretrievable magic of life. The calming tendency in Impressionism came from the choice of subject matter which left the problems of the industrial age untouched and treated life as though it were a jolly picnic, a perpetual holiday, a lovely still-life posed by nature and man.

This realism of subject matter should not be confused with the realism of brush technique and manner of observation. Although not entirely lacking in French art, the latter found its chief representatives in England and, strangely enough, allied itself with a movement which we think of as part of the late idealistic trend, the Pre-Raphaelite. Exactness in the observation and representation of naturalistic detail was the common trait of all its phases; the strangeness and preciousness of the last phase, as in Dante Gabriel Rossetti and Edward Burne-Jones, were chiefly the result of treating an ideal world, a *world of the mind,* in a painstakingly realistic way.

It was John Ruskin, the early champion of the pre-Impressionist J. M. W. Turner, who expounded veracity in the art of the Pre-Raphaelites. In his *Ruskin Today,* however, Kenneth Clark pointed out that it was the brotherhood's combining of *detailed truth* in their rendering of objects with quattrocento form or style which made Ruskin their defender.[11] This contradiction of faithfulness to detail, in the sense of imitation or *mimesis,* to *idealistic* Christian style or form is also at the core of Ruskin's esthetics. Ruskin, who had read little philosophy, would probably have objected to the very term; his thoughts never achieved the coherence of a single system. Yet, basically he was like Henry Adams an *aesthete* in the Kierkegaardian sense of the *Either-Or.* Like Adams, he tried to reconcile his estheticism with his moral sense. Kenneth Clark says in this connection: "The central drama of Ruskin's life [is] that of the pampered aesthete who gradually becomes aware of social injustice."[12] Ruskin is like Adams not a logical and consistent writer but in his prose an artist-poet. Like Adams, "Ruskin continually and increasingly found his dogmatic statements falsified by his experiences, and not being a philosopher but a poet, he changes the definition of his terms to suit the flow of thought."[13]

To Ruskin and Adams can be applied the often quoted lines from the former's *Stones of Venice:* "The whole function of the artist in the world is to be a seeing and feeling creature."[14] With this in mind, the inconsistencies in his writing, so blatant from an intellectual standpoint, become at least understandable.

Two such apparently contradictory statements, chosen from Clark's selection, follow. Ruskin's probably most dogmatic statement about *veracity to nature* occurs in his *Modern Painters:* "Every alteration in the features of nature has its origin either in powerless indolence or blind audacity."[15]

On the other hand, he defends Albrecht Dürer, whose engravings were to his contemporaries the apogee of *Dutch realism*. Writing about Dürer's "Virgin and Child" (1518) he remarks: "The head of a Dutch girl with all the beauty left out is [not done] with the mechanical dexterity of a watchmaker but with the intellectual effort and sensitiveness of an artist. . . . The engraving is full of the painter's higher power and wider perception."[16] This *wider perception*, this *Duererism*, as Ruskin loves to call it, is then not identical with ocular truth since it suggests more than the vague and superficial looking for identification can register. Pre-Raphaelite art thus provides a link between the art of the Flemish and German masters of the late Middle Ages and the art of modern magic realists and Salvador Dali.

Both varieties of realism, that of subject matter as well as that of technique, were indigenous to America, products of the history, manner of life, way of thinking, and economic conditions of this country. Alfred H. Barr called it the result of the "much advertised American love of fact and detailed local color."[17] In spite of, or because of the youthfulness of her art life, America was in certain aspects ahead of Europe in the appreciation of European realism. Charles H. Sawyer has pointed out that as early as 1869 James Jackson Jarves likened Courbet's qualities to those of Walt Whitman, calling him an American Courbet in verse; that Millet and Courbet were both accepted in Boston at a time when their names were anathema in Paris; that in 1866 the Allston Club in Boston, under William M. Hunt's leadership, bought Courbet's "Quarry" for $5,000; and that Millet's work was frequently exhibited in Boston during the fifties.[18]

But New England, especially Boston and Cambridge, was also the center of the dispersal of Ruskin's idealistic ideas and the work of the Pre-Raphaelites through Charles Eliot Norton's activity (D. G. Rossetti wrote to him as early as 1858), and Oscar Wilde lectured to an enthusiastic public in New York on the "English Renaissance" (the Pre-Raphaelites) in 1882.

The American art market and American collections, both private and public, in the last decades of the nineteenth century were already swamped by the landscapes of the Barbizon school, to which John La Farge devoted a series of lectures inaugurating the Scammon course at the Art Institute of Chicago, probably the first systematic course on modern European art offered in this country. They were published in 1908 under the title *The Higher Life in Art*, thus indicating that American artists did not look upon realism as a low movement, or upon reality as base, but as being permeated with a higher meaning, with idealism. It is for that reason that no other Barbizonist became so popular, and indeed popular with the American masses, as Jean François Millet, whose work was fundamentally biblical and synthesised the rival movements, realism and idealism.

William Morris Hunt, the oldest member of the Adams circle, and as a pupil of Millet, likewise a link between the camps of idealism and realism, became the French painter's champion in America. He explained Millet's credo, "the drama of labor surrounded by beauty," in his teachings, lectures, and writings; he was also an early collector of Millet's work. Van Wyck Brooks noted a deeper reason for this affinity, the magnetic *occult relation* between New England and Barbizon in the combination of landscape and the Bible as it was not merely painted but lived in the settlements of Barbizon as well as Brook Farm.[19] Thus idealism and realism did not appear pure or dogmatically separated in America, but were combined— though not always successfully—as classicism and romanticism had been earlier.

Though conditions for a fusion of idealism and realism seemed to be favorable in American art, a true synthesis was rarely achieved, as the work of La Farge and Saint-Gaudens proves, and to a lesser degree that of H. H. Richardson. This will be considered further in the chapters devoted to the artists of Adams' inner circle. Adams himself rarely took part in the *battle of the schools*, at least not explicitly in his writings. Yet we may safely assume that his sympathies, so far as he had any for contemporary art, were with the works of his artist friends, and therefore with later idealism. Since he detested naturalism in literature, loathing Zola's novels, he must also have disliked nineteenth century realism of the Courbet variety in the visual arts. He treated the polarity of idealism and realism in the arts as part of the greater polarity in the field of thought, that of idealism and materialism (e.g. his wife's monument by Saint-Gaudens).

There, in the realm of thought and beliefs, the dichotomy existed as sharply as that between idealism and realism in the work of Adams' artist friends. But equally great, if not greater, was the desire for final unity. Adams' mental climate was that of the second half of the nineteenth century. The idealism of Kant, Schopenhauer, and especially Hegel, largely eighteenth century in its roots, was confronted by the materialism of the nineteenth century. Of the three varieties of materialism—substance (*Stoff*), senses or sense experience, and force—Adams was drawn most strongly to the latter, in which matter is treated as the secondary product of energy. The attractiveness of determinism, which allied itself with materialism, was known to him through the writings of Darwin, Comte, and Marx.

Idealism appealed chiefly to the artist and seeker after faith in Adams and was later strengthened through his study of St. Thomas Aquinas' *Summa Theologiae*, whereas materialism and physical determinism attracted the scientist in him. He once called himself "a dilution of Lord Kelvin and St. Thomas Aquinas."[20] The systems of both idealism and materialism, however, concerned the artist-writer Adams more as form and structure than as content or truth. The conflict between idealism and materialism, faith and force, the Virgin and the dynamo, was realized and unified by Adams in the art of the written word.

II
Henry Adams' Writings
on Art and Artists

2. Harvard and Berlin

(First Contacts with Art;
German Idealistic Philosophy: Hegel)

*H*enry Adams' relations to art and artists were those of a *dilettante*, of an *amateur* who, in the true sense of the terms, takes delight in art and loves it. Indeed, he was fond of referring to himself generally as a dilettante and to his occupation with art as dilettantism. Interest in art was a means of developing that quality which he called *taste and dexterity*. Adams used art as a rampart erected between himself and the world's demands for profitable activity in order to live for his *own satisfaction*.[1] Art was also part of that complex of luxury in which he believed as a steady business.

To become a writer-artist, to use art as a screen to be protected from life and action, that was a question of temperament to the very young graduate from Harvard, as well as to the very old man who drew his life's balance. Two passages from the pen of Henry Adams, separated by fifty-seven years, are in essence identical. We read in his "Autobiography" in the *Class Book of 1858*, "My wishes are for a quiet literary life, as I believe that to be the happiest,"[2] and to Henry Cabot Lodge he wrote on the occasion of his brother Charles' death in 1915, "he was a man of action, with strong love of power, while I, for that reason, was almost compelled to become a man of contemplation, a critic, and a writer."[3]

Adams did not cease to be surprised, however, that art could have taken hold of him and have influenced him in fields of thought, scientific as well as historical. His love for line, form, and quality, and the impact of art, predominantly visual art, upon his thought were realized in the arrangement of ideas into structurally built systems, and also in his choice of root metaphors such as the *Virgin* and the *dynamo*. These images of polar character and significance were both artefacts. Both were born of visual experiences, impressions undergone by the visitor to cathedrals and world's fairs.

The almost physical appeal of Adams' thoughts, the architectural quality of his system, the manner and form in which his ideas were expressed, his subtle, rhythmical style, his use of innuendo and sardonic irony, all these, rather than truth or the consistency of specific ideas, make for the attraction and the value of his writings.

A letter to William James seems to prove this statement. Comparing the great autobiographies of world literature to his *Education*, Adams said: "Of them all, I think St. Augustine alone has an idea of literary form, a notion of writing a story with an end and object, not for the sake of the object, but for the form, like a romance."[4] Elizabeth Stevens cites an unpublished exchange of letters between Henry and Brooks Adams in the Adams papers in the Houghton Library at Harvard. Most characteristic is a passage in a letter by Henry to Brooks: "I have no scruple, in my own theories, about handling my material in view of a climax, and for artistic purposes, the climax must always tend to tragedy."[5] Here Adams revealed himself as the esthetic type; his receptivity was a matter of sensitivity rather than of rationality, his mind was impressionable rather than logical. Yet visual art was not so much discovered or loved for its own sake but for its application to the formulation of thought; it was one of the feeders for that consummate craftsmanship in writing in which Adams most completely realized his artistry.

The awareness of art and its function in the formulation of his thoughts increased during half a century, from his Harvard years (1854-58) and his postgraduate study years in Germany (1858-59), to his years as an art collector in London (1861-66), and finally to his cathedral tours in France at the end of the century. The culmination came in his book *Mont-Saint-Michel and Chartres* and its sequel *The Education of Henry Adams*. The first was dedicated to the Virgin as the visual symbol of the glorious manifestation of medieval unity, the other to the dynamo as the menacing demonstration of modern multiplicity.

In our investigation of Adams' writings on art we shall follow the historical method of evolution so dear to Adams himself, stressing different aspects of his relations to art as we proceed. We shall occupy ourselves first with his philosophy as the basis of his thinking about art, then go to his activity as an art collector, and afterwards follow his descriptive and critical remarks about art objects written during his travels. In connection with his trip to the South Seas, we shall deal with his attempts to draw and to paint watercolors. From these occasional incidental occupations with art we shall proceed to the most serious of his writings on art, *Chartres*, and end with his relation to contemporary art and artists.

Adams' first mention of art occurred in his letters of 1858 from Berlin. Twenty years old and fresh from Harvard, he wrote: "Here one is surrounded by art, and I defy anyone but a fool to feel ennuyeed while he can look at the works of these old masters."[6] This was evidently written in self-defense both against critical voices at home and his own scruples, the result of a Puritan upbringing. Later in the same letter he said, "I must work, work, work; my very pleasures are hurried, and after all, I shall get most pleasure and (I believe) advantage, from what never entered into my calculations: Art."[7]

That might be called Adams' first awakening to the role art was to play in his life, an experience which had never entered into his calculations before.

In the Berlin chapter of his *Education* he did not grant the same importance to the arts during those years. "His sense of line and color remained as dull as ever, and as far as ever below the level of an artist," he said, but this remark, written so many years later than the Berlin letters, smacks of his usual self-depreciation.[8] Then too, the intervening years might have dimmed his awareness.

During the Berlin years and the subsequent European *Wanderjahre*, art meant chiefly pictures, old masters in the museums: "I am also busied during my leisure odd minutes or hours in studying art and reading and studying theoretically painting."[9] The book Adams was reading was Kugler's *History of Painting*, as we learn from a letter to Charles Sumner written a few days before.[10] It might have had a lasting effect upon the forming of his taste.

Adams' admiration for art, then, still resembled that of a very young man in quest of education during a grand tour, and followed the conventional taste and the conventional itinerary. The "Sistine Madonna" in Dresden was called "the most exquisite of all exquisiteness," and medieval Nuremberg was *fascinating*.[11] During the same years in Berlin, Adams also discovered music, chiefly German, the music of Beethoven. His *Education* tells us about what he called "a revival of an atrophied sense," but it was "something apart, accidental and not to be trusted."[12] One thinks of Plato's suspicion of music or the reaction of some of the characters in Thomas Mann's novels to this unhealthy intoxication. It blossomed into a sweet-melancholy interest in Adams' last years when, after his eyes had begun to fail, he delighted in French twelfth and thirteenth century music which was sung to him.[13] Yet even before this, chamber music had been performed in the Hay-Adams house.[14]

With the notable exception of medieval French music based on Gregorian chants, Adams' musical taste inclined towards the classical, to Mozart, "very pretty, and easy, and familiar, and gentlemanly." He never was a Wagnerian. From Nuremberg—he had just attended the *Ring* in Bayreuth—he wrote: "My conviction that such a monstrosity of form is simply proof of our loss of artistic sense, is stronger than ever."[15] He was finally able to grasp the new form in Debussy's music, but he barely tolerated *Pelléas and Mélisande*.[16] A more detailed investigation into Adams' relation to music must remain outside our scope, as must that to literature, a subject to which alone a whole book could be devoted. His interest in literature as revealed in his writings ran the gamut from the *Chanson de Roland* to the verses of his contemporaries Swinburne and Verlaine.

As for Adams' own novels, detailed references will be made later to *Esther*, the best one, which in its psychological realism resembles the novels of Henry James. Yet *Esther* is of importance here, too, not because of his form and manner of writing, but as a source for the opinions on art held by Adams and his friends. The novel contains, only slightly veiled, descriptions of some of the members of the circle in the setting of a newly built St. John's Church, which was modeled after Richardson's Trinity Church in Boston. Of his poems we shall deal with *Buddha and Brahma*, and specifically with the hymnical *Prayer to the Virgin of Chartres*, which anticipated the dialectic antithesis of the Virgin and the dynamo further developed in his *Education.*

One matter, however, should be discussed while we are dealing with Adams' student years: his relations to German idealistic philosophy. It is our contention that it was especially his interest in Hegelianism which helped to provide the framework and the method of his thoughts on the evolution of history and art. When this interest started can only be conjectured, and that it was based on a thorough knowledge of Hegel's writings seems very doubtful. Around the middle of the nineteenth century dialectics was *in the air*, as is relativity today.[17] Francis Bowen, who taught metaphysics at Harvard when Adams was a student there, must have further strengthened Adams' then anti-materialistic bent of mind through his attacks on the "justly called 'dirt-philosophy' of materialism and fatalism."[18] But we have no direct proof of the influence of Bowen's metaphysics on Adams.

It was certainly James Russell Lowell who, as professor of *belles lettres*, planted the seedling of respect for German thought and taste into mind, eyes, and heart of the young Harvard student. "German thought, method, honesty and even taste became the standards of scholarship . . . Kant ranked as a law giver above Plato."[19] Thus Adams wrote in his *Education.* From this, one would assume that he must have become very familiar with German philosophy and poetry at that time, though the 1858 catalog of his library contains relatively few German authors, such as Goethe and Schiller, all in English translations, and no books on German philosophy and esthetics at all.[20] Yet there were the university library and probably Lowell's books to draw on, since this inspiring man encouraged contact between student and teacher outside the classroom. Lowell influenced Adams' choice of Germany for postgraduate study.

The descriptions of Adams' student years in Berlin (1858-59), where Hegel's courses on esthetics had drawn huge crowds thirty years before and where his influence had survived and was steadily growing, give no clues to Adams' study of Hegel or any other German philosopher. He found Berlin University *mediaeval* (scholastic) and the study of law there did not interest him: "His first lecture was his last. . . . What sort of instruction prevailed in other branches, or in science, Adams had no occasion to ask."[21] He concentrated therefore on learning the German language the hard way, attending classes in a Berlin high school. He wrote about *Preussisches Schulwesen* for the American press and met some celebrities, among them Alexander von Humboldt. Later, in 1872 he came in contact with the great German historians Theodor Mommsen, Ernst Curtius, Heinrich von Sybel, and Hermann Grimm.

In his *Education* there is only one direct mention of Hegel in connection with the Berlin study years.

> His metaphysical sense did not spring into life, so that his mind could leap the bars of German expression into sympathy with the idealities of Kant and Hegel. Although he insisted that his faith in German thought and literature was exalted, he failed to approach German thought and he shed never a tear of emotion over the pages of Goethe and Schiller.[22]

This negative reference to German thought and Hegel sounds discouraging enough for our investigation into a possible relationship between German idealistic philosophy and that of Adams; but we shall not drop it as fruitless.

In 1869, the year before Adams joined the Harvard faculty, William T. Harris began to publish a translation of Hegel's *Aesthetics* in his *Journal of Speculative Philosophy* which, as Horace M. Kallen noted, "signaled the appearance at last, in the United States of a professional dialectic of art," and "pointed to the initiation of esthetics as a separate and distinct discipline at the American colleges."[23] But it is improbable that Adams took notice of it; his previous contacts with the arts had been practical or historical rather than theoretical. After his return to Harvard as assistant professor of history he gave courses on the Middle Ages and specialized in the legal aspects of that period, on early German, Anglo-Saxon and Norman institutions.[24] In his teaching he followed what was then known as the German historical method and the seminar procedure, which he is credited with having established in American colleges after his teacher Lowell had taken steps in that direction.[25]

That Adams included art in his teaching of medieval history is clear from a passage in his *Education*: "Adams was glad to dwell on the virtues of the Church and the triumphs of its art."[26] But a more direct proof of the fact that art if not esthetics found its way into Adams' courses, is given in a letter to Charles Milnes Gaskell, in which Adams expressed regret for not having "a good historical collection of cathedrals in photograph. My trouble here is in getting this sort of illustration. You can imagine me giving lectures on medi- aeval architecture cribbed bodily out of Fergusson and Viollet le Duc."[27] Yet only English and French books are mentioned. The only clue, and rather a weak one, to any specific contact of Adams with German art is found in a letter to his friend and pupil Henry Os- born Taylor acknowledging a complimentary copy of his *Classical Heritage of the Middle Ages*. Some lines in the letter deal with the combination of his historical and esthetic interests during the Har- vard teaching years and might help to throw light upon the paradox of how the teaching of the history of English law could have led him to German art. "Never did any man go blind on a career more vir- tuously than I did, when I threw myself so obediently into the arms of the Anglo-Saxons in history and the Germans in art."[28] The refer- ence to the Germans in art is unfortunately not specific and in this connection quite puzzling. Yet Adams can hardly mean a thorough study of German art history, of the existence of which he remained quite ignorant, with the exception of Kugler's *History of Painting*. Nor can he allude to German art of the Middle Ages, to which even later there is only one short reference in *Chartres*. Least of all, could he be alluding to German contemporary art, of which there is no mention in all his writings.

Thus it remains only to interpret the passage as alluding gen- erally to a German outlook or taste in art. That Hegel's *Aesthetics* in translation had become known to him during his Harvard teach- ing period cannot be proved, as has been noted. Whatever he knew of Hegel's system in general at that time must have been received at secondhand. The German scholar Ernst Gryzanowski, whom Adams esteemed as his best contributor to the *North American Review*, might have kept the name and philosophy of Hegel before him, as Samuels suggests.[29] Gryzanowski called upon the Adamses when they stopped on their wedding journey at Florence in 1872 and talked metaphysics to them—"enough to last for a long while," Mrs. Adams wrote.[30]

The outcome of our investigation into Adams' relation to Hegel's philosophy, and more specifically the German philosopher's esthetics, has so far been negative and has resulted in no documentary evidence. Yet *Chartres* and his *Education* are so impregnated with Hegelianism that we continue the search into the new century.

In Paris in 1901 Adams became a kind of mentor to two young American poets and bohemians, George Cabot (Bay) Lodge, the son of the senator, and Trumbull (Joe) Stickney. They formed what Adams jokingly called the Conservative Christian Anarchist Party "to restore true poetry under the inspiration of *Gotterdämmerung*," something smacking of the then so current *l'art pour l'art* creed, even of *fin de siècle*. The anarchistic wing in it, however, limited only to Adams and Bay Lodge, "as a party drew life from Hegel and Schopenhauer, rightly understood."[31] This bantering remark points, if nothing else, to Adams' discussing the German philosophers with his bright young friend, whose biography he wrote after his untimely death in 1909.[32] So after 1900—at last—Hegel is often mentioned in Adams' writings.

Reviewing his state of mind in 1903, Adams wrote in his *Education*: "Often deceived by the intricacies of thought hidden in the muddiness of the medium, one could sometime catch a tendency to intelligible meaning even in Kant or Hegel."[33] What appealed to the determinist Adams was the law of contradiction or opposites and Hegel's determinism: "Doubtless this law of contradiction was itself agreement, a restriction of personal liberty, inconsistent with freedom."[34] The law of contradiction was then resolved in the *synthesis*, which is the unification of contradictions. Here Adams concurred with Hegel, who offered him a way out of his personal dilemma and permitted him to be positive, even mildly optimistic. "Even Hegel, who taught that every notion included its own negation, used the negation only to reach a 'larger synthesis,' till he reached the universal which thinks itself, contradiction and all."[35]

This unification of thesis and antithesis in the synthesis was for Adams certainly one of the greatest attractions in Hegel's system, a counterweight to Calvinistic-Puritan dualism, which was in so great a degree responsible for his innate, calamitous pessimism, as Yvor Winters has shown.[36]

A reference to Adams' pessimism and its relation to the thought of another German philosopher, Schopenhauer, might be inserted here before we return to his relation to Hegel. Adams environmental Puritan pessimism must have early drawn him to Schopenhauer, of whom he wrote in a letter to Gaskell:

> Throughout all the thought of Germany, France and England—
> for there is not any thought in America—runs a growing stream
> of pessimism which comes in a continuous current from Malthus
> and Karl Marx and Schopenhauer in our youth, and which we
> were taught to reject then, but which is openly preached now
> on all sides.[37]

This pessimism seems finally to triumph in the thirty-third chapter of his *Education*, "A Dynamic Theory of History," and in the essays collected by his brother Brooks under the title *Degradation of the Democratic Dogma*.[38]

The idea of decline or fall, early kindled through the study of Gibbon's *Decline and Fall of the Roman Empire*, fused with Calvinistic as well as Hegelian determinism and reached Spenglerian proportions of doom and destruction. Adams did not, however, accept Hegel's positive, absolute belief in the state or its glorification as the consummation of finite or material life. Again, one would hardly expect consistency in the application of what Adams knew of Hegel's ideas, since quite evidently it was not the substance but the method, the form of Hegelianism, which attracted a mind so eager for unifying congealing generalizations. Most of all, it was the use of contradictory or polar images which Adams learned from Hegel.

There are lines in his *Education* obviously written in defense of the use of opposite images, such as the *Virgin* and the *dynamo*. The two terms were evidently chosen more for the sake of lively dramatic method, of chapter-headings necessary in the intellectual game called dialectics, than for their strength as argument or proof:

> Images are not arguments, rarely even lead to proof, but the
> mind craves them, and, of late more than ever, the keenest ex-
> perimenters find twenty images better than one, especially if

contradictory; since the human mind has already learned to deal in contradictions.[39]

Thus we are now prepared for the final proof of Adams' relation to Hegel. It is found in a letter from Paris to his brother Brooks, dated 5 November 1899, written after his reading of Eduard Bernstein's *Die Voraussetzungen des Sozialismus und die Aufgaben der Sozialdemokratie* (1899):[40]

> Bernstein has taught me, too, what Hegelianism is. I knew I was a Hegelian, but never knew what it was. Now I see that a Hegelian is one, who agrees that everybody is right, and acts as if everybody but himself were wrong. What a delightful idea—so German—that Karl Marx thought himself a Hegelian. It is equal to Wagner's philosophy.[41]

Henry Adams *was a Hegelian* who *never knew what it was!* That explains satisfactorily why we could find few if any direct traces of Adams' firsthand study of Hegel, despite our awareness of a Hegelian scent or flavor in his writings.[42] The result again is that for Adams, a predominantly visual or esthetic type, it was not so much thought-substance or thought-content but thought-structure or thought-form which proved attractive.

Hegel's dialectic procedure, his use of contradictory terms, his application of the tripartite system to all branches of human culture, his mystical belief in the spirit of an age (*Zeitgeist*) and in the soul of a nation, and finally his emphasis on the dynamic concept of becoming—there are traces of all of these in Adams' contradictory terms and images, like the Virgin and the dynamo, unity and multiplicity, Romanesque and Gothic, and also in his dynamic theory of history, with its emphasis on flux and transition. Hegelianism possibly also reinforced Adams' belief in the *rule of phases*, though here the direct inspiration came from Comte's *three stages of the human mind.*

As a true child of his period, Adams was as equally attracted and repelled by Hegelianism as he was by Darwinism; he was a follower and a critic at the same time. Both systems are dynamic: idealistic Hegelianism had its concepts of becoming and of the world process, while materialistic Darwinism had its natural selection, survival of the fittest, and evolution from lower to higher. Adams felt the structural resemblance of these systems. In spite of their difference in content, Hegelianism and Darwinism both seemed to guarantee uniformity and unity; both had the character of inevitable destiny, predetermined sequence, and charted direction. They were a substitute for faith and religion. For Adams, Darwinsim "had the charm of art";[43] he was a "Darwinian for fun."[44] Here the esthetic type reveals itself fully! Adams wonders why, for the same reason, he had not become a Hegelian Marxist, since "by rights, he should have been also a Marxist, but some narrow trait of the New England nature seemed to blight Socialism. . . . He did the next best thing, he became a Comteist, within the limits of evolution."[45]

Hegelianism and Darwinism unite in their attractiveness of structure and finality of form which, at least temporarily, stilled the thirst of man's quest for unity. Thus the change from the German to the English cultural scene is by no means an abrupt one.

3. London
(The Pre-Raphaelites; Art Collecting)

A s far as Henry Adams' art education is concerned, his English years (1861-68), which coincided with the critical years of the Civil War and during which he served as secretary to his father, the American minister to England, were notable for his somewhat tenuous relations to Pre-Raphaelitism and more positively for his activity as an art collector. This latter occupation was so amalgamated and synchronized with his interest in geology, paleontology, anthropology and prehistory, the whole complex of scientific investigations into origins, freshly stimulated by the appearance of Darwin's *Origin of Species* in 1859, that the artistic cannot entirely be separated from the scientific. Certainly art collecting was to Adams not strictly an esthetic interest in the modern sense. It still resembled somewhat the accumulating of curios as pursued in previous centuries. Collecting was then focused on objects, on their artful *make*, on how forms and shapes were created by nature and by man.

We note during Adams' English years the bipolarity of his interests, his being at home in the world of idealism—the Pre-Raphaelites—as well as in that of scientific observation, which contributed so widely to the materialism of the period. Certainly his art interests in general lacked unity of purpose and did not follow a preconceived plan. For that reason his art collection must at all times have looked somewhat confusing. James T. Adams, who visited Henry Adams towards the end of his life, described his own impressions: "Things which he had brought from Europe and the East were everywhere and though they were beautiful, their total effect was not beauty but miscellaneous."[1]

Sir Cecil Spring-Rice, poet and British ambassador to the United States, stressed in a letter the curio flavor of Adams' collection and mentioned specifically "a precious idol given him by the Japanese minister."[2] But the Oriental objects were later additions to the collection, largely acquired after the death of Mrs. Adams, with whom he had done most of his collecting in London.

Harold Dean Cater, who reconstructed the appearance of the contents of the house in Washington from interviews with Adams' relatives and friends, found the general character of the collection to be a combination of English eighteenth and nineteenth century paintings and Japanese art.

> The furniture was English, low and comfortable. . . . On the walls were Turners, De Wints, Constables, Blakes, and many other choice paintings. . . . On the cases were jades, porcelains, and bronzes, several Kwannons and one statue of the Oriental god of happiness. Oriental design could be seen on screens, cushions and a few lacquer pieces.[3]

In her *Education by Uncles* Abigail Adams Homans describes the Henry Adams collection:

> There were shoulder-high book cases around his living room hung with pieces of Chinese brocade and above were some of his collection of pictures, which were scattered everywhere all over the house. There were many examples of English eighteenth and nineteenth century watercolor—De Wint, Cotmans, Coxes and Girtins—while the dining room had two notable Turner oils—an early one of Norwich cathedral over the fireplace and on the opposite wall a later one of a characteristically luminous whaling ship. In his study were many drawings including . . . Blake . . . of Nebuchadnezzar on all fours eating grass.[4]

The paintings mentioned by Cater were chiefly works of the English romantic watercolor school, to which Ruskin and the Pre-Raphaelites had opened the English public's eyes. Adams' interest in the then not too popular medium of watercolor antedated the general trend in England and certainly in his own country. It was, among other factors, his connection with the Pre-Raphaelite circle which introduced him to it. Though this connection served foremost the practical end of art collecting, it also brought him in contact with the progressive English set in literature and art to whom ideas counted most.

The man who introduced Adams to Pre-Raphaelitism was Thomas Woolner, the sculptor of the circle. He gave a thumbnail sketch of Woolner in his *Education*:

> Woolner's sculpture showed none of the rough assertion that Woolner himself showed . . . but his busts were remarkable. . . . He took the matter of British art—or want of art—seriously almost ferociously, as a personal grievance and torture; at times he was rather terrifying in the anarchistic wrath of his denunciation.[5]

Little can indeed be seen of Pre-Raphaelitism in Woolner's sculpture, but one can assume he acquainted Adams with the rebellious, antiacademic trend in the movement.

None of the other members of the brotherhood were mentioned by Adams, except Holman Hunt in a very casual way.[6] As personalities they could hardly have appealed to him. Adams had an instinctive fear of what he and his time called the decadent, probably because he thought himself mentally to be one. He came closest to the brilliancy and the decadent eccentricities of Pre-Raphaelitism—here used as the name of a movement and not as that of a brotherhood—in the person of Charles Algernon Swinburne, whose poetic faculty he admired immensely but whose "wildly eccentric personality it took him twenty years to get over."[7] Swinburne's intimate friendship with Dante Gabriel Rossetti fell into the years of Adams' stay in England. But the main inspiration from this side and from Richard Monckton's circle in Fryston Hall, through whom he came to know Swinburne, must have been literary or literary-critical.

Among his acquaintances who belonged to the world of literature, as well as to that of art, should be mentioned Francis Turner Palgrave, critic, poet, educator (later professor of poetry at Oxford), and brother-in-law of Adams' most intimate English friend Charles Milnes Gaskell, a member of Parliament and a writer. Palgrave had just published his *Golden Treasury of English Songs and Lyrics* (1861). He is important to us here, however, as Adams' chief mentor in the world of auction rooms and art collections. A friend of the poet laureate Tennyson and an art collector in the old style by family tradition ("as an art critic . . . too ferocious to be liked"[8]), Palgrave certainly did not make Adams buy Pre-Raphaelites—and neither did Woolner. On the other hand he was not so old-fashioned in his taste as to limit his advice to the purchase of established old masters, but combined it, therein meeting Woolner's taste, with a lively interest in Blake and Turner and other English watercolorists of the eighteenth and nineteenth centuries. We are reasonably certain to see in this inclination the result of Rossetti's artistic rediscovery and rehabilitation of Blake, and Ruskin's worship of Turner.

This purchase of English romantic art marked the limit of Adams' concessions to the more advanced taste in art and art collecting then found in London. His father, from whom "he inherited a certain taste" for the pursuit of collecting, disapproved of this type of art and insisted Henry had no taste, "because he could not see what his son thought he saw in Turner." It was here that the representatives of two generations differed, but the son continued to carry quite a bit of the odd assortment of his father's "aesthetic ragbag . . . regarded as amusement and never called art"—collecting old coins and engravings, for instance, and a sporting interest in attending sales at Sotheby's and Christie's.[9] In their taste for English architecture, however, father and son differed entirely. While the still largely classical taste of the former was partial to Christopher Wren's London churches, the son's romantic leanings favored the Middle Ages.

To Henry Adams' interest in the Middle Ages, Ruskin's writings, though not Ruskin's personality, contributed in some measure. We have proof in a letter written by Adams from Harvard College to Charles Milnes Gaskell, another of the Yorkshire Milnes and a distant cousin to Monckton. In this letter he recommended "Viollet le Duc's essay on military architecture in the middle ages" and expressed surprise that "he did not tumble over it, while . . . mousing about in England, or that Palgrave did not call his attention to it, when [he] was reading Fergusson and Ruskin."[10] It is regrettable the title of Ruskin's book was not given. It might have been *The Seven Lamps of Architecture* or *The Stones of Venice*; the coupling of Ruskin with Fergusson and Viollet le Duc suggests a work dealing with architecture. The one by James Fergusson might have been his *Illustrated*

Handbook of Architecture (1855) or *A History of Architecture in All Countries from the Earliest Times to the Present Day*; the first volume of the latter appeared in 1865 while Adams was still in England, the last in 1876. The relationship between Adams and Ruskin has been stressed by Walter Fuller Taylor, who states that "both treat art as a product of the whole life of a people."[11] Yet Adams himself seems to have mildly criticized Ruskin in his *Education* for holding a too purely esthetic, isolated view of medieval sculpture, and for failing to detect in it "the force, that created it all—the Virgin, the Woman."[12]

All in all, the occasional mention of Ruskin in his *Education* contributes little to Adams' relation to the Englishman's writings. Adams' and Ruskin's Middle Ages were by no means the same thing, in the way that Charles Eliot Norton's and Ruskin's Middle Ages were identical. Adams neglected the arts of the Middle Ages in Italy, which Ruskin stressed.[13] He found their finest examples in France in the transitional Norman style of the twelfth century, not in the Gothic of the thirteenth century favored by Ruskin and his followers. Adams' interest in Ruskin's writings during his earlier years and his later criticism are most clearly indicated in a letter to Gaskell. Writing about Horace Walpole and "his ridiculous affectations of age," Adams said, "I pardon nobody for bad Gothic and Venetian taste. Yet I once read Ruskin and admired! . . . Lord but we date!"[14]

Yet while in England, Adams had not progressed to such heights of independence in judgment. His relation to the Middle Ages was still that of an occasional sightseer. This attitude and that of the roving collector are typical of the young amateur, and it is to Adams the art collector that we now turn, tracing that activity back to its beginnings and also pursuing it beyond Adams' stay in London.

Adams' first interest as a collector was in engravings. In a letter written during his first days in Berlin he exclaimed, "Lord such engravings."[15] And while in Dresden he begged his brother Charles to compare prices of the print of Raphael's "Sistine Madonna" by Müller, which had "the highest reputation" in Dresden, with those to be had in Boston.[16] He meant "to devote a few hours to engravings this winter," and for this purpose tried to get an introduction to the

overseer of the royal collection. Yet he felt himself not expert enough
to buy without advice as to their states, confiding to Charles, "I know
nothing about these things as yet."[17] The buying of prints was a family interest, and furthermore, at a time when photography was still
in its infancy, it was a way for the educated traveler to keep a visual
record of what he had seen.

The real initiation to the world of art collecting, and to Sotheby's,
Christie's, and Agnew's auction rooms, took place in London. In his
Education the greater part of the fourteenth chapter, entitled "Dilettantism," was given to the recording of these experiences. Adams
considered art collecting to be an important formative factor in the
process of his education. Following the general keynote of the book,
he found in this activity only questionable enjoyment and final failure. It failed to lead to correct identification and reliable standards
of evaluation which, as the long story of the purchase of a so-called
Raphael drawing was supposed to show, did not exist even among
experts. It was this personal disappointment which led him to the
conclusion, as Yvor Winters has shown, that one cannot form any
valid judgments about a work of art and that judgments are wholly
relative.[18] Art collecting seemed to Adams the very demonstration
of all that was scrappy, spotty and aimless in the English character.
By indulging in the national vice of the upper classes, he made himself an accomplice in the sport of antique hunting, largely a privilege
of the English aristocracy.

"Of all supposed English tastes, that of art was the most alluring
and treacherous. Once drawn into it, one had small chance of escape, for it had no centre of circumference, no beginning, middle or
end, no origin, no object, and no conceivable result as education."[19]
This was written in retrospect many decades later as another contribution to the history of failure, his personal failure as well as that of
his generation in the quest for unity, in the search for the meaning of
life and art, and for absolute values. Yet during these English years
he followed willingly his mentors Palgrave and Woolner:

> Adams went to the sales and bought what he was told to buy;
> now a classical drawing by Rafael or Rubens; now a water-
> color by Girtin or Cotman, if possible unfinished because it was
> more likely to be a sketch from nature; and he bought them not

because they went together—on the contrary they made rather awkward spots on the wall as they did on the mind—but because he could afford to buy those and not others.[20]

Accordingly his main interest was old master drawings, and second, English watercolors. It seems that for the latter he relied chiefly on Woolner; "he trusted Woolner implicitly about a Turner." Palgrave was his chief adviser in the field of old master drawings.

Both Woolner and Palgrave figure in the purchase of the Raphael. It was in a lot of drawings formerly in the possession of Sir Anthony Westcombe of Liverpool, whose collection had a good eighteenth century pedigree.[21] Although much overworked, the small red chalk drawing was recommended by Palgrave. Woolner too approved of it as a genuine Raphael. Reed, the curator of drawings at the British Museum (which had a superb example of the same subject, a study of a young poet, the so-called Horace in the "Parnassus"), rejected it as a Raphael, but discovered later that the watermark on the paper was the same as the one used by the Raphael engraver Marc Antonio. The lines of an Italian sonnet on the reverse of the sheet were finally read, but proved nothing as to its authenticity. Adams placed it over the mantelpiece of his living room, where it hung for some forty years as another trophy dedicated to the cult of the ignoramus. Modern Raphael scholarship does not even mention it as a schoolwork.[22] It seems to have been at best a contemporary copy; yet Adams, not knowing that Raphael drawings were copied during the painter's lifetime and that a relatively large number of such school drawings exist, arrived through his own ignorance and through the disagreements of experts at the conclusion that judgment in art is a dubious business and generalized here as in so many other instances only his own doubts.

Palgrave was better equipped for judgment than either Woolner or Adams and was a notable collector of drawings. According to a letter to Gaskell, Palgrave gave Adams "three of his drawings to [his] great delight."[23] In another letter to the same friend Adams jokingly puts the blame for this weakness on Palgrave who "has instigated me into going to an auction sale and giving £12 for a Cuyp. He swears it's dirt cheap at the price. You shall see it when you come up. I've sent it to be framed and shall hang it in my room. I fully expect to be ruined by him ultimately, for drawings are my mortal point and I can't resist."[24] This very drawing turned up recently on the New York market and is now in the Fogg Art Museum, Harvard University, the gift of John S. Newberry. It is an exceptionally beautiful ink and wash drawing by Aelbert Cuyp, "A View of Rhenen," measuring 7 x 9½ inches. Its backing bears the characteristic copperplate handwriting of Henry Adams but is so faded that only the date of the purchase (1867) is still legible. It is the best documented drawing from the Henry Adams' collection, being mentioned by Lugt as in the collection of Dr. Wellesley, principal of New Inn Hall, Oxford, which was sold in 1867 at Colnaghi's, where Adams bought it.[25] After Adams' death it was owned by Mrs. Arthur Adams, Dover, Massachusetts. The quality of this drawing speaks well for Adams' taste as a collector.

Although Adams disavowed repeatedly all claims to be or ambition to become a connoisseur or art critic, since "for some things ignorance is good, and art is one of them,"[26] he was in turn asked for advice by Gaskell when the latter put some of his pictures up for auction at Agnew's, among them a Boucher and rather obscure Italian masters like Cignani and Padovanino. Adams advised him to sell them without reserve. As his only yardstick for doing so, he mentioned his personal likes and dislikes: "I am no judge of market values, as you know, and have only one principle to go on, which is to make up my mind whether or no I want a given thing at all."[27]

The activity of Adams as a collector of drawings and watercolors continued for a long time after his stay in London, and Palgrave and Woolner remained the connecting links between him and the auction rooms. While his *Education* considered activity in this field as a more or less closed chapter after the London years, the letters of Mrs. Adams to her father gave much valuable information about Adams' interest in art and art collecting during the following years.[28] Belonging to a family of collectors and patrons of the Boston Museum of Fine Arts, Mrs. Adams enthusiastically shared her husband's interests and activities in the arts. Her taste ran generally parallel to his, so the judgment offered in her letters about works of art might very well be taken as in conformity with that of her husband. Still, she did not completely succumb to his superior taste;

her criticism appears often to be more conventional than his. Certain of her interests, for instance in eighteenth century English portraits, did not appeal to Adams and were pursued by her alone.

Old master drawings, Blake, and English watercolors are the interests to which the young bride was exposed on the first trip to London with her husband in the summer of 1872. She wrote that Palgrave "had a new lot of original drawings collected for Henry from time to time at sales," and specifically mentioned "one by Rembrandt; a sketch in red chalk, by Vandyke of children of Charles I—very charming; a Raphael and some others." The names appear almost to be too important—and we have been warned by Adams' disappointing experiences with the first so-called Raphael. Mrs. Adams noted somewhat later that they went to "a sale of some old drawings . . . one very spirited figure by Hogarth, in red and blue chalk, and a lady in sepia by Sir Joshua R . . . twelve illustrations of Milton by Blake . . . six of a hymn," but they did not buy any.[29] On her trip to England in the next year (1873) she recorded that Palgrave had collected "some more nice things for us," and mentioned "a sweet little drawing by Veronese." To the acquisitions of this year, all presents from her husband, belonged "a charming little sketch in red and black crayon by Watteau—a girl lying asleep on a couch, bare feet etc."[30] She noted in the same letter, "we are pausing over a rough sepia sketch by Sir Joshua."[31]

Hand in hand with the collecting of old masters went that of Blake and English watercolors. The letters by Mrs. Adams quoted above also allude to this interest. At their visit to Palgrave in early August of 1872, when the drawings with the important names were handed over "as a wedding present to Henry," there was a William Blake "in India ink—Ezekiel, I think weeping over his dead wife, and three or four other mourners." Among the things in Palgrave's own collection, Mrs. Adams especially mentioned in the same letter another Blake "about 18 inches by 12, Nebuchadnezzar, untrammeled by clothing, on his hands and knees, eating grass,—I took it for Caliban, until corrected. The whole figure and background very strangely coloured and tout ce qu'il y a de plus Blake."[32]

The Nebuchadnezzar turned up again in the correspondence of the next year (1873). Mrs. Adams tried through her father to interest

her brother Edward W. Hooper in the purchase of this famous monotype or color printed drawing at a low price. This brother, as Mrs.
Ward Thoron informs us, was "one of William Blake's earliest American admirers"; his excellent Blake collection is now scattered.[33]
Marian Adams wrote:

> Ask Ned if he would like a water colour by Blake of Nebuchad-
> nezzar eating grass—about 18 x 9 inches—which F. T. Palgrave
> owns and is willing to let us have for ten pounds; Mrs. Palgrave
> hates it and they are not opulent. We think it very striking
> though quite ghastly, but Ned's enthusy-musy for Blake may
> extend to this. Tell him I looked through a little note book of
> William Blake yesterday meaning to buy it for him if it seemed
> worth while but I did not think it was.[34]

The Nebuchadnezzar was finally bought by the Adamses themselves.
Mrs. Adams added to the announcement of the purchase, "It is fear-
ful!"

On the *water-colour line*, as Marian called it, there was always
fullest harmony between husband and wife. They sought watercolors
in little shops in London. Mrs. Adams wrote on Sunday, 27 July 1879:
"Yesterday, tell Ned, acting on his advice, we bought a charming
water colour—a De Wint, rare and much sought after here; picked
it up in a little shop near Covent Garden. Our lodging house parlor
[at 17 Half Moon Street, Piccadilly, W.] looks very nice with our
first six all framed and hanging up."[35]

But Palgrave and Woolner contributed most to that part of the
Adams collection. There was a watercolor by Samuel Prout, "in his
earlier style before he got architectural," secured for them by Palgrave. Marian noticed "some Cotmans and Turners at the sculptor
Woolner" during her visit in the summer of 1873, and she assured
her father that his Turner "holds its own."[36] Six years later the
Adamses purchased from the sculptor's collection "water colours
which Mr. Woolner prefers to sell to us rather than a dealer; two
David Cox, one Girtin, three Mulready."[37]

This purchase must have pleased Woolner because later he sent
pictures by Bonington to the Adamses "as an expression of gratitude
for kindness."[38] The Adamses came to own four Boningtons, two of
which were presents from Woolner, who called the first one "the

largest small picture you ever saw."[39] Mrs. Adams described it in a letter to her father as "an oil painting about eight by ten inches . . . very delicious," and added, "as Bonington ranks with Turner in England, and higher in Paris, I'm rather staggered at so valuable a gift."[40] Woolner also sent "a charming little engraving . . . an artist's proof" of this Bonington, "adding much to the value of the picture."[41]

Two years later arrived the second Bonington, which Woolner begged them "to accept . . . found in an old shop in Highgate suggesting Bonington." He had "cleaned it himself and to his great joy found Bonington's monogram under the dirt and varnish." Again Mrs. Adams rejoiced that "in Europe Bonington is heads even with Turner in reputation. We shall at this rate leave fine pickings to our heirs."[42] The collection must indeed have been considerable. Mrs. Adams wrote proudly and somewhat whimsically to her father: "Mrs. Bancroft [the wife of the historian] said the other day, 'My dear, I dislike auctions very much, but I mean to go to yours after you die.' "[43]

It is very much to be regretted that "no inventory of the Adams' library and art objects exists," as his nephew Charles Francis Adams noted in a letter. Only relatively few drawings and watercolors can be identified as coming from the Adams collection.[44] Adams himself gave some drawings to the Boston Museum during the last years of his life. The inventories list, as gifts of Henry Adams in 1917, a "Crucifixion" attributed to Murillo and a "Religious Subject" attributed to Cirro Ferri. Six drawings came from the estate of Henry Adams as a lot without titles or attributions. The inventories list further drawings, a "Neptune" attributed to Rubens and a "Nun" attributed to Van Dyck, as having been in the Adams collection. In 1920 the Boston Museum acquired from an Adams relative, Mrs. Henry C. Quincy, a "Descent from the Cross" of the school of Rubens, with a lion and wolf on the same sheet, a "St. Francis" by Murillo, and a "Landscape" by Salvator Rosa. These attributions to famous old masters, however, have still to be examined.

English watercolors apparently from the Henry Adams collection were lent to the Fogg Art Museum of Harvard University. Miss Agnes Mongan cited a group of watercolors, including examples by Girtin and Cotman, belonging to Adams' niece Mrs. Robert Homans.

Another group was described as coming from the *H. Adams Collection* by Richard C. Morrison of Boston. They included works by Cotman, De Wint, and Mulready; one was a colorful "Sunset," signed and dated J. S. Cotman 1830, another was a "Farm Scene," neither signed nor dated but very characteristic of De Wint's style.

Other art objects that were brought together around the nucleus of drawings and watercolors can be reconstructed from their mention in Adams' writings. There were oils and pastels, antique furniture, textiles, rare books, ancient coins, Greek vases and Tanagra figurines, silver work from the Near East, and a rather large number of objects from the Far East. With the exception of the last named category, which will be dealt with in connection with Adams' critical mention of East Asiatic art in the countries of its provenance, Japan, China and India, we shall now take them up item by item as they appear in the correspondence of the Adamses. The majority was picked up by Adams during his travels or longer stays in Paris, while Marian did some antique hunting on her own in Washington, D.C.

The collecting of paintings with the names of great artists attached to them never appealed to Adams. Through his association with the English aristocracy he could have had his pick of the finest, but he felt rather ashamed of the snobbism of his wealthy countrymen who ransacked English castles with the help of dealers.[45] After having helped to obtain from Castle Howard for the Boston Museum one of the finest paintings by Velasquez now in this country ("Infant Don Balthasar Carlos and his Dwarf") he felt apologetic to Carlyle "for the eighteen thousand pounds."[46] The "Entombment" by Delacroix is another important picture acquired for the Boston Museum with Adams' help. It was bought as a memorial to Martin Brimmer, a president of the museum, from funds to which Henry Adams contributed generously. In a letter to his brother Brooks he joked about this magnanimity shown to the memory of that *Bostolistine*.[47]

Of even greater importance for the history of art collecting in Boston was Adams' connection with Isabella Stewart Gardner. He advised her from Paris concerning books on cathedrals and her purchase there of "the sculptured Lady of Etruria," an Italian marble in which he noted *Phenician* influence.[48] Adams was directly responsible for her acquisition of a thirteenth century stained glass window, allegedly from the church in St. Denis, which depicted scenes from the life of St. Denis or King Dagobert. He saw it at the Bacri Frères shop in Paris, and not being able to buy it for himself, brought it to Mrs. Gardner's attention. It was placed in her private chapel in Fenway Court, her Venetian palace in Boston, now a public museum.[49] About her very personal creation of Fenway Court, Adams wrote to Mrs. Gardner after his first visit in 1906 (one is not quite sure that a grain of Adamsian irony is not mingled with the praise): "You have given me a great deal of pleasure and greater astonishment. . . . As long as such work can be done, I will not despair of our age, though I do not think anyone else could have done it. You stand quite alone."[50]

So far as his own purchases were concerned, Adams was satisfied with smaller things more in harmony with his collection of drawings and watercolors, and was delighted to find in Paris "a little Boucherian pastel-girl smelling a carnation" because he wanted "something decadent and refined and soft and pretty."[51] A portrait of Mme de Prie, done in crayons and attributed to one of the Van Loos, was purchased chiefly because he erroneously believed it had once belonged to Horace Walpole at Strawberry Hill.[52]

In general Marian Adams' taste in painting followed the conventional and fashionable trend. As a present on their seventh wedding anniversary she received from her husband "a charming little portrait by Zoffany, court painter to George III, of Princess Charlotte," and for the occasion she gave him "a wee little Turner watercolour about five inches by three.[53] Marian Adams was fond of eighteenth century English portraits, but "Henry hates" them. She rhymed:

> Jack Sprat dislikes portraits,
> His wife dislikes paysages,
> And so betwixt them both
> The choice is very large.[54]

The great scoop in Marian's career as an independent collector was the purchase of a pair of portraits by Sir Joshua Reynolds, undertaken by her in spite of Henry's initial skepticism. The story, recorded triumphantly in letters to her father, unfolds like a detective thriller: how the pictures were offered to her by an impoverished old lady as having been sent to her grandparents from England, how she first saw them in a gloomy Washington house, how she finally bought them, not out of "charity, far from it," but taking "a gambler's chance,"[55] and how her confidence in their genuineness and in the old lady's tale was proved beyond doubt by restoration and research. The two kit-kat size (36 x 28 inches) portraits turned out to be those of Mrs. and Mr. Groves. Groves, "to whom they consigned tobacco from their plantation," was the London agent of Samuel Galloway of Tulip Hill, West River, Maryland.[56] Galloway sent his own and his wife's portraits to London as return compliments and was the grandfather of the old lady. The authenticity of the portraits was clinched by the listing of "Mr. and Mrs. Groves" in Sir Joshua's memoranda under August 1765, evidence supplied by Henry himself, who by chance came across it in the *Life and Times of Sir Joshua Reynolds* by Leslie and Taylor.

The portraits were hung side by side in the library between the windows, and even Henry said, "Yes, they are charmingly modelled and very dignified."[57] Richardson too "was much pleased with the Sir Joshuas and has inspired the Andersons [for whom he had just built a new house in Washington] with wrath at their blindness in rejecting them as rubbish offered to them at the same time they were offered to me."[58] They were given by Adams to the Corcoran Gallery of Art in Washington, D.C., as a memorial to his wife, but were later returned to the Mrs. Hughes in whose house Marian had discovered them.

Other paintings came by inheritance, such as a Teniers sent to them by Henry's aunt Mrs. Chardon Brooks, "as a memorial of Uncle Chardon."[59] The collecting of antique furniture was carried on by both with the aim of furnishing and decorating their home. "Old Moorish writing tables" were most "fascinating" to Marian on their trip to Spain, as she wrote to her father.[60] In Washington she bought a seventeenth century Flemish wardrobe chest and an inlaid *escritoire* from the estate of an American who had been *chargé d'affaires* in Belgium.[61] A natural outgrowth of the collecting of furniture was that of textiles. Mrs. Adams mentioned in her letters a corslet, "bought in Naples, two-hundred-years-old Persian."[62] In an "antiquity shop" in Granada she bought "a charming mantilla of black blonde, about two yards long and very fine."[63]

Marian Adams was also very much interested in "old tapestry from Spain . . . offered for sale here by the butler of the British Minister who brought it from Madrid." She wrote to Richardson about it and also tried to interest her brother Edward for an eventual purchase by the Boston Museum.[64] After his wife's death, Adams continued the collecting of furniture. His taste inclined to the low pieces he had seen in the Far East, since they accommodated his short legs, and the comfortable French *dix-huitième*. His friend John Hay teased him about this passion in a letter: "As to you, your disorderly and sensual dallying with Louis XV furniture is becoming a world scandal."[65] This refers to the fact that Adams had decorated his apartment in Paris at 88 Avenue du Bois de Boulogne in the Louis XV style, which Cater described:

> The furnishings were chiefly French, tied in with Chinese pieces that he bought from two shops which he loved to haunt: Chines's and Mme. Langweil's. His library was long and narrow, between a big salon and his bedroom. There were books in eighteenth century lacquered cabinets. His desk was a Louis XV table, with drawers, and on it he kept alternately a pair of Yung Cheng ginger jars or an exquisite Greek figure in a glass case. There was usually a slight look of disorder about the room.[66]

The apartment was dismantled in 1912 and its contents shipped to Adams' brother Brooks at Quincy,[67] "where the Old House was being prepared for exhibit to the public."[68] Thus, by a whim of fate the products of Adams' "sensual dallying" joined the heirlooms of his Puritan ancestors in the old family manse.

The tendency towards luxury, even the luxury of decadent periods, was one of the many paradoxes in Adams' personality, which on the other hand shows so many characteristics of stern frugal Puritanism. In the world of his father and grandfather collecting was permitted chiefly under the educational flag. The collecting of books, coins, Piranesi prints, and eventually of small ancient objects, was in the good old New England tradition. Adams continued this older tradition, and after his wife's death we see the widower filling the rooms of the Richardson house with these objects.

Adams' collection of fine books, of rare and illustrated editions, must have been considerable. As a bibliophile he was probably best understood and encouraged by his friend Gaskell, who shared this interest. Adams mentioned, in a letter to him from Italy, a "Dante printed in 1502" by the illustrious Venetian printer Aldus Manutius.[69] Gaskell gave him a copy of the 1762 edition of the *Contes et Nouvelles* by La Fontaine with the exquisite engravings by Charles D. J. Eisen.[70]

In no other field was Adams closer to his father's interests or hobbies than in numismatics. Greek and Roman coins were his special delight. In Athens, Egypt, Syria, and all over the Balkans, he haunted "low quarters [to] bargain for coins with dirty pawn brokers and greasy Greek peddlers." He bought "more than a hundred since Assouan and they afford . . . not only much amusement but lots of instruction,"[71] and praised especially the beauty of the coins from Syracuse, which indeed belong to the finest in Greek design and workmanship, but he fell occasionally for clever forgeries, of which he was "curious to get a complete set . . . for protection and comparison."[72]

Greek art appealed to him in the small, intimate size. Of all the treasures of the Hermitage in St. Petersburg he was most attracted by a "little Greek sphinx with an Aphrodite beside it" found in Kertch, a "coloured Greek jibe at the usual Sèvres or Saxe figures."[73] While with his wife in Naples he bought Tanagra figurines.[74] He also owned some Greek vases, which he showed to Palgrave in London, and to which Mrs. Adams referred in a letter to her father: "Frank Palgrave admires our Greek vases, but thinks them not very old— two hundred years B.C., but that will do."[75]

Of ancient Egyptian art the usual scarabs were offered to him by native peddlers on his trip along the Nile, but it is not certain what he bought there. As already noted, Adams pursued chiefly the collecting of ancient coins while in Egypt and Syria. Pieces of Islamic art are rarely mentioned. Only once did Oriental silver strike his fancy, though he was aware of being taken in by the dealer. One of these pieces was an Armenian (?) wrought silver cream jug "with weird little naked figures . . . dancing about like mad," the other was a large jar, "a crusader's piece [or a] reproduction of such things as old Khayyam would have drunk from."[76] He bought only the first, since he thought one forgery was enough.

The picture of Adams as a collector is further rounded out by information gleaned from the letters of John Hay, with whom Adams shared a house in Washington built by Richardson in 1885. Though the two friends occupied separate quarters, the decoration of the house both inside and out was a task of common interest. Hay shared Adams' interest in old master drawings. In a letter from London of 25 August 1887, he told Adams: "I bought at the R— sale a nice lot of old Master drawings—which I tard to show you."[77] From Amsterdam on a trip in 1896, after a visit to the Museum Fodor, which has a fine collection of drawings, Hay reported on 28 June to his friend: "Then we went to the F. Museum, mostly modern French, with one room of old drawings just about as good and as many as we have."[78]

The greatest event in Hay's activity as a collector was the purchase of a Botticelli. To Adams, then on his second trip to the East, he wrote from Cleveland: "My visit to that capital [Washington] is attended by some palpitation, as my Botticelli has arrived and is at my house as yet unhonored and unsung. I am half afraid to see it, yet I wish to know the worst. But of the misery, the misery of the empty house next door."[79] And two months later: "My big Botticelli has come and is hanging on the stairs. It is a beautiful thing— a picture of first importance."[80]

Love for art and the collecting of art was a trait all the members of Adams' intimate circle had in common. It was not restricted to the artists among them, for it was shared by the statesman as well as the geologist. Adams' novel *Esther* reflects that group interest, and though it is a fictional report, it is nevertheless realistic enough to serve as a reliable source for the artistic interests of the Adams group in general and also for many details.[81] The hero, the Reverend Stephen Hazard (notice the name so characteristic of Adams' skeptical attitude towards world and womanhood), though in some respects recalling Phillips Brooks (1835-93), minister at Trinity Church in Boston and later Episcopalian bishop of Massachusetts, has more than one trait in common with Henry Adams, especially Adams the art lover: his educational background (German university), his dilettantism (he has studied a little of everything), and his residence in Paris, where he discovered Wharton (La Farge). Adams also had him go to the Far East at a time when he himself contemplated such a trip but had not yet realized it.

The library of the Reverend Hazard accords perfectly with Adams' many-sided interests in the arts, "an elaborate collection of illustrated works on art, Egyptian, Greek, Roman, Mediaeval, Mexican, Japanese, and whatever else had come in his way."[82] East Asiatic, especially Japanese, art was collected by the group in the novel, as it had been by Adams, King, and La Farge at the time the novel was written. Wharton (La Farge) bought a "bit of Japanese enamel," while Strong (King), Adams' ideal American, declared he had a better piece, "given to him by a Daimio of Kiusiu." Strong also owned the "most perfect bit of Japanese lacquer."[83] The general trend towards *Japonism*, which had as many enthusiastic followers in the United States, especially in Boston, as it had in Europe, was also reflected in the manner in which the studio of the amateur artist Esther was decorated "with the regular supply of eastern stuffs, porcelains . . . one or two ivory carvings . . . some Japanese screens and eastern rugs."[84]

In the book the interest in the art of East Asia rivaled the interest in the art of the Middle Ages, of which, characteristically, Hazard was the chief champion.[85] These interests were expressed in discussions on art which will be drawn upon later in dealing with Adams' medievalism. But it may be mentioned here that East Asiatic and medieval art evolved as the two strongest interests in his art education.

Just as the geologist Strong (King) of the novel became interested in the arts, so the fundamentally artistic Adams was drawn to geology.[86] Since Adams' interest in the origin and the making of things was inseparable from his relation to art, his activities as a collector in the field of natural sciences must be considered briefly, leaving it to specialists in the field to deal with it extensively. Adams' interest dated back to his years at Harvard where the Swiss professor of zoology Louis Agassiz gave lectures on the "Glacial Period and Palaeontology, which had more influence on his curiosity than the rest of the college instruction altogether."[87]

Louis Agassiz's son Alexander, one of Adams' intimate friends, combined his great achievements in the natural sciences with his interest in the antiquities of Peru, and brought together a considerable collection of Pre-Columbian Peruvian art, later given to Harvard. He was also mentioned as an "early and ardent collector" of Japanese art among the Boston *Japonists*.[88] Since Adams took Alexander Agassiz as a model from the time they were co-students, their mutual interest in affairs does not need to be proved.

Thanks to his article on Sir Charles Lyell, the geologist protagonist of Darwin, "Adams passed for a friend of geologists."[89] He transmitted this enthusiasm to his friend Gaskell, on whose estate, Wenlock Abbey in Shropshire, he carried on some geological and paleontological observations, like "every curate in England who dabbled in geology and hunted for vestiges of Creation."[90] Twice Adams visited that grandiose prehistoric monument, Stonehenge, first in 1865, "a second time from Norman Court" (Wenlock Abbey) ten years later.[91]

Adams kept this interest in prehistory and prehistoric art until his old age. Several of his letters indicate that he put some money into the excavations carried on by Henry Hubert, director of the St. Germain-en-Laye Museum and an authority on French Celtic art, in a region near Les Eyzies in the Dordogne, where splendid examples of the art of Cro-Magnon man had been found.[92] Adams planned to accompany Hubert to "dig bones in the Dordogne," but ill health kept him from it. He continued, however, to toy with the idea, for "going down" held a macabre as well as a soothing attraction for the old man. He wrote to John F. Jameson: "I am trying to dig for a primitive bone in the cave of Eyzies. I adore hairy elephants."[93] After Hubert discovered the remains of a child in one of the caves Adams wrote to Mabel La Farge from Washington: "Any day I may be forced to quit, and in that case, I've nothing to fall back upon. As far as I can see, I must go down to live with my 30000-year-old baby in

1. "Old House," Adams National Historic Site, Quincy, Massachusetts. West Side. Photographed by Charles E. Peterson. Reproduced from the Collections of the Library of Congress.

2. "Old House," Adams National Historic Site, Quincy, Massachusetts. Northwest View, Rear. Photographed by Charles E. Peterson. Reproduced from the Collections of the Library of Congress.

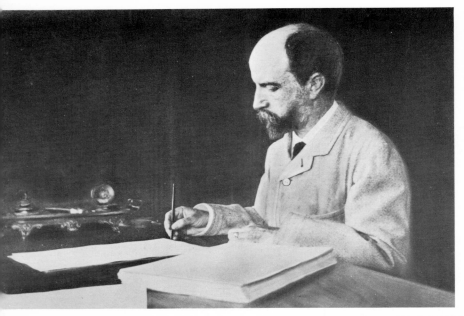

3. Henry Adams in his Study during his Harvard Professorship. Photographed by Mrs. Adams in Beverly Farms. Collection of the Massachusetts Historical Society. The Bettmann Archive.

4. Henry Adams in his Washington Home. Photographed in 1899. Collection of the American Academy of Arts and Letters. The Bettmann Archive.

5. Henry Adams after 1900. Drawing by John Briggs Potter. Location Unknown. The Bettmann Archive.

the Dordogne. I might have worse company, but hardly worse trouble."[94]

The circle of existence was complete to Adams, and always being aware of its roundness, of its having no beginning and no end, he divined the sameness of the spiritual motivation behind the art of prehistoric man, expressing itself in fertility idols, and in the art of the Middle Ages, which created the *Virgin Mother*. In this sense he wrote to Margaret Chanler from South Lincoln, Massachusetts, where he was recovering from a stroke: "I shall expect you to carry me over and put me into an automobile at Cherbourg, and take me straight to the Dordogne to see my infant of the pre-glacial period. I am looking forward to it as the last pleasure I shall have in life. Don't disappoint me. We shall worship the Virgin in any cave that happens to come handy, for I am sure she will be there."[95]

One of his charming notes to Elizabeth Cameron is worth quoting in full, since it illustrated what kind of amateur in the arts and sciences Adams was: "Hubert came to dine and talk about my Dordogne baby, which he is to accoucher. I have given him a thousand francs to start on and he is to boss the job. I am very slowly worrying through the last pages of the new imprint of Chartres. I am loaded with thirteenth century MSS and meditate vast erudition."[96]

4. Travels

(Europe, America, Africa and Asia;
Observations on Art;
the South Seas and
Attempts at Watercolor)

*H*enry Adams' occupation with the arts was limited in neither time nor space. As he traveled around the globe from west to east, from south to north—more specifically from Massachusetts to Japan, from Polynesia to Scandinavia—so his interest in art encompassed works from many different regions and of many different races. His interests were equally vast in time. They stretched from the Old Stone Age to his own period: "I have gone round the whole circle of arts and tastes . . . and have pursued the imagination into its remotest haunts."[1] Yet he was not an impartial lover; he had favorites.

Adams moved far from his beginnings. His New England education, his home background, and his father's interests furnished only the limited basis of the classical; and that was chiefly Rome. "The American parent, curiously enough while bitterly hostile to Paris, seemed rather disposed to accept Rome as legitimate education, though abused."[2] He devoted the sixth chapter of his *Education* to Rome, but little or nothing was said about the city's monuments and its art. The Forum and St. Peter's merely illustrated history, symbols of rise and fall, emotional embodiments of two failures of western civilization. The fact that twice the climax of that tragedy of failure had taken place in the same place gave a special aura to the town, but it was an aura of decay. He never failed to sit on the steps of the church of Ara Coeli, the old Christian basilica on the Forum, partly built of material from ancient Roman temples, performing there a memorial rite for the ghost of Gibbon, the eighteenth century high priest of *the fall*, by quoting passages from the historian's *Autobiog-*

raphy: "In the close of the evening as I sat musing in the Church of the Zoccolanti or Franciscan Friars, while they were singing Vespers in the Temple of Jupiter, on the ruins of the Capitol."[3]

All these were historical-intellectual associations. Visually the Rome of the 1860s was medieval. The pictures were uncleaned, the churches unrestored, the ruins unexcavated. "Mediaeval Rome was sorcery."[4]

Rome and Italy held Adams for a long time, but he never studied its art monuments and objects thoroughly. He found Italy, however, less and less enjoyable, and his enthusiasm faded with the dream of youth. Rebellion against the cult of antiquity, performed so loyally by his elders, announced itself early in the closing passage of a letter written to his friend Gaskell from Rome, 23 April 1865, though there might be much youthful boasting behind the pronouncement: "I am coming back to write a new work on art, which is to smash the Greeks."[5] In the light of the later development of Henry Adams' taste, this passage gains significance as an early symptom of esthetic unorthodoxy and independence. The term *Greeks* was probably merely a synonym for antiquity as he understood it then, before he actually knew Greece and Greek art.

Whatever esthetic disapproval existed, it did not hinder his return, since Italy and Rome remained "a pure emotion," a historical relic—a relic also of his own youth. Rome remained to mean the Forum and St. Peter's, and "one never forgot to look and it never ceased reacting."[6] Rome widened into the Mediterranean area, "where for nearly forty years I have meant annually to come."[7] That was written in 1899 during his last trip to Italy, to Sicily, when old age and disgust with the Italy of the tourists made him decide never to return.

Previously Adams had been to Italy eight times, between 1860 and 1896, and had seen all the famous towns and sights, but little mention was made of them in either his *Education* or letters; no reference can be found in them to a single building, statue or picture of Roman antiquity, and little to its offshoot, the Italian Renaissance. Only Michelangelo was mentioned several times, but as a great personality chiefly; few references were made to his works.

Passages in one of his *Letters to a Niece* are the most specific illustrations of his attitude towards Roman antiquity and the Italian Renaissance. The young woman had written him exuberant letters from Rome, and the ironical uncle poured cold water on her enthusiasm;

> but of Rome, as in Rome, there is almost nothing of the very first quality. Even the Michael Angelos and the Vatican marbles do not appeal to me as intensely as the Slave or the Venus of Milo in the Louvre, and Byron's description of the Gladiator is finer than the Gladiator himself. Roman architecture is very far from the first class. Saint Peter's reeks of money and infidelity. The best things are always Michael Angelo and the Campagna.[8]

A short time later he wrote to the same niece:

> That Rome and Michael Angelo should at first knock one silly, is proof of sense. The world contains only one or two great tragic motives in the historical drama and Rome concentrates them [the imperial and the papal failures] as Michael does, so that they strike any-one with imagination almost a physical blow. Florence is not tragic at all, and in spite of Dante and all the rest never counts for a tragic motive . . . Florence was always mercantile;—never imperial or spiritual,—and I think that was really what worried Dante. I feel it even in the mosaic marbling of the Campanile; and [*Michelangelo's*] Penseroso seems to me to be pondering what it means. Evidently he is in a mess, and cannot for his life understand it. So I think Michael felt in Florence that his style of art was out of place, as Dante's was in the earlier time. Florence is a place to play in. Tuscany always was peaceful, fat and sensual. You see it in the decorations of the early tombs and Vergil taunts the Etrurians in the Aeneid with caring for nothing but wine and music and love-making . . . Venice is still more so, and to my mind, too much so. Florence is a pleasant medium between the shop and the camp and the court. It has just a fair share of all, and just enough religion to be graceful.[9]

Adams recommended, however, the small, largely still medieval places in Italy to his niece:

> Yet I would like to be with you, and read Dante, and see who sleeps in the Campo Santo, and go down to Pisa, which is to me finer than Florence, and almost the only interesting architecture south of the Appenines. Florence is charming. I have nothing to say against it; but Pisa and the older cities appeal to my archaic

sympathies more. There is always an odor of spice and brown sugar about the Medicis. They patronised art as Mr. Rockefeller or Mr. Havemeyer does. They are not Dantesque. Still, Florence is charming in its way, and has literature, which cannot be said of Venice with all its beauty. But the little places are the best, just as the old parish churches in England and France are often more sympathetic than the big cathedrals. I used to like Perugia, and was awfully disappointed to miss Assisi.[10]

Adams' judgment of the Italian Renaissance, though in many details exaggerated, is indeed astonishing when we consider that all through the latter part of the nineteenth century Roman antiquity and the Italian Renaissance were *de rigueur* for the educated as well as the uneducated traveler. Then American skyscrapers were hidden behind classical veneers and the lobbies of Fifth Avenue mansions were turned into fake Florentine halls. Adams classified this as *goldbug taste*. To Adams the Roman Empire and the Italian Renaissance of the popes and the Medici were infested by the same goldbug. The term *goldbug* had been coined by Horace White, editor of the Chicago *Tribune*. The noisy enthusiasm of his traveling countrymen was indirect proof of it. Pompeii and the temples were contaminated by them, and their swarming presence made him see the more clearly that Italian art was decorative and the expression of historical decay. Adams was always searching for sources, the springs of youth and purity.

Contrary to the fashion prevailing in New York and Boston, Adams was little interested in Italian art. This lack of deeper interest separated him most definitely from his younger contemporary, the fastidious esthete, collector, and writer on art, Bernard Berenson. This might have been the chief reason why, in spite of repeated invitations, he never visited I Tatti, the great art expert's Italian villa between Florence and Settignano. The story of the somewhat ambiguous relationship between the two men will only be fully told when the Berenson-Adams correspondence in the I Tatti archives, not yet fully published, becomes available. Berenson acknowledged in his *Sketch for a Selfportrait* that he owed his friendship with Edith Wharton to Adams, while the latter revealed in a letter to Elizabeth Cameron that he occasionally asked Berenson for expert information on Italian art. But as an agent for art dealers Berenson catered to the American goldbug and seemed to Adams as contaminated by it as the pictures he dealt with.[11]

Adams was cynically humorous and certainly prejudiced when he was confronted with the derivative of the derivative, namely the Renaissance in France and England. To him they were the triumph of the goldbug: their art as showy, tasteless, monetary, and inwardly as rotten as the taste of his contemporaries. Whatever existed of quality in the castles of the Touraine was still connected with the medieval fortress; the rest was frosting. He made an exception of the château of Blois, which "is very beautiful. At least, the fragment which contains the staircase, making one side of the court." But in spite of Blois and Chaumont, Touraine could not compare with Normandy: "It leaves a greasy taste; a mercantile and gold-bug trail, even on the architecture and the murders." "I turn back," he wrote, "to my dear Coutances and my divine Mont St. Michel with the relief of an epicure who has had to eat pork."[12] Adams' most violent physical distaste centered around Fontainebleau:

> The "goldbug" style is fit to express Francis I and Henry VIII with their Field of Cloth of Gold, and their sensual appetites; the life that Brantôme describes, and Diane de Poitiers and Anne Boleyn decorated. As the decoration of appetites it is often very beautiful, as in the old parts of the Louvre and great artists, like Jean Goujon, could often hide its innate vulgarity of wealth; but between it and the religious-military art of Mont St. Michel and the Hôtel de Cluny is a gulf where I break my neck.[13]

And in the same vein:

> I do not love the Valois or their art . . . They are very earthy. They feel gilded, and smell of musk. They strike attitudes, and admire themselves in mirrors. Francis I and Henry VIII are brothers and should have been cooks. They look it. Their architecture looks it, just in proportion as it loses the old military character. In soul, it is mercantile, bourgeois and goldbug. When I look at it, I am homesick for Mont St. Michel and Coutances. The ancient Gauls were noble in comparison, and I yearned to live in the stone-age.[14]

This was written in 1895 after the discovery of twelfth century art had prejudiced his eyes, and when his mind had already formed the theory of the dissipation of creative energy and the inevitable decay of the later phases of western civilization. This dissipation manifested itself in all fields, especially in those of art and religion.

But he was fair and just enough to realize that he himself and his own taste had been contaminated by this disease. Where decay demonstrated itself frankly, gracefully, and cynically, he enjoyed it frankly and cynically. This *dix-huitième* side of his taste was mentioned in connection with his art collection. When he met that weakness for bric-a-brac, "rococo fun" and "Chinese pleasantries," lacquers, Ming porcelain, and tapestries in the palaces of such eighteenth century collectors as Frederick the Great's sister Wilhelmine at Bayreuth, or in the rooms of Catherine the Great at Petershof and Czarskoe Selo, he rejoiced in it.[15] Of all the art he had seen in Sweden, he found only the eighteenth century tapestries in the Stockholm royal palace worth mentioning.[16]

Certainly it was also the distinctly feminine character of the eighteenth century which attracted him. Marie Antoinette's garden around the Petit Trianon in Versailles "is beautiful in its desertion." "Certainly it is not a religious repose, but it is painfully human and pessimistic. I was greatly touched by the little old, opera-comical hameau of Marie Antoinette which is prettier now in its abandonment than ever it can have been when new."[17]

The princely galleries, however, "the cemeteries of art, the Louvre and other museums" and their pictures rarely excited him.[18] But of course he visited them. In the Hermitage he found "nothing first-rate . . . except the Dutch."[19] Stockholm had "one, or even two excellent Rembrandts."[20] Of all the museums he saw, he was most impressed by the Prado in Madrid. "As for the gallery here, I can't deny that it knocks all my expectations flat. Never did I dream of such Titians." But the general impression was "Spain is a hole."[21] The celebrated cathedral at Burgos, which influenced his friend Richardson so much, was disappointing. It was only Moorish Spain which delighted him. "Cordova was fascinating. The great mosque was glorious. The little houses and especially their hammered iron gates, were adorable." And further, "Granada ranks with the first class places, and for beauty stands only second to Naples."[22]

Thus the Mediterranean, amalgamated with the dark-skinned, colorful Oriental, was judged more favorable than *marble-white* an-

cient purity. He found *charm* even in the fusion of the Spanish-Medi-
terranean with the native Indian in the Churrigueresque Baroque
of the churches in Mexico.[23] He wrote: "There is in Guadalajara,
alone, more good art than in all our cities together, putting museums
and collections out of the question; but it is baroque and Spanish and
altogether sweet and decadent, while ours is dead and dried."[24] And
he summarized: "Artistically the old Mexico, both ecclesiastical and
secular, was charming and astonished me much.[25] From Havana
Adams wrote in 1894 to John Hay about the merits of colonial Spanish domestic architecture: "The look of the houses shows that once
good things were understood here. They knew and still know how
to make arches. Every old building has a fine arched court. Here and
there one sees a good façade."[26]

Adams came to know the Orient first in Egypt. He visited the
Nile twice, in 1873 and 1898. At that time historians looked upon
Egyptian culture chiefly as preliminary to the early European.
Adams showed no specific enthusiasm. He dutifully did the sights,
Luxor, Karnak, Philae. The great impression was Abu Simbel. He
photographed the colossal sculptures there to "catch their spirit."[27]
"As a sight, there is nothing I have seen in the world equal to this
temple, and on coming to it, I sat down mildly and forgave my poor
old Ramses all his architectual sins in Egypt."[28] The general impres-
sions from the second trip were described in a letter to Mabel
Hooper:

> One does the usual temples, and, by way of a change one resorts
> to the usual tombs. . . . Egypt interests me always, of course, but
> that is because it is a kind of compendium or Century Diction-
> ary of History, and I get the cosmos in a nut-shell here. Rome
> fades off into a passing blizzard; western civilization becomes a
> rather gross misapprehension; and even oriental enormities count
> only as a more or less labored variation on an originally simple
> theme.[29]

On this second trip to Egypt, which he "cared little to see
again,"[30] he visited the excavations at Saqqara, Medinet Abu, and
the Ramesseum, but Islamic Egypt held his interest, rather than that
of the pharaohs. He was "playing with the Khalifs and the Sultans."

He bought some silver and became interested in the "wonderfully cheap process and the lovely effects of the Cairene glass," chiefly for the sake of his friend La Farge.[31] He went on to Syria where he visited Damascus and Baalbek. Then he traveled to Smyrna and Ephesus in Asia Minor, and finally to Greece. Yet it was a sentimental journey through history, leading to reflections on the laws of history and the fate of civilization and empire, rather than an art trip.

Greece, however, offered an esthetic challenge and became a touchstone for his taste, which at this time (1898) had undergone the revolutionizing experience of East Asiatic art and that of the Middle Ages. "After seeing Egypt and Syria, Italy and Japan, Greece shrinks; and after living in French Gothic and Michael Angelo Renaissance, Greek art has less to say to the simple-minded Christian," Adams wrote from Athens to his Grecophile friend Gaskell.[32] He saw Greece with new eyes, disdaining the classical as well as the Hellenistic Greece of his school and English years, and discovering the early phases, the Aegean and archaic. He wrote that Attica was a "droll little amusing fraud of the imagination."[33]

> Athens was always a fraud, and Aristophanes and Socrates and the rotten and impudent scepticism and cynicism and sophism of the schools expressed the character of the place very much more successfully than the artists ever succeeded in expressing religious majesty in Zeus or religious emotion in the Parthenon. Peace to the ashes of poor Palgrave! Athens leaves me cool![34]

Adams looked upon art as a product of society and philosophy, and he decidedly was not a lover of the Athenian shop-keeping bourgeoisie. That was expressed in a letter to his brother Brooks:

> By way of variation, I would provide myself with an Aristophanes. The contrast between the shop-keeping bourgeoisie of Athens, with their so-called wit, and their damnable scepticism and their idiotic Socratic method, on the one side; and the dignity, grace, decorative elegance, and almost complete want of religious depth or intensity of Eleusis, Delphi, and their symbol the Parthenon, on the other, is what I felt most strongly on the Acropolis.[35]

Delphi was different from Athens. He discovered it as the artistic manifestation of a people of northern mountaineers and compared its spirit and character to the forested hilly temple precincts of Japan:

> Delphi is better. There the Greeks evidently put all they had
> of faith and soul. Delphi did not leave me cool. Its religiosity is
> very Japanese, to be sure, and singularly Greek and graceful in
> its grandeur; but it is those, though the theatre and the race
> course, as usual, dispute victoriously both the place and the in-
> terest with the temple; and Apollo was evidently more con-
> cerned with statues and decorations and lines of columns than
> with oracles. Still, the Greeks certainly felt their Delphi. The
> place has quality of its own, unlike anything else in the world,
> and one hardly misses the buildings because clearly the religion
> of the place must have been anterior to them and rather les-
> sened than heightened by them. In what is left of them and of
> the statuary, I was glad to find that the very archaic character
> was general. At Delphi one does not want Greek cleverness;
> one wants a little Greek intensity. Beautiful as Apollo and
> Hermes and Aphrodite are, in the later time, they much too evi-
> dently know it. At Delphi the finest bit they have discovered is a
> bronze statue, provisionally named Hiero of Syracuse, so
> straight-forward, so simple, so intensely realistic, and yet so
> beautiful.[36]

This bronze statue was the well-known "Charioteer of Delphi," as
the editor of Adams' letters W. Chauncey Ford noted. It is one of the
finest works of the early fifth century B.C. transitional style marking
the end of the archaic and the beginning of the classical period. The
piece had been excavated by the French just two years before Adams
visited Delphi.

Adams was far ahead of his time in his appreciation of the
archaic style, then almost exclusively of interest only to the learned
archeologist. This passage on Delphi is by far the most perceptive in
the whole travel literature on Greece up to that time, and anticipated Gerhard Hauptmann's similar description in *Der Griechische
Frühling* (1907). The Greek temple, however, which he had been
taught to worship and was the foundation of all New England public
architecture, was dealt with very critically:

> Greek temples are never religious, mysterious, or very serious,
> and they are not even—don't quote me—very imposing. At a

small distance they look small. Unlike Egyptian temples or
Gothic cathedrals, they suit very well as jewel-boxes for Aphrodite . . . There is no excess at Delphi. The horror of the priest-
ess' cavern is unseen and quite imaginary. . . . I was immensely
pleased with the wonderful taste of it, as I always am with
everything Greek.[37]

In Sicily, too, it was less the Greek temple as architecture than
the taste of its setting which he admired. Although he called the temple at Girgenti "the most beautiful Greek ruin," he was even more
enthusiastic about the Greeks as landscape gardeners:

Girgenti and Syracuse were interesting studies in that profession, but yesterday came the climax in Taormina. . . . the Greek
is the only man who ever lived that could get the whole value out
of his landscape, and add to it a big value of his own. His share
counts for almost as much as the share of nature. The wretch
was so complete an artist that big or little was equally easy for
him to handle and he took hold of Etna just as easily as he did
of the small lump of gold or silver to make a perfect coin.[38]

Although Adams went to Sicily chiefly to see the Byzantine mosaics of Monreale, he was happy to discover in the Palermo museum
"some Greek metopes from Sergeste [*sic*] or some other old ruin
which . . . seemed to me of the very first class. To bag two first-class
art-works in one place, when I knew so few in the world, was a
triumph."[39] These sculptures from the temple in Segeste were even
older than those he had seen in Delphi. They were of the time when
the Greek genius had just emerged from that of the Mediterranean
Orient. And he was more aware of these Asiatic and African roots in
the art of Mycenae and Tiryns than their discoverer Schliemann.
This was also before Evans had published his discoveries which revealed Crete as the island focus of a Bronze Age civilization of which
Mycenae and Tiryns were merely later colonial branches. Adams
wrote that Mycenae

is the citadel of a highland chief whose tastes are developed by
contact with Indian Moguls. I was glad to clear my mind about
it. Homer became easy, and even a little modern, as though he
knew rather less about his ancient predecessors than I did. After
my winter's travels Mycenae seemed neither very old nor very
difficult to understand although its forms are different from

those of Egypt and Asia Minor. . . . Then we drove down the valley to Argos, which is nothing, and to Tiryns, which is Mycenae over again as a sea-port, with only the changes which a sea-port would make.[40]

And he was even more definite as to the part-oriental origin of Mycenae and Tiryns:

They are worth seeing, for they bring one's Homer quite down to fact, and they belong to the time of the Pyramids when the dead lived on earth, before the age when it was found cheaper to invent another world for them. The vaulted tombs at Mycenae belong to the same stage of thought as the Pyramids of Gizeh and the tombs of Beni Hassan. . . . the clan-chief of Mycenae got his ideas of art from the Tyrians and Asia Minor. . . . Agamemnon was in Egyptian pay. As for Tiryns it is merely another Scotch fortress . . . with store houses for imported wares—bonded warehouses in short.[41]

Through his ability to perceive connections, to envision in a global way, Adams established not only the unity of the pre-Greek Mediterranean civilization, of which Mycenae was a part, but extended its radius to the Americas, in this respect similar to Sir Grafton Elliot Smith's theory in *Culture, the Diffusion Controversy* (1927). Adams used pottery ornament as proof of this theory. He wrote to Brooks Adams from Washington in 1901:

I cannot resist the suspicion that the Phenicians reached Brazil, as early as the Mycenae period. The pottery is even Greek, which makes the case worse. If the Brazil Indian came in contact with Phenician commerce a thousand years B.C.; and the Malay civilization came in on the west coast a thousand years A.D., the development of the North American Indian becomes less certainly isolated. . . . The Phenician extension is another matter, and requires very careful study indeed. On one side it possibly touches Brazil, and on the other it involves England, on a third it raises all sorts of questions about the Etruscans, Greece, the Black Sea and the Homeric poems. Who were the Mycenaens and who were the Dorians? How far back does Cypriote commerce go? Who were the Hittites? Who were the Trojans of the lowest tone?[42]

Adams saw more clearly than his contemporaries that Greek art not only emerged from but finally became submerged in the Orient, bringing about the birth of medieval art. His interest in prehistoric and archaic Greece developed hand in hand with that in Byzantine art. This love for another type of nonrealistic, stylized art was also ahead of his time. He began even to question the theory of his brother Brooks, of decay and degradation of civilization, which he had made his own as far as these last phases of the Roman Empire and Hellenistic civilization were concerned. In this too he was a bold anticipator. The following lines were written before Alois Riegl in *Spaetroemische Kunstindustrie* (1901-23) challenged the theory of decay which had dominated art history since Winckelmann:

> Ravenna was my personal circus. It was what I came for. . . .
> As you may remember, or forget, my brother Brooks and I, in
> our historical discussions of theory of his book, have been greatly
> exercised by the fact, that the Roman Empire, one day, about
> the year 400, dropped to pieces without any apparent cause. It
> decaded. Everybody says so. The fact may be considered as
> accomplished. By universal consent, its art decaded with its
> politics. Yet it showed very curious energy for a corpse. It
> adopted a new and very strong centralised religion just at that
> time. At Byzantium, which happened to survive, Justinian, a
> hundred years later, codified the law in a way which still serves
> as the foundation for European jurisprudence. He also built the
> church of Saint Sophia in an entirely new form of architecture
> which is still our admiration. The Empire did many other things
> not usual for corpses to do, and among the rest, built Ravenna,
> which was the reason I wanted to see it. So we went there, and
> I found what I wanted. Ravenna is a startling discovery to a
> poor American searcher for conundrums. Except the great
> Gothic churches like Chartres and Amiens, with their glass and
> sculpture, I know nothing to compare with the religious splendor
> of the Ravenna churches with their mosaics. They are a revela-
> tion of what can be done by an old civilization, when the gold-
> bug breaks down, and Empires expire.
>
> To complete the study, I came here [Venice] and once
> more inspected St. Marc's. This afternoon I chartered a gondola
> and cruised far over the wide lagoon a dozen miles north to
> Torcello, and stopped at Murano, always after Byzantine re-
> mains. It is a lovely excursion as dreamy and weird as the
> Apocalypse; and the churches told me the same story as at Ra-
> venna. There are two mosaic Virgins over the apsis of Torcello
> and Murano, as splended as anything Gothic or Greek. Yet they

are five hundred years later than Ravenna. For a dead Empire, I hold this to be a phenomenon quite peculiar.[43]

Adams pursued the Byzantine phenomenon to its root in Constantinople and its far reaching branches in Russia and Sicily. St. Sophia's priceless mosaics were then still covered with whitewash, so "the old walls are about the only antiques left visible."[44] He correctly classified the late Byzantinism of the Kremlin in Moscow as barbaric:

> The Kremlin is more than half barbarous, but is not strong; it is Byzantine barbarized. The bulbous domes are weak. The turnip with its root in the air is not so dignified as the turnip with its root in the earth. The architecture is simply ignorance. The builders built in 1600 as they built in 1200 because they knew no more. They had no building stone. Gold was their only idea of splendour.[45]

Monreale in Sicily capped it all. "At last I saw Monreale and the mosaics, and, for a wonder, these were worthwhile. They make even Ravenna modest."[46]

Three roads lead from the great mosaics of the Byzantine Virgin; all were traveled by Henry Adams. The first leads back to Greece, the second to eastern Asia, and the third to the western Middle Ages. It was at the end of the last one that Adams found unity. We shall follow him first to the East, to Japan, the South Seas, and India. The journey was only apparently a detour in the wrong direction. The roads from the east and west came together in Adams' later writings, and the quest for unity materialized in Saint-Gaudens' Adams Monument in Rock Creek Cemetery, in which Greek *Charis*, Buddhist *Nirvana*, and the Virgin Mary met in the Great Mother, the final ground of all life and energy.

As we have seen, East Asiatic art was for Adams and his companion La Farge first of all that of Japan before it came to mean that of China and India. It stood for the small object—the blockprint, lacquer, netzuke, and sword guard, in short for *Japonism*—before it meant architecture and sculpture. It grew out of their collector interest in Japanese bric-a-brac, which had its American center in Boston and Cambridge. As mentioned before, Van Wyck Brooks has given a fine description of these activities and the men interested in them, Alexander Agassiz, Raphael Pumpelly, Edward W. Hooper (Adams' brother-in-law), Edward Morse, and Percival Lowell, and of the two men who first led and finally defeated them by going back to the true and early sources of Buddhist art, William Sturgis Bigelow and Ernest Fenollosa.[47] Adams and La Farge had the advantage of the advice of the latter two in Japan, and also that of Okakura Kakuzo during the stay of that great scholar in the United States. La Farge especially was close to Okakura, who later dedicated his charming and profound *Book of Tea* to the painter.

Yet the lure of *Japonism* was not so quickly overcome. We shall meet with its lingering spell in Adams' letters from Japan and in La Farge's *An Artist's Letters from Japan* (1897). But their trip to Japan was not merely a hunt for collector's items. They were both seekers after *Nirvana*. It was not merely a joke when La Farge gave that magic word in reply to a journalist's inquiry as to their common purpose in visiting Japan. La Farge touched on that episode in the words with which he ended the dedication of the aforementioned book to Adams: "If only we had found Nirvana—but he was right who warned us that we were late in this season of the world."

In that cult of Nirvana too they followed esthetic Boston, where even the millionaire sportsman Appleton named one of his yachts *Nirvana*, and from where the two friends Bigelow and Fenollosa had started their pilgrimage to Buddha.[48] Adams was early affected by it. During one of the happiest periods of his married and professional life, when teaching at Harvard, he wrote from his summer cottage near Boston to Charles Gaskell: "One year resembles another and if it weren't for occasional disturbing dreams of decay, disaster or collapse, I should consider myself as having attained as much of Nirvana as a man of my trade and temperament can expect to do."[49] And forty years later there was still the same search, as he confided to the Bostonian high priest of Buddhism, William Sturgis Bigelow, who had sent him his *Buddhism and Immortality*: "I will as usual, take refuge in the Lotus. There we will meet. We shall not be alone."[50]

Adams and La Farge had their very personal reasons for starting a pilgrimage to the land of Nirvana. Adams had just lost his wife under tragic circumstances and the house in Washington, just completed for them by Richardson, stood empty and deserted. His trip was a flight from the Western world, a flight almost from life, and it was not accidental that Adams read Buddhism on the train which carried him to the port of embarkation.[51] "I was myself a Buddhist when I left America," he wrote to John Hay.[52] James T. Adams was certainly right when he assumed that "the Buddhist mood and thought for his wife's memorial had come to Adams in Japan on his first trip with La Farge."[53]

And La Farge too was a seeker for inspiration. "I had a vague belief that I would find there certain conditions of line in the mountains which would help me," he wrote in an autobiographical sketch.[54] The reference was to the landscape setting for the figures in his "Ascension" mural, which should look natural and still be fitting for "what the mystic people call levitation." His *Artist's Letters from Japan* was the outcome of the common search for the Oriental spirit. The dedication to Henry Adams showed that the book was the brain child of the two friends:

> If anything worth repeating has been said to me in these letters, it has probably come from you, or has been suggested by being with you—perhaps even in the way of contradiction. And you may be amused by the lighter talk of the artist that merely describes appearances or covers them with a tissue of dreams. And you alone will know, how much has been withheld that might have been indiscretely said.

The last sentence hints at the friends' deepest aims, the expression of which was discreetly withheld here and in Adams' letters. Their interest as collectors while in Japan was chiefly in curios, yet there was from the beginning a note of disappointment in Adams' letters. In one to John Hay from Yokohama he wrote:

> I am trying to spend your money. It is hard work, but I will do it, or succumb. Kaki-monos are not to be got. Porcelain worth buying is rare. Lacquer is the best and cheapest article. Bronzes are good and cheap. I want to bring back a dozen big bronze vases to put on the grass before our houses in summer, for palms or big plants, so as to give our house the look of a cross between curio shops and florists. Tokio contains hardly anything worth getting except bronzes. A man at Osaka has sent up some two hundred and fifty dollars worth of lacquers, sword-hilts, inlaid work, and such stuff. As he has the best shop in Japan, we

took the whole lot, and have sent for more. Inros are from ten
to fifteen dollars. I shall get a dozen for presents. Good cloisonné
either Chinese or Japanese, is most rare. Fine old porcelain is
rare and dear. Embroideries are absolutely introuvable. Even
books seem scarce. Japan has been cleaned out. My big bronze
vases will cost from fifty to two hundred dollars apiece, but
these will be good.[55]

Later he wrote to Hay from Nikko:

Yesterday arrived from Osaka a large lot of kaki-monos, sent up
by the great curio-dealer, Yamanaka. I gleaned about two
dozen out of the lot. They are cheap enough, but I fear that
Fenollosa, who is in Tokio, will say, they are Tokugawa rot,
and will bully me into letting them go. He is now trying to prevent my having a collection of Hokusai's books. He is a kind of
St. Dominic and holds himself responsible for the dissemination
of useless knowledge by others. My historical indifference to anything but facts, and my delight at studying what is hopefully
debased and degraded, shock his moral sense. I wish you were
here to help us trample on him. He has joined a Buddhist sect;
I was myself a Buddhist when I left America, but he has converted me to Calvinism with leanings towards the Methodists.[56]

The struggle between the *Japonists* and the true connoisseurs
of Buddhist art started on the day the four men met in Yokohama.
The first letter written from Japan by Adams to Hay referred to it
already:

Sturgis Bigelow acts as our courier and master of ceremonies
. . . Fenollosa and Bigelow are stern with us. Fenollosa is a ty-
rant who says, we shall not like any work done under the Tokugawa Shoguns. As these gentlemen lived two hundred and fifty
years or thereabouts, to 1860, and there is nothing at Tokio except their work, La Farge and I are at a loss to understand why
we came.[57]

Gradually, though grudgingly, Adams accepted Fenollosa's view, or
at least became more than doubtful of the purchases made for himself and his friends. He wrote to Elizabeth Cameron:

I have bought curios enough to fill a house, but nothing that I
like, or want for myself. The stuffs are cheap and beautiful, but
I have found no really fine embroidery. The lacquer is relatively
cheap, but I do not care for it. I can find no good porcelain or

bronze, and very few wall-pictures. Metal work is easy to get, and very choice, but what can one do with sword-guards and knife handles? I am puzzled to know what to bring home to please myself.[58]

And he wrote to Hay in the same vein:

I have still to report that purchases for you are going on, but more and more slowly, for I believe we have burst up all the pawnbrokers' shops in Japan. Even the cholera has shaken out the little that is worth getting. Bigelow and Fenollosa cling like misers to their miserable hoards. Not a kakimono is to be found, though plenty are brought. Every day new bales of rubbish come up from Tokio or elsewhere; mounds of books; tons of bad bronze; holocausts of lacquer; I buy literally everything that is merely possible; and yet I have got not a hundred dollars' worth of things I want for myself. You shall have some good small bits of lacquer, and any quantity of duds to encumber your tables and mantles [sic], but nothing creditable to our joint genius. As for myself, I have only one Yokomono—or kakimono, broader than long—and one small bronze, that I care to keep as the fruit of my summer's perspiration.[59]

Adams "bought about 2000 dollars worth of curios, half for Hay," according to a letter from Yokohama[60] to his factotum Theodore F. Dwight, to whom he wrote further: "Although I have bought what seems to me an enormous mass of things not more than a tenth part of them are intended for our own establishment. The rest are commissions or presents. Only half a dozen pieces of bronze, porcelain or kakimonos, are to adorn our charms."[61]

By the end of their stay in Japan the two friends were nauseated by curios. Adams had learned that most of the stuff he once cherished "is made for export and not true Japanese," and he summed it up:

Only one lesson was impressed more deeply than ever on my heart; which was that if I want good things, I must buy Chinese. In porcelain there is no comparison; in embroidery, none; in kaki-monos not much; the best Chinese is always out of sight ahead, as in cloisonné, and, I think, even in bronze, though bronze is *the* Japanese metal. Only in gold lacquer and small metal work, like sword-guards, or perhaps small ivories, like netsukes, where Japanese humor and lightness have the field to themselves the Japanese excel. They are quite aware of their own inferiority, and the prices they pay for good Chinese or Corean work are out of all proportion to their own.[62]

He noted the superiority of both Chinese art and culture over those of Japan and wrote to John Hay from San Francisco on 21 October 1886 after his return:

> There are no good curios for sale in Japan, and it is cheaper and quicker to buy them in New York or Paris. Another nugget of golden learning acquired by me, is the certainty that Japan and its art are only a sort of antechamber to China, and that China is the only mystery left to penetrate. I have henceforward a future. As soon as I can get rid of history and the present, I mean to start for China, and stay there. . . . In China I will find bronzes or break all the crockery.[63]

For the time at which it was written, that is a remarkably correct estimate of the relative values of Chinese and Japanese art and culture, and it represents, after a stay of only three months in Japan, a considerable growth in understanding, almost an about-face of taste.

That Japan is a "country of small things" came to him immediately, and was stated in the first letter to John Hay: "This is a child's country. . . . The whole show is of the nursery. Nothing is serious: nothing is taken seriously. All is toy."[64] He found that nursery size also in Japanese architecture. The first trip led them to Nikko with the shrines of the Shoguns Iyeyasu and Iyemitsu. Here Adams and La Farge set up housekeeping in a Japanese *doll's house*. La Farge painted the miniature garden with the miniature waterfall, while Adams occupied himself with reading and writing.

Adams began to appreciate the highest expression of that minuteness, the tea ceremony, of which Bigelow had become *Professor*, and which, "held in a bare little room . . . with walls of Chinese simplicity," determined the size and character of the "best and choicest [Japanese] work . . . little things to be worn or to be shown to guests at the Cha-no-yu."[65]

Nothing, however, was said about the functionalism of the Japanese house and its superb handling of space which roused the enthusiasm of the later American traveler Frank Lloyd Wright, but much praise was given to the skill in blending architecture with landscape: "Nikko is after all, one of the sights of the world. . . . Without forgetting the fact that the temples are here and there rather cheap grotesque, the general result of temple and tomb, architecture, ornament, landscape and foliage, is very effective indeed." In the same letter he said, "I admit to thinking it a bigger work than I should have thought possible for Japs. It is a sort of Egypt in lacquer and greenth."[66]

Adams called Kyoto a *Japanese Granada*.[67] It is strange that Nara, with its much older and grander architecture and sculpture, a bit of T'ang China in Japan, was only barely mentioned. The giant bronze Buddha at Kamakura was more fully appreciated. Using the words of La Farge, Adams called it "the most successful colossal figure in the world." The final verdict was: "Japan is not the last word of humanity, and Japanese art has a well developed genius for annoying my prejudices."[68]

Did Adams then hope to find *the last word of humanity* in the South Seas? Was he still in search of Nirvana, of "the life behind a veil," as he called it in his poem *Buddha and Bramah*? His *Education* is reticent about the years between 1871 and 1892, the suppressed years in Henry Adams' life. His letters, too, reveal little, and the only direct answer is given by Mabel La Farge in "Henry Adams: A Niece's Memories," introducing *Letters to a Niece*: "Overtaxed and overstrained by sorrow, as well as by his efforts to surmount it, to Henry Adams the year in the South Seas was a reparation of mind and body. Sleep, which had nearly deserted him, returned once more."[69] Then it was Nirvana, or something close to Nirvana, that he attained. Lines in his *Education* devoted to the South Seas in retrospect breathe Nirvana:

> Adams would rather, as choice, have gone back to the east, if it were only to sleep forever in the trade-winds under the southern stars, wandering over the dark purple ocean, with its purple sense of solitude and void. Not that he liked the sensation, but that it was the most unearthly he had felt.[70]

It was flight out of time and space, but it was not flight from Western civilization. Adams did not intend to go primitive in the South Seas, like Paul Gauguin, not even like Robert Louis Stevenson, whom he met there. He barely missed Gauguin in Tahiti—it was a matter of three days—but even if they had met physically, they would never have understood each other spiritually.[71] This is clearly stated in a letter from La Farge to Adams about the "wild Frenchman," which will be noted later. While Gauguin was anti-Greek, Adams and La Farge saw Homer and his heroes or Greek mythology and its naiads in the divine bodies of the Polynesians, their bearing, and their dances. Stevenson too was reminded of Western art and civilization; he thought Samoa "full of Rousseaus," by which he meant motifs from the paintings of the Barbizon Théodore Rousseau.[72]

While Gauguin almost succeeded in shaking off the West, and in doing so opened up a new path for Western art, La Farge spoiled his South Seas paintings and watercolors with his too well-measured figural compositions, smacking of the plastercast Greeks as taught at the Ecole des Beaux-Arts. La Farge's color looks civilized and tame compared to Gauguin's burning palette. And yet color was for La Farge, as well as for Adams, the lasting gain from this trip. La Farge's work done in the South Sea islands will be dealt with later; Henry Adams' *education of the senses*, as Mabel La Farge calls it[73] —his discovery of pure color, his going artist in his watercolors— will be discussed immediately after considering his critical pronouncements on Polynesian art in Hawaii, Samoa, Tahiti, and the Fiji Islands. Little enough is found in his letters, little also of true appreciation of the native crafts. Adams' taste for the archaic did not reach that far.

For native dance and poetry Adams had a deep understanding. Before Gauguin too did so in *Noa Noa* (1895), Adams collected the legends of Tahiti and incorporated them in his privately printed *Memoirs of Marau Taaroa, Last Queen of Tahiti* (1893), enlarged and again privately printed as *Memoirs of Arii Taimai* (1901), the old chieftess of the Tewa clan, into which Adams had been adopted. But references to the visual arts are lacking in this book, which compares in this respect unfavorably with Gauguin's writings in which, probably for the first time, Polynesian art was treated as an esthetic object and not as an ethnological curio.

Only one passage in Adams' letters deals with Polynesian art more or less extensively: "They have no other arts worth mentioning. Some day I will tell you of their straw mats, their chief artistic pride; their houses, too, are artistic in their way, and their taste in colours is splendidly bold; but their real art is social."[74] Fine *mats* —Adams purchased one—were mentioned again in another letter; he received some as presents, as well as a tapa and wooden bowls, as a matter of courtesy.[75] He was "surprised to find the Fijian native house quite the finest yet seen . . . the decoration shows taste, and the dignity of it is really something pretty effective."[76] He compared it to the Samoan house, which he fittingly described as a "turtle-back on posts."[77] That is all there is about art!

It can hardly be said that Adams turned painter in the South Seas; at least such a contention would be a gross exaggeration. His attempts to draw and to paint in watercolor were likewise strictly those of a dilettante. Yet, through the desire to master the dazzling phenomenon of color by means of brush, paper, water and pigment, however inadequate, he came to experience color. One has the impression that up to this time, despite his interest in English watercolors, he had seen the world and its reflection in painting chiefly as line and mass. He started out as a print collector, in the black and white manner of photography, the art he mastered so well himself. From now on color became the prime motor of his esthetic sense, and led him to the miracles of Byzantine mosaics and medieval stained glass. He shared this enthusiasm for pure and intense color with his contemporaries, the Impressionists; but since he saw in the art of his own time only decadence, he failed to acknowledge it. Only in the watercolors and gouaches of his mentor La Farge, done before his own eyes in the South Seas, did he appreciate that phenomenon.

Adams' lessons in watercolor started as early as the railroad trip to San Francisco for embarkation to the South Seas. He wrote to Mabel La Farge:

I am trying to learn something about watercolours, so that I can sketch with you when I come home. La Farge instructs me, and I dabble already in blues and browns. All yesterday I labored to attain sage green for the sage-brush. Of course I do not try yet to draw; all my ambition is limited to finding out what the colors are. I think I know cobalt and indigo as the result of one lesson, but am not quite sure, for La Farge seems to use any color that comes handy, and it always turns out purple.

He discussed his teacher's color sense and enthusiasm in the same letter: "La Farge does nothing but ejaculate 'By Jove,' and 'Adams, look at that!' and 'Just see the color of that pig-stye' or 'Now we're getting into yellow again' or 'What is the color of that sky,' just when I think it's pure cobalt, and he sees sixteen different shades of red in it."[78]

But Adams did not take up the brush in earnest before they reached Honolulu. "My sketches are very funny," he wrote. "The only trouble is that no painter that ever lived could begin to catch the lights and colors of this island. I have learned enough to understand what can't be done, but La Farge makes wonderful purple attempts to do it, though he knows how absurd it is."[79] "Our Garden in Honolulu," one of the few of these sketches by Adams still in existence, was formerly in the possession of Mrs. Mabel La Farge at Mount Carmel, Connecticut, who wrote that it was "almost painfully, historically labored, not the work of an artist but of a historian." Adams himself described his watercolor diversions in a letter to Elizabeth Cameron as looking "like young ladies' embroidery of the last generation," and added ironically, "I cannot reach so far into high art, and only try to do like Turner or Rembrandt, or something easy and simple, which ends in my drawing a very bad copy of my own ignorance; but it has the charm that I felt as a boy about going fishing; I recognize that I am catching no fish on this particular day, but I feel always as though I might get a bite to-morrow."[80]

He included small drawings in his letters to his niece; of a beach scene in Samoa he wrote, "If I dared, I would stick in a native or two, or some children playing." But the dilettante was afraid to tackle figures. With the same letter he inserted a watercolor ("after a small photograph") of two girls in a canoe and admonished his niece, "but don't you show my colored things! If you let them be seen by anyone . . . I will never write you another line. I let you have my pictures because you children show me yours, which is fair exchange; but other people would think I was seriously intending to paint, and I don't want other people to think anything about it."[81]

In the letter Mrs. La Farge mentioned another drawing, "a very small thing of palm trees in the middle of the writing," and noted, "this one I like the best though it is the least." It was probably freer in technique and not so labored. Adams must have made progress as a painter, despite his testimony to the contrary, at least in the handling of the watercolor medium and in dealing with color under La Farge's guidance: "He has taught me to feel the subtleness and endless variety of charm in the colour and light of every hour in the tropical islands day and night."[82] He joked that in the future art experts might attribute his work to La Farge:

> I painted her [Haapi's] native house or hut [at Tautira], and tacked my picture on the wall of our residence, where it was vastly admired by the whole village, and will, I am sure, be sworn to be a genuine La Farge whenever they find out that La Farge's pictures are more esteemed than mine. La Farge was jealous of my popularity, and so he set to work and painted a big pandanus fruit dropping to pieces so naturally that the whole village flocked to see it, and never looked at my picture any more. He will be sorry when my picture is bought by a New York picture dealer as a La Farge for a thousand dollars. Still, I don't paint as well as I did. I do less well all the time, since my first little sketch that I sent to you. By and bye I hope to paint badly enough to be a professional and exhibit my pictures though it is very hard to paint as bad as that.[83]

What Adams had gained from his experiments in watercolor was stated in all sincerity in a letter to Elizabeth Cameron:

> My own calm has not been much disturbed of late, and I go on, trying every day to make pictures, and every day learning, as one does in a new language, a word or two more, just to show that the thing is laughable. Still, I have learned enough, from La Farge's instructions, to make me look at painting rather from the inside, and see a good many things about a picture that I only felt before. Perhaps this is worth while. Perhaps it isn't. I don't know, and think I don't care.[84]

If and in what manner Adams continued to paint in watercolor is not certain. He seems to have lost his enthusiasm while on his trip through the South Seas. He wrote from Papeete to Mabel La Farge, "La Farge is hard at work painting; but I have got tired of trying to sketch what I don't know how, and so I do nothing at all."[85]

Only once again was a desire to sketch mentioned in his letters, while staying in Dos Bocas, Cuba: "As for sketching, everything is so picturesque that I cannot begin. I need something simple, with broad lines, and no drawing. . . . My attempts are more humorous than ever."[86] Yet, though no evidence of later work by Adams can be ascertained, uncle and niece talked and wrote about watercolors like two professionals. La Farge's *Considerations on Painting* (1895) prompted him to write to Mabel Hooper, "I have read La Farge's lectures and I am going straight down to buy a new watercolor outfit."[87] Finally, in the letter to her of 8 July 1894, Adams gave technical details about the selection and mixing of watercolors as he had seen La Farge do it.[88]

It is very probable that Adams destroyed his drawings and watercolors and that only the few given away as presents to his friends might be still in existence. His nephew Charles Francis Adams wrote: "To the best of my knowledge and belief Henry Adams never painted any watercolours which could be called works of art. He may have made a few sketches and given them away during his lifetime but there was nothing of this sort divided after his death." Mabel La Farge, who owned a few of the sketches, graciously wrote me about them:

I remembered my uncle showing me his watercolors a few years before he died and telling me about the circumstances of doing some of them very shyly. The first ones, that he tried, were very labored and meticulous, trying conscientiously to get in everything—then through my father-in-law's influence he gradually limbered up a bit and did some nice things in the South Sea. If you will read things he said to me about painting in his "Letters to a Niece" you will get some idea of his tender encouragement, to the budding young in the arts. There was no one like him for encouragement and understanding. I brought him all my youthful things, and he in return showed me his. He put some of his with mine meaning, I supposed, that after his death they would be returned to me with mine—none of them came, so I suppose the Adamses had them, but Mr. [Charles Francis] Adams writes me that they have none, so I suppose, he must have destroyed them after he had shown them to me. Neither he nor I think Henry Adams ever intended or would care to have his things seen and their destruction seems to prove this. I feel somewhat the same way and the three tiniest things, he sent me from the South Seas in letters, I would feel disloyal to his trust to show. One, of their garden in Honolulu is almost painfully, historically labored, not the work of an artist but of a historian, another tiniest, two girls in a canoe, and the only remaining one in the letter itself of a very small thing of palm trees in the middle of the writing—this one I like the best though it is the least.

I remember a little bunch of violets he had received from a child, painted as a memory—labored too thus, but touching in sentiment. And I remember the words he said when I showed him a childhood's effort of mine of a sea in purples and blues: "Thou little child on whom those truths do rest that we are toiling all our life to find."

You can imagine how stimulating such encouragement, such humility from a very great man, was to a child.

I think that is almost all I can tell you. I wish it were much more. Such a combination of heart and mind I never expect to experience again.

It is evident that sketching was not much more than a diversion to Henry Adams, and that not too much importance should be attached to it.

All the time the search for *the last word in humanity* went on, and it brought Adams ever closer to the home of Buddha. The travelers returned from the South Seas via Java and Ceylon, both islands in which the style of the Gupta period, spreading from India, created some of the greatest examples of religious sculpture of all times. But strangely enough, Adams failed to mention important examples of Buddhist sculpture in his letters, though his mind was presumably then occupied with the memorial figure for Rock Creek Cemetery, the realization of which under the hands of Saint-Gaudens absorbed so much of his thoughts about Buddha and Nirvana. Perhaps the lack of time—they spent only about two weeks in Java—accounts for the fact that they did not visit Barabudor, certainly the most grandiose architectural-sculptural symbol of Buddhism in East Asia. La Farge alone went ashore to visit the island of Bali. But Bali was then not yet the over-advertised beauty spot in the Indian Ocean.

Adams disliked the colonial Dutch and the colonial style in

Batavia, which he called "The Hague overrun by hordes of Malays —Buitenzorg the Sans Souci of Batavia." His judgment was certainly incorrect when he wrote: "I expected signs of old civilization, but not a bit. Not a temple or a shrine or a trace of thought; no architecture except huts less interesting than the Fijian or Samoan; no nothing. . . . Java is Japan without everything that makes Japan interesting." La Farge bought silks, cloths, and costumes, but even the superb Javanese textiles failed to impress Adams, who referred to his friend's "coveting any rubbish he sees."[89]

Ceylon had preserved Buddhism in its purest form. Henry Adams called it "the most interesting and beautiful island we have seen, taking its many-sided interests into account. . . . Ceylon is what I supposed Java to be, and it was not—a combination of rich nature and varied human interest, a true piece of voluptuous creativeness." Yet the art of the island did not fulfill his expectations. The temple of the Sacred Tooth in Kandy was a "sad disappointment after the Japanese temples," and he continued: "The art is poor, rather mean, and quite modern, and even the golden shrine of the Tooth had little to recommend it except one or two cat's eyes. Occasionally a refined piece of stone carving—a doorway or threshold—built into a coarse plaster wall, shows where some older temple has been used for modern ornament, and gives an idea that Ceylon had refinement in the thirteenth century."[90]

They went to Anuradhapura to study the remains of that older, "more refined" civilization, where Buddha "flourished two thousand years ago":

This then was Anuradhapura; the bo-tree; six dagobas with relics; and one or two temples more or less Brahmanic, that is, rather for Siva and Vishnu than for Buddha, though Buddhism ran here a good deal into Brahmanism. As long as Buddhism flourished, Anuradhapura flourished, and the kings went on building tanks, both for bathing and for irrigation, some of the irrigation tanks being immense lakes, with many miles of embankment. When Buddhism declined, the place went gradually to pieces and nothing but what was almost indestructable remains. Of course we cared little for the historical or industrial part of the affair, but came here to see the art, which is older than anything in India [which is incorrect] and belongs to the

earliest and probably purest Buddhist times; for Anuradhapura was the centre of Buddhism even then. I expected—
never mind what—all sorts of things—which I have not found.
To my surprise and disappointment, all the art seems to me
pretty poor and cheap. Compared with Egypt or even with Japan, Ceylon is second rate. The huge brick dagobas were laid out
on a large scale, with a sense of proportion that must have been
artistic, but the want of knowledge or use of the arch makes the
result uninteresting. The details are not rich; the stone carving
is not fine; the statues are not numerous or very imposing even
in size; and all the stone-work, even the bathing tanks, is so
poorly and cheaply done, without mortar, riveting or backing,
that it can't hold itself up. I have hunted for some-thing to admire, but except the bigness, I am left cold. Not a piece of work,
big or small, have I seen that has a heart to it. The place was a
big bazaar of religion, made for show and profit. Any country
shrine has more feeling in it than this whole city seems to have
shown.[91]

This criticism, too, went beyond the mark. Not only was it incorrect to blame the Indians for lack of knowledge of the arch, but
most of the destruction was due to the terrific force of jungle growth
and not to bad workmanship. The sculpture, which was later removed
to the museum in Colombo, is of the very finest quality. Here again
the expectation was so great, the hope to find "all sorts of things" so
intense, that reality remained behind it. And he went through the
mock ceremony of "sitting under the sacred bodhi tree for half an
hour, hoping to attain Nirvana," but "left the bo-tree without attain-
ing Buddhaship." There were also bitter words in the same letter:
"I have no longer any hope of finding real art in Ceylon; even the
oldest looks to me mechanical, as though it were imported, and paid
by the superficial area; but we want to be sure, we have seen all the
styles, and the rock temple is a style."[91] He described the rock temple
in another letter. Probably because of his disappointment in Buddhist art, which he undervalued, he then overvalued that of the so-
called Hindu Renaissance:

To me the only interesting remains in the place were not Buddhist at all, but a very old rock-temple of Brahma, where the
artists had made some really well-felt attempts to please and
honour their favorite deity Siva—either him or some other in-

carnation, I think it matters little what. I regret to say that artistically, in Ceylon, unlike Japan, Buddha is a bore and a big one. More than that, he always was a bore.[92]

The last part of the statement about Buddhist art in Ceylon has to be taken in the sense of Adamsian irony, and it is certainly not consistent with his earlier statement from Singapore about the superiority of East Asiatic over Western art. That remark was made on the occasion of a comparison between Chinese architecture and a neo-Gothic stone church there "with one or two bronze statues of English art" which "showed how bad our art is." He continued: "One always doubts a little in Europe or America, whether a statue, a picture or a building may not, after all, have some good point that might save it from sweeping damnation; but here one feels without reasoning or wasting time about it—that our art is wholly, in big and small, artificial and hopeless."[93]

Should one take this damning judgment of Western art at its face value, or see in it just another of Adams' quick and sweeping generalizations? Its sincerity, however, need not be questioned. Such statements were products of the emotions felt then and there. Furthermore, it is not clear whether by *our art* he meant merely the European and American art of his own time, or the whole of Western art. Were the latter true, it must look strange, indeed, that on his very first trip to Europe after the Asiatic journey, he should finally come in Normandy face to face with *the last word in humanity*, revealed to him in medieval art of the eleventh through the thirteenth centuries.

The revelation, though sudden, came not quite unexpected and not without preparation. Adams' relations to the Middle Ages go back to his very first trip to Europe, to his first stay in Antwerp and in medieval German towns. It is certain, however, that he needed the detour via Asia to become aware of certain values he had never been so conscious of before; the greatness of an archaic, generally non-realistic art, and its ground in a profound spirituality—in religion.

5. Mont-Saint-Michel and Chartres

(Medieval Art as
Manifestation of the Spirit;
Published Sources)

*T*he trip to Normandy was undertaken with the family of Adams' former pupil Henry Cabot Lodge, the historian and senator, in the late summer of 1895. It led from the Norman churches, especially Mont-Saint-Michel, to Chartres. The impression was immediate and strong, and started Adams, then on the threshold of old age, on the road to a new interest, a new goal for the remaining years of his life. The tourist's interest grew into the plan for a book, *Mont-Saint-Michel and Chartres* (hereafter called *Chartres*), which became the final confession of a life's search for unity, for the meaning of life and the universe. His letters and *Education* register the growing realization of his having found at least a new focus for the search. He wrote to Charles M. Gaskell in September:

> The Normandy trip turned out well . . . I am sure that in the eleventh century the majority of me was Norman . . . Going back now to the old associations seems to me as easy as drinking champagne. All is natural, reasonable, complete and satisfactory. Coutances and St. Michel show neither extravagance nor want of practical sense. They are noble . . . but they are not like later Gothic, self-conscious or assuming. They knew their own force, perfectly well; measured it to a hair; gave to the ideal all it had a right to expect, and looked out for the actual with a perfectly cool head.[1]

A long letter to John Hay from Paris later in September reiterated these ideas.[2] He had written to Elizabeth Cameron in August,

"I worshipped at last before the splendor of the great glass Gods. Chartres is a beautiful gate by which to leave the Norman paradise."[3] Adams' *Letters to a Niece* contains the most enthusiastic and most personal lines about the new esthetic thrill or shock which comes only rarely to a man and opens new vistas, gives new directions:

> We thought Coutances the most charming of all these places, but perhaps it was only a surprise. The Norman cathedral there was something quite new to me, and humbled my proud spirit a good bit. I had not thought myself so ignorant or so stupid as to have remained blind to such things, being more or less within sight of them now for nearly forty years. I thought I knew Gothic. Caen, Bayeux and Coutances were a chapter I never opened before, and which pleased my jaded appetite. They are austere. They have, outside, little of the vanity of Religion. Inside, they are worked with a feeling and devotion that turns even Amiens green with jealousy. I knew before pretty well all that my own life and time was worth, but I never before felt quite so utterly stood on, as I did in the Cathedral at Coutances. . . . On Saturday we came on to Mont-Saint-Michel . . . It is the Church Militant, but if Coutances expressed the last—or first— word of Religion, as an emotion of self-abasement, Mont-Saint-Michel lifted one up to a sort of Sir Galahad in its mixture of sword and cross . . . and, last of all, two long hours at Chartres on a lovely summer afternoon, with the sun flaming behind St. Anne, David, Solomon, Nebuchadnezzar, and the rest, in the great windows of the north transept. No austerity there, inside or out, except in the old south tower and spire which still pro- tests against mere humanity.[4]

Quite a few of the leading ideas of the future book were touched upon in these letters and will be referred to later in the analysis of *Chartres*. Adams reviewed these summer weeks of happy discovery in his *Education*:

> Where Mrs. Lodge summoned, one followed with gratitude, and so it chanced, that in August one found one's self for the first time at Caen, Coutances and Mont-Saint-Michel in Normandy. If history had a chapter with which he thought himself familiar, it was the twelfth and thirteenth centuries; yet so little has labor to do with knowledge that these bare playgrounds of the lecture system turned into green and verdurous virgin forests merely through the medium of younger eyes and fresher minds. His

German bias must have given his youth a terrible twist, for the Lodges saw at a glance what he had thought unessential because un-German. . . . One could not at first see what this novelty meant; it had the air of mere antiquarian emotion like Wenlock Abbey . . . but it expelled archaic law and antiquarianism once for all, without seeming conscious of it; and Adams drifted back to Washington with a new sense of history.[5]

In both his letters and *Education* Adams stated he knew the Middle Ages before, or ought to know them, but that from then on he not only saw them and history, but also life with new eyes. It seems worthwhile, therefore, to review the medieval monuments, especially architectural, that Adams had seen prior to his first Norman trip in 1895. To the young student fresh from Harvard and attuned to teutonic romanticism, Antwerp, his first European town, seemed medieval in 1858:

The thirteenth-century cathedral towered above a sixteenth-century mass of tiled roofs, ending abruptly in walls and a landscape that had not changed. The taste of the town was thick, rich, ripe, like a sweet wine; it was mediaeval, so that Rubens seemed modern; it was one of the strongest and fullest flavors that ever touched the young man's palate . . . He merely got drunk on his emotions, and had then to get sober as he best could. He was terribly sober when he saw Antwerp half a century afterwards.[6]

In rich, compressed language, strangely anticipating Thomas Wolfe's style, Adams tried in these lines of his *Education* to evoke what was forever lost, and unable to do so, at least caught its flavor —*thick, rich, ripe, like a sweet wine*. He discovered the Middle Ages even in predominantly baroque Antwerp because he wanted to find them there, because he expected them there. It was the same with Germany: "Until coal power and railways were created, she was mediaeval by nature and geography, and this was what Adams under the teachings of Carlyle and Lowell, liked."[7]

A few pages later in his *Education* he noted that he "conscientiously did his cathedrals, his Rhine."[8] On a hiking tour through Thuringia, "his heart singing like a bird,"[9] he visited Eisenach and the "Old Wartburg above . . . covered with romance and with history until it's as rich as a wedding cake."[10] He traveled in Franconia,

6. Adams House, 1603 H Street, N.W., Washington, D.C., in 1907. Reproduced from the Collections of the Library of Congress.

7. Entrance Hall, John Hay House, Washington, D.C. From a photograph in Mariana G. van Rensselaer's *Henry Hobson Richardson and his Works*, 1888. Reproduced from the Collections of the Library of Congress.

"with old road-side saints, crucifixes and Madonnas," and saw Bamberg and its cathedral.[11] He went to Nuremberg, "to Duerer and old Peter Vischer, the churches and the streets, the glorious old windows and the charming fountains."[12] On a visit in 1901 he recalled this first one nostalgically—"This was one of my first delights in art way back in '59."[13]

Adams was eager to show his young bride the medieval sights of Germany and took her on a Rhine trip in 1872, and from there via Bavaria into Switzerland. Yet, as she wrote in a letter to her father, Marian Adams thought celebrated Cologne Cathedral "extremely ugly, the only impressive part being the size."[14] In Augsburg they "take first a church, then an antiquity shop, next a museum";[15] in Basel they saw the Holbeins.[16]

On his later trip to Germany in 1901, when he visited Heidelberg, Würzburg, and Rothenburg, Adams summed up his earlier impressions of Germanic towns. From Bayreuth, where he had gone to hear Wagner, he wrote to Elizabeth Cameron after a visit to Rothenburg:

> When I came first abroad in '58 all the towns were Rothenburgs. Antwerp, Nürnberg, even Strasbourg, looked just as mediaeval or nearly so. Inside, they were much more so. I felt as though I must have been really thirteenth-century and all but me departed . . . Really, too, there is some very excellent carving in astonishing good condition, at Rothenburg, in the churches, and even three large windows of good fourteenth century glass. There are some interesting houses, and bits running back to the 12th and even to the 11th, so that I was not wholly abandoned. —To be sure, it is not French, but very near it; and it made me wonder once more that in my own golden day, even Germans and English were almost as artistic as other people, and in the same exact simple style which I was wont to delight myself.[17]

The next in time to offer an education in medieval art was English Gothic. But Adams, as previously noted, seems to have been little impressed by it, possibly because so many of his countrymen were overwhelmed by the Gothic of their forebears. It was certainly not caused by lack of knowledge or encouragement, since his most intimate English friend, Charles Milnes Gaskell, was an enthusiastic connoisseur and owner of a medieval place, Wenlock Abbey in Shrop-

shire, which Adams often visited, first in 1864. It included several
monastic buildings, among them "the Prior's house, a charming
specimen of fifteenth-century architecture."[18] In a letter to her father
Marian gave a detailed description of Wenlock Abbey, calling the
Norman wing eight hundred years old.[19] In connection with restoration work at the abbey, the two friends corresponded about the construction of medieval roofs, yet English medieval art somehow
failed to click with Adams.[20] But this was originally also the case
with French medieval architecture, as indicated in the letter to a
niece quoted above.

Adams' next contact with the art of the Middle Ages occurred
when he was teaching at Harvard. In a much later letter (1912) to
Raymond Weeks, professor of Romance languages and literature at
Yale, he spoke of his "interest in mediaeval matters which was neces-
sarily active when [teaching] mediaeval history at Harvard College
in 1872," but was "now merely dilettante."[21] He was referring to
those interests which lay outside political, ecclesiastic, and juridical
history, and concerned the arts. Mention should also be made of
Lowell's long poem *The Cathedral,* a glorification of Chartres, the
publication of which fell into Adams' early Harvard teaching years
and which he doubtlessly knew. But though its mood strongly pre-
sages that of Adams' own *Chartres,* as Samuels noted, the poem can
have affected Adams only years later, if at all.[22] In his article "The
Mediaevalism of Henry Adams," Herbert L. Creek was undoubtedly
correct about Adams' teaching at Harvard; "this early excursion into
the Middle Ages left no real monument and apparently had little
immediate effect on the intellectual and emotional life of the man."[23]
Adams was then and during the following years engaged in writing
his monumental *American History.*

Adams did not begin his researches on the art and philosophy
of the Middle Ages in earnest until four years after he had received
the initial stimulus of the Norman trip. The gestation of *Chartres*
can be followed step by step in his letters and *Education.* It was the
fruit of his "Indian Summer." In the fifteenth chapter of his *Education,* which bears that appealing title, he described the circumstances
under which the book was born:

> Solitude did what the society did not—it forced and drove him
> into the study of his ignorance in silence. Here at last he entered

the practice of his final profession. Hunted by ennui, he could no longer escape, and, by way of a summer school, he began a methodical survey—a triangulation—of the twelfth century. The pursuit had a singular French charm which France had long lost—a calmness, lucidity, simplicity of expression, vigor of action, complexity of local color, that made Paris flat. In the long summer days one found a sort of saturated green pleasure in the forests, and gray infinity of rest in the little twelfth-century churches that lined them, as unassuming as their own mosses, as sure of their purpose as their round arches; but churches were many and summer was short, so that he was at last driven back to the quays and photographs. For weeks he lived in silence.[24]

These art trips were taken with friends, with Henry Cabot Lodge into the immediate surroundings of Paris, with Saint-Gaudens to Amiens to view the sculpture, and with La Farge to Chartres to study the glass. He probably owed most to La Farge's guidance. Elizabeth Cameron's house in Paris, which was at his disposal for a while, turned into "a gay library of twelfth century architecture."[25] He described his studies in a letter to her: "My photographs too are an occupation, and by the way a fairly expensive one. The mere clochers and flèches number hundreds in the Monuments Historiques series alone. Your rooms are becoming a school of romanesque architecture. Volumes lie about the floor."[26] Similarly he wrote to Gaskell:

> While you have been doing your Houses, I've not yet got lower than twelfth-century churches. It will take me a year or two more to get back to the last century. I am making a collection of twelfth-century spires. They are singularly amusing, and, for afternoon walks or drives in summer, are quite delightful. There are dozens within easy reach of Paris, all culminating in the Chartres spire. I find that I always get back to the twelfth century when left to myself. It is like the Greek in the Mediterranean. One finds nothing else in the long run which supplies mass with quality to make a long run.[27]

The winter of 1899-1900 was spent in Washington. In a letter of the first of February to Cecil Spring-Rice he looked back on the preceding summer and the work done at that time:

> As for myself, after passing the summer in the twelfth century, thinking only of Norman clochers and flèches and of choirs and

glass; after scouring the country round Paris for twelfth-century churches, and after attending service at Chartres most of the Sundays, I was rudely disturbed by the return of winter and Mrs. Cameron, who ejected me from my summer-quarters and drove me across the winter-ocean.[28]

During the summer of 1900 studies were resumed in France. They were devoted chiefly to the writings of St. Thomas Aquinas.[29] Adams read metaphysics and called the study of St. Thomas "a side-play to my interest in twelfth-century spires and Chartres Cathedral."[30] We shall see how this *side-play* occupied the center of the stage more and more, and finally became the spiritual spire which rose from the foundations of twelfth century architecture. The sources are silent about the subject for the next two and a half years. Then a letter of February 1903 to Elizabeth Cameron noted:

[The] twelfth-century manuscript has swelled and swelled to the size of an ox, so that I can't afford to print it, as I meant. A private edition of fifty copies could cost at least fifteen hundred dollars, and I prefer Ming potiches. Think of giving up twenty Ming potiches for the vanity of a twentieth volume! As for publishing it at the expense of a thief in calf-binding, the idea is worse than shameful. My only hope of heaven is the Virgin. If I tried to vulgarize her and make her as cheap as cow-boy literature, I should ask for eternal punishment as a favor. Magazine literature would be noble, compared with mine.[31]

Thereafter the writing progressed rapidly and was finished in March 1903, according to a letter of the fifteenth to Elizabeth Cameron: "My great work on the Virgin is complete even to the paging, and I have no occupation."[32] And he wrote to her on 31 January 1904, "I am going to put my Chartres into type; it will serve to amuse me till May."[33] Yet adverse circumstances delayed the printing. Adams had sent manuscript and money to Baltimore, where both apparently suffered from fire.[34] As it turned out, he "lost only a few chapters and a month's time."[35]

The impressions derived in the summer of 1904 on his first motor tour of the French cathedrals could not have appeared in the original version of the book, yet the purchase of an eighteen-horsepower Mercedes and "the mad run through the centuries"[36] marked a turning point in his approach. (A second motor trip to the familiar places was taken in June 1908.[37]) In December 1904 he wrote to Gaskell:

Talking of Thomas Aquinas, I have just finished printing my Miracle de la Vierge. The book will run up to a pretty bulky size, but I print only a hundred copies, one of which will be for you. It is my declaration of principles of the Conservative Christian Anarchists; a party numbering one member. The Virgin and St. Thomas are my vehicles of anarchism.[38]

As to its character and aim, he denied it was a book, claiming "it is only a running chatter with my nieces and those of us who care for old art." But that was definitely an understatement, or as he called it in the same letter, "self-depreciation."[39] He held to his role of an uncle to nieces, however, when he wrote to Gaskell again:

I will send you the volume you want. I had quite forgotten having mentioned it to you, since showing you the Abelard chapter. It was meant only for nieces and women, for men no longer read at all, and I've given only to men who asked for it. Indeed I've not given it even to my brothers and nephews. They borrow it from their women-folk, if they want it. Of course it is not for the public.[40]

But secretly he seems to have been proud of *Chartres.* He was more satisfied with it than with any of his earlier writings and he preferred it by far to his later *Education.*[41] He confirmed that preference in a letter to Raphael Pumpelly, geologist and collector of Japanese art, who had asked for a copy of *Education*:

The only book I ever wrote that was worth writing was the first volume of the Series—the Mont-Saint-Michel. The volume began the demonstration of the law which this "Letters [to American Teachers of History]" announces, and the Education illustrates. Unluckily the women took a fancy to the Mont-St.-Michel, and begged the whole lot.—I've given them all away, and barely had enough to supply a few libraries besides.[42]

And when the public began to clamor for *Chartres*, Adams wrote to Gaskell: "Having given away all my copies of my volume on 'Chartres,' I am now reprinting it, for it has become a favorite book with the Professors of Middle-age art and literature, so that they worry me for copies . . . so I spend my vast wealth lavishly on printing as a form of senile vice. It comes high, so I don't keep an auto."[43] One of those *Professors* was Frederick Bliss Luquiens of Yale, to whom he explained he did not care "to make the 'Chartres' volume a mercantile affair . . . because the inspiration of the period is religious and therefore not possible to teach."[44]

The first reprinting of the volume in 1912 was—as a compromise—done "secretly." Before Adams attempted it he tried "to find out what now has been learned in seven years" since the first printing, and went on to say, "this really amuses me, and of course leads to long correspondence."[45] The letter to Luquiens showed Adams' anxiety to be correct in the matter of Thomist philosophy: "I care far more for my theology than for my architecture, and should be much mortified if detected in an error about Thomas Aquinas or the doctrine of universals."[46]

The completion of the revised edition was announced in a letter to Elizabeth Cameron of January 1912. "At last I've finished! My final proof-sheets are sent off; my final occupation is ended."[47] And later he wrote to her in the same vein: "Having sent off thirty copies of my new 'Chartres' to public libraries and universities, I feel as if my last peg were driven into life, and nothing remains to do."[48]

Yet there was a postlude: the final publication in 1913 for the use of the general public, undertaken by the American Institute of Architects, and prefaced by Ralph Adams Cram. Adams *complained* about this to Elizabeth Cameron.[49] He called it *theft*[50] and he *kicked*,[51] but he was amused by his late literary fame and by the fact that the papers reviewed him as a youthful beginner,[52] since "not one has yet been aware that [I] ever wrote anything else."[53] The book turned out to be a popular success. More than any other art book published in the United States, it made the public conscious of the Middle Ages. Even at the time of the Normandy invasion, American war correspondents visited the Mount with *Chartres* in their pocket. Noting the great influence of the book upon the American reading public, Van Wyck Brooks wrote, "Adams was astonished to find himself 'a leader of a popular movement with [his] Chartres as Evangel and Ralph Adams Cram for St. John Baptist.'" The same author explained its great success in the years following World War I: "A younger generation has risen, who shared the despair of the present, and thousands who, like him, had lost their faith, were turning, as he turned, to the Middle Ages."[54]

The preceding account of the gestation of *Chartres* and its final writing and publication has already introduced some of its material, its leading ideas, its aim and character, and even to some extend its structure. We shall now deal with all these aspects more extensively and critically, reviewing the first ten chapters of the book, those concerned with the visual arts.

Chartres as a whole is difficult to classify. It definitely is not, as has often been assumed, a book on art history, although it has been included in the selected bibliography of one of our most popular art history texts, since the knowledge of the facts of art history and art historical research are avowedly not its objective.[55] *Chartres* does not even attempt to offer absolute accuracy in this specific field. It certainly cannot compete with the very specialized publications on the art history of the Middle Ages, especially with those published since 1913. It is not even an up-to-date monograph on the abbey church of Mont-Saint-Michel or the cathedral of Chartres. Neither is it a comprehensive history of medieval literature, art, philosophy and religion. It is less and more than all this. It might be characterized as offering some ideas on the interrelationship of French medieval art and religion from the eleventh to the thirteenth century. It has two heroes—or heroines—art and religion, which are supposed to make up a perfect unity during the period in question.

One has the feeling that during the process of writing, the book grew way beyond its original plan and intention to be the informal travel talk of an art tourist, or an art-uncle for nieces with Kodaks. At a certain point it almost ceases to deal with esthetic experiences and becomes a confession of a seeker after unity, of a pilgrim who hopes to find in the Middle Ages an emotional repose—peace—Nirvana.

And just this breaking through by breaking away, its very apparent elusiveness and ambiguity of purpose, make for the attraction, the uniqueness of *Chartres*. It is a book which all the time pretends to be light while it is not, a piece of writing which presents itself informally as a running chatter while it is firmly and formally constructed. Although there are fissures in the construction—after the tenth chapter and again after the thirteenth—the building remains standing aloft. The visual arts, although done with after the tenth

chapter, supply the socle for the remaining parts. Had *Chartres* remained only a book on some phase of the visual arts, had Adams
stuck to his guns, the book would have lost its value today. The
fifth and seventh through tenth chapters, in which the book (made
heavy by too much description and secondhand dispensing of ar-
cheological information) loses momentum, alone would probably be
found boring. But since it goes on to religious-philosophical heights,
even the barren but often indispensable facts and dates of these
weaker chapters take on an afterglow of value and meaning.

Although Adams deviated from his initial plan, he must have had
the ideas which were developed in the last three philosophical
chapters at the back of his mind, as the letters written immediately
after his first Normandy trip indicate. Thus, using philosophy in the
approach to esthetic objects guarantees the final unity of content and
form of *Chartres*. The *leitmotiv* of the book, that art and religion
are really states of mind (*Kunstgeschichte als Geistesgeschichte*, as
the Austrian Max Dvorak formulated it later and independently),
was conceived even before the Normandy trip.[56] In *Esther*, Adams'
novel written more than a decade before that trip, the Reverend
Hazard, who bears a marked spiritual kinship to Adams himself, "in
regard to art was so full of its relations with religion that he would
admit of no divergence between the two."[57] And he entertained
thirteenth-century ideas; this is the phrase Adams used so often,
after he had taken up his studies of the Middle Ages, to describe
his own mind—if he did not call it *eighteenth-century*.

The theme of *Chartres*, that art and religion are one or become
one in the Middle Ages, is clearly stated in a letter to Albert S. Cook:
"I wanted to show the intensity of the vital energy of a given time,
and of course that intensity had to be stated in its two highest terms
—religion and art."[58] The same idea is expressed in the book itself:
"Religious art is the measure of human depth and sincerity."[59]

Representing the esthetic type, Adams first experienced religion
through the medium of the visual and tactile art object. Yet in the
process of the book's writing, all that is matter evaporates into pure
spirit. In that way *Chartres'* building stones, its foundations and
façades so to speak, selected by the chance process of very personal
interests, not to say prejudices, lead up to the convergent lines of the

religious-philosophical steeple of immaterial thought. There, in the last chapter on St. Thomas, they touch the infinite. This process of transformation of matter into spirit takes place by grace of the Virgin who, being both body and spirit according to Adams, acts as the main support, as the middle pillar, as the *trumeau* at the cathedral's gate.

To Adams the cathedral is the embodiment and realization of medieval thought. The summit of medieval systematic thinking in St. Thomas' *Summa Theologiae* reveals itself to him in the shape of a cathedral. Part of the medieval synthesis is just this interdependence of art and religion. Thus one may be justified in observing that Adams' book *Chartres* is structured like the cathedral of Chartres. (See Chart I.)

Adams himself came to the conclusion that the whole book culminates in the final chapters. He wrote to William James: "The three last chapters are alone worth reading, and of course are never read."[60] As the skeleton outline shows, the book is far from treating the Middle Ages or even the medieval humanities in their entirety, yet it deals with them as an entity or synthesis. It is, however, questionable whether such a synthesis can be presented without dealing with the entirety of the given period. On the other hand, emphasis or selection of the essentials is the privilege of an author who does not intend to be encyclopedic.

In *Chartres* the Middle Ages are limited in time, including only the eleventh through the thirteenth centuries. This selection not only was an unusual one, for previously the medieval periods of interest ranged from the thirteenth to the sixteenth centuries, but also provided a better focus for the understanding of the true Middle Ages of feudalism and the Crusades.

As for limitations in space, *Chartres* deals with France almost exclusively and only in the last three chapters includes the Italian Saints Francis and Thomas without, however, stressing their origin. The English, German, Scandinavian, or Spanish Middle Ages are barely mentioned or ignored. During the period covered in *Chartres*, European culture was international rather than national, and important contributions were certainly made to it by all its nationalities. On the other hand, France acted as a catalyst of all of them, and it can hardly be denied that statistically or quantitatively the highest flowering of medieval art took place there. But Adams' point of view was a novel one for an author who was neither French nor writing in

---

ORGANIZATION AND CONTENT OF
MONT-SAINT-MICHEL AND CHARTRES

A. Mont-Saint-Michel

    I. *Saint Michiel de la Mer del Peril* (general introduction)
   II. *La Chanson de Roland* (literary counterpart to the Mont)
  III. *The Merveille* (northern part of monastic compound)
  IV. *Normandy and the Ile de France* (their churches)

The first chapters provide the 11th century *Romanesque foundation* or *crypt*, strongly masculine, belonging to Michael and God the Father. IV leads to the façade, which is erected in subsequent chapters.

B. Chartres

    V. *Towers and Portals* (exterior)
   VI. *The Virgin of Chartres* (interior)
  VII. *Roses and Apses* (compared to those of other churches)
 VIII. *The Twelfth-Century Glass*
  IX. *The Legendary Windows*
   X. *The Court of the Queen of Heaven* (later glass at Chartres)

These six chapters constitute the *12th Century façade* of Chartres, the church of the Virgin built in the style transitional from Romanesque to Gothic.

C. History and Literature

  XI. *The Three Queens* (Blanche of Castile, Eleanor of Guienne, Mary of Champagne)
 XII. *Nicolette and Marion* (worldly literature)
XIII. *Les Miracles de Notre Dame* (ecclesiastic poetry and miracle tales)

These three chapters might be compared to the *nave roof and flanking clochers*, dealing with history as well as 12th century worldly and ecclesiastic poetry, stressing the female aspect.

D. Religious Philosophy

 XIV. *Abélard* (the great 12th century schoolman)
  XV. *The Mystics* (chiefly St. Francis)
XVI. *Saint Thomas Aquinas* ("Summa Theologiae")

The last three chapters provide the surmounting *steeples* of religious philosophy, representing the fully developed Gothic, belonging to the Trinity.

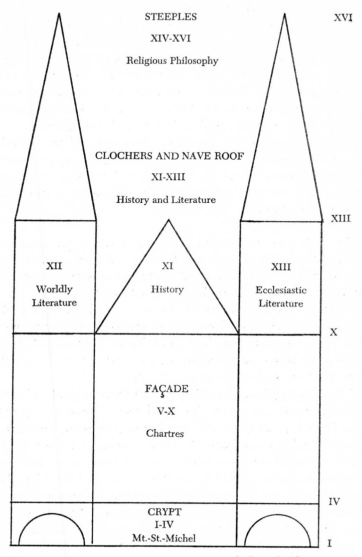

I. Organization of *Mont-Saint-Michel and Chartres*

French. Italy was the gateway to the art of the Middle Ages used by
English writers such as Ruskin and Norton.

A particular stroke of luck was Adams' arrival at Chartres by
way of the churches of Normandy. Although accidental, this turned
out to be a most fruitful approach to the evolution of medieval architecture from the Romanesque to the Gothic. The recognition of the
formative role of the Norman Romanesque element in the creation
of the French Gothic of the Ile-de-France is Adams' lasting contribution to the history of medieval architecture. Hans Sedlmayr, an in-
ternationally acknowledged expert on the origins of the cathedral,
wrote of *Chartres*: "It is questionable whether the spiritual difference between the Norman Romanesque and the Gothic has been
anywhere so profoundly and clearly seen. Knowledge is gained here
far ahead of its time."[61]

The fortunate and fruitful discovery of the importance of the
soldierly Romanesque is announced in the first chapter of the book,
"Saint Michiel de la Mer del Peril." It is effectively introduced in the
very first sentence, "The Archangel loved heights," which has the
simplicity and monumentality of the opening chord in a prelude
to an organ fugue. It is characteristic also of what was called the
visual bias in Adams' style. The short, lapidary, and yet lofty sentence sets the stage for a situation of formidable masculinity which
is not, however, without grace or airiness.

"The Archangel stands for Church and State and both militant."[62]
And the Archangel, as well as the casual visitor, "from the top of this
Abbey Church . . . looks across the bay to Avranches, and towards
Coutances and the Contentin."[63] These names, and those of other
Norman cathedral towns such as Caen and Bayeux, are now memorable to Americans since D-day of the summer of 1944. Mont-Saint-
Michel in particular became, to the American soldier who saw it for
the first time, the very embodiment of the Middle Ages. Like a plate
from a picture book turned into a visible three-dimensional reality,
it was the complete Middle Ages. There it stood, all piled on a rock
and emerging from the sea, a symbol of strength and victory. In this
respect, as in so many others, Adams possessed prophetic vision.

The factual side of the description does not interest us here; it follows closely Corroyer's monograph on the Mount and is adequate. Throughout the book Adams used easily accessible sources. He hardly ever turned to rare books and articles, and even less to original documents. (A reconstruction of the publications used for the art parts of *Chartres* is appended at the end of this chapter.) Original research, the digging for unknown facts, so masterly handled in his *American History,* was not his procedure in this book. About his use of sources he wrote to Luquiens: "We want to get at the atmosphere of the art, so we translate; but once we feel at home there, we throw away our scaffolding."[64] And in the book itself Adams repeatedly expressed his method and his aim in a similar way:

> We have set out to go from Mont-Saint-Michel to Chartres in three centuries, the eleventh, twelfth and thirteenth, trying to get on the way, not technical knowledge; not accurate information; not correct views either on history, art or religion; not anything that can possibly be useful or instructive; but only a sense of what those centuries had to say, and a sympathy of their ways of saying it.[65]

"For us, the world is not a schoolroom or a pulpit, but a stage."[66] "A tourist never should study, or he ceases to be a tourist."[67] And finally, since he saw he could not entirely get along without facts and dates and the atmosphere of the schoolroom, he broke into the apologetic remark: "Dates are stupidly annoying;—what we want is not dates but taste;—yet we are uncomfortable without them."[68]

The phrase, "a sense of what those centuries had to say," smacks somewhat of the Hegelian *Zeitgeist.* The evaluation of taste is the artist's approach, rather than that of the student of history: "True artists, turned critics, think also less of rules than of values."[69] In view of these warning statements, it would be unfair to search for small technical errors in fact and hold them against Adams. Robert A. Hume, whose *Runaway Star* contains the most understanding analysis of *Chartres,* supports this opinion by observing that it is not "offering a painstaking chronology of exact historical data," but recaptures "the vital, unified spirit of a lost age." He said further, "Artistically it matters little whether the unity of that previous age be real or mythical."[70]

Adams grasped connections of meaning and understanding intuitively after the most necessary facts had been supplied to him through books, and even more through personal observation on the spot. He found the cause for his immediate familiarity with Norman landscape and architecture in a mystical connection with blood and soil: "The hills and woods, the farms and fields of Normandy . . . so familiar, so homelike are they, one can almost take oath that in this, or the other, or in all, one knew life once and has never so fully known it since."[71] To explain this familiarity he said: "If you have any English blood at all, you have also Norman . . . helping to build the Abbey Church at Mont-Saint-Michel." And he addressed the Virgin in his *Prayer*:

> You, who remember all, remember me;
> An English scholar of Norman name,
> I was a thousand who then crossed the sea
> To wrangle in the Paris schools for fame.[72]

Since Adams' mind was attuned to the coordination of facts to ideas and memories, he saw immediately the connection between Mont-Saint-Michel and Monreale, the (holy) mount of St. Michael and the (royal) mount of the Viking-Norman kings, between North-west and Southeast, between the Viking in France and the Viking-turned-Arab in Sicily. Instead of the currently held nebulous ideas about the influence of the Orient on the Gothic, specifically the pointed arch, brought about by the Crusades, he stated clearly that this contact between West and East, Viking and Arab, actually took place at the beginning of the twelfth century in Sicily, in the churches and castles of Monreale, Palermo, and Cefalù: "Down nearly to the end of the twelfth century the Norman was fairly master of the world in architecture as in arms, although the thirteenth century belonged to France, and we must look for its glories on the Seine and Marne and Loire."[73] To Adams the eleventh and twelfth were the Norman centuries, the thirteenth the French century, and he saw the styles of these nationalities and centuries as distinguished from each other. They met in Chartres Cathedral. Thus he establishes the starting point of the evolution of northern French art a hundred years earlier than was usual, and moved it also a considerable distance to the northwest:

The west porch of Chartres, which is to be our peculiar pilgrimage, was a hundred years later than the groundplan of Mont-Saint-Michel [1020], although Chartres' porch is the usual starting-point of Northern French art. . . .

Compared with the great churches of the thirteenth century, this building [the abbey church of the Mount] is modest, but its size is not what matters to us. Its style is the starting-point of all our future travels. Here is your first eleventh century church![74]

A hymn on the Romanesque style follows:

Serious and simple to excess! is it not? Young people rarely enjoy it. They prefer the Gothic. . . . No doubt they are right, since they are young: but men and women who have lived long and are tired—who want rest—who have done with aspirations and ambition—whose life has been a broken arch—feel this repose and self-restraint as they feel nothing else. The quiet strength of these curved lines, the solid support of the heavy columns, the moderate proportions, even the modified lights, the absence of display, of effort, of self-consciousness, satisfy them as no other art does.[75]

It is probable that Adams arrived at these evaluations of the architectural phases of the Middle Ages through the experiences of his own life, its youth, maturity, old age. Jacob Claver Levenson is of this opinion. In *The Mind and Art of Henry Adams* he states: "The naiveté of the Romanesque, the refinement of the Transition, the scientific modernity of the Gothic all had their appeal to him because he saw them as phases of life, which he had experienced."[76]

This appreciation of the Romanesque in preference to the fully developed Gothic was in general ahead of Adams' time. Among the very few who shared this view was his friend H. H. Richardson. The passage just quoted reads, in fact, as though it had been inspired by the architect, and indeed, Adams gave Richardson credit for his understanding of the Romanesque. At the time these lines were conceived he wrote to Elizabeth Cameron: "I caught the disease from dear old Richardson, who was the only really big man I ever knew; and as I grow older the task becomes a habit, like absinthe, and I crave my eleventh-century Norman arch."[77] Other passages breathe Richardson's spirit—the architect was dead at the time of writing—

"Taking architecture as an expression of energy" and "Mont-Saint-Michel throughout . . . is built of granite," for example.[78]

Throughout the book Romanesque construction, simplicity, and energy remain yardsticks of excellence. Adams saw very well that "the thirteenth century did not build so. The great cathedrals after 1200 show economy, and sometimes worse. The world grew cheap, as worlds must."[79] His brother's theory of the application of physics to history and his laws of acceleration and retardation were influential here. Brooks Adams' *Law of Civilization and Decay* was published in 1895, the year of Henry Adams' first Normandy trip. Henry wrote to Brooks from Paris on 8 September:

> Of all these familiar haunts the one that moved me most with a sense of personal identity with myself was Coutances. A great age it was, and a great people our Norman ancestors . . . Since then our ancestors have steadily declined . . . The Gothic always looks to me a little theatrical and false, like its roofs. The Gothic church, both in doctrine and in expression, is not my idea of a thoroughly happy illusion. It is always restless, grasping and speculative; it exploits the world and makes profits . . . The pointed arch is cheap. Still, it had very great beauties in its best time, and, as an artistic form of illusion, it gives me a sense of reflecting my own ideals and limitations. It is human.[80]

Adams used the eleventh century Romanesque and the thirteenth century Gothic dialectically as thesis and antithesis throughout the book, the result of Hegel's influence. Synthesis was provided, accordingly, by the transitional style of the twelfth century, which Adams called the style of the Virgin. This correlation of style to religion and also to *types of society* seems likewise to be distinctly Hegelian. Adams associated the eleventh century Romanesque, the thesis, with aristocratic society, with the soldierly archangel and the God of the Old Testament, while the fully developed thirteenth century Gothic, the antithesis, was called *bourgeois*, belonging to the Trinity of the schoolmen. But not only Adams' mind but his sensuosity also reacted keenly to the antithetical character of Romanesque and Gothic. Correlating the experiences transmitted through the eyes to those of the palate, he wrote: "The heavy round arch is like old cognac compared with the champagne of the pointed and fretted spire."[81] The Romanesque appeared to Adams to be the most unified of the three styles: "Church and State, Soul and Body, God and Man are all one at Mont-Saint-Michel, and the business of all is to fight, each in his own way, or to stand guard for each other."[82] The form in which this statement is cast is likewise rhythmically-dialectic, and once discovered, one meets that method of writing often in the book, whose very title *Mont-Saint-Michel and Chartres* is dialectic. The interior of the abbey church supplied another antithetical experience:

> Through the Romanesque arches of 1058 [in the crossing of the church, built on the very top of the rock] you look into the exuberant choir of latest Gothic, finished in 1521. Although the two structures are some five hundred years apart, they live pleasantly together. The Gothic died gracefully in France. The choir is charming—far more charming than the nave, as the beautiful woman is more charming than the elderly man.[83]

This statement of esthetic tolerance or relativity is actually a denial of absolutes in matters of taste or artistic judgment. Adams also expressed it, almost frivolously: "Taste is free, and all styles are good which amuse."[84] But this is inconsistent with his and Brooks' degradation theory which operates with the terms *stronger* for what is earlier and *weaker* for what is later in time. It is an inconsistency frequently met in *Chartres*, and less often in Adams' letters which, being more informal and originally not written for publication, took a more decided stand for the Romanesque and against the Gothic. Adams must have felt this lack of consistent judgment as an embarrassment, since he tried to overcompensate for it with a most passionate plea for style tolerance. This passage follows immediately after the allusion to the graceful death of the Gothic in France cited above:

> One need not quarrel about styles of beauty, as long as the man and woman are evidently satisfied and love and admire each other still, with all the solidity of faith to hold them up; but, at least, one cannot help seeing, as one looks from the older to the younger style, that whatever the woman's sixteenth-century charm may be, it is not the man's eleventh-century trait of naïveté;—far from it! The simple, serious, silent dignity and energy of the eleventh century have gone. Something more complicated stands in their place; graceful, self-conscious, rhetorical, and beautiful as perfect rhetoric with its clearness, light and line, and the wealth of tracery that verges on the florid.[85]

In this manner the first chapter sets the stage for the whole book and presents, like a classical overture, most of the major motives of the book. The remaining art chapters deal with development and sometimes drag.

The second chapter "La Chanson de Roland" may be skipped here, since it deals chiefly with a literary work, but nevertheless it demonstrates one of the first attempts at the humanities approach, the comparison of one type of art with another. The *tertium comparationis* was introduced in the first chapter as the military masculinity of the Romanesque style: "With Mont-Saint-Michel the 'Chanson' is almost one. The 'Chanson' is in poetry what the Mount is in architecture. Without the 'Chanson' one cannot approach the feeling which the eleventh century built into the Archangel's church."[86] A richer restatement of these ideas follows in the second chapter: "The poem and the church are akin; they go together, and explain each other. . . . Their common trait is their military character, peculiar to the eleventh century. The round arch is masculine. The 'Chanson' is . . . masculine."[87]

Chapter III "The Merveille," the name for the buildings at the north side of the Mount, deals with the transitional style of the twelfth century. It was the century of the first three Crusades which alone, among these religiopolitical as well as economical exploits, might be looked upon as true expressions of the religious energy of the Middle Ages. By the thirteenth century, on the other hand, the Crusades had become habit and bad business. They could no longer be counted on seriously as offering inspiration to the architects and the communities which built the huge cathedrals. This viewpoint runs counter to the widely held and still popular theory that the thirteenth century, the century of the great cathedrals of Paris, Reims, and Amiens, is the highpoint, the consummation of the Middle Ages. Adams placed the highpoint more than a hundred years earlier and therefore closer to that focus of medieval energy, the first three Crusades. Medieval knighthood still formed an international European unity, and the idea as well as the reality of the Holy Roman Empire, although challenged, was still intact, while the thirteenth century brought about both the disintegration and the end of international European knighthood and *Kaisertum*. Adams' comments on the results of the *outburst* of the first Crusade can be applied only to the twelfth century, especially to its beginning. "It was splendid even in a military sense, but it was great beyond comparison in its reflection in architecture, ornament, poetry, color, religion and philosophy."[88] He noticed, as few had before, that then Mont-Saint-Michel and Byzantium were still close to each other, resulting in the "famous period of Transition, the glory of the twelfth century, the object of our pilgrimage."[89]

As the book unfolds, it becomes increasingly clearer that Henry Adams esthetically favored the eleventh century Romanesque as an expression of the archangel and God the Father, while emotionally he was a partisan of the Virgin and the Gothic. The transitional style gave him a chance to solve the dilemma, since it presented a synthesis of the Romanesque and Gothic styles, similar to the way in which the mysticism of the same period resolved the antithesis of faith and reason. Although Hegel was not specifically mentioned here or anywhere else in the book, this chapter dealing with the transitional style seems to be more permeated with Hegelian thought than even the first one. We have further seen how Adams tried to avoid absolute standards of taste and how uncomfortably he felt doing so. Yvor Winters summed up the situation: "Throughout *Mont-Saint-Michel* he insists that the judgment of art is wholly relative, at the same time, that the insistence causes him deep regret."[90]

Yet the transitional style, being the synthesis of two opposed styles, seemed to offer the way out, and although Adams called his exalting of the transitional merely a *preference*, one is aware that the occupation with that style brought him deep relief and that his true sympathies and his *faith* in things esthetic were realized in it:

> Art is a fairly large field where no one need jostle his neighbour and no one need shut himself up in a corner; but, if one insists on taking a corner of preferences, one might offer some excuse for choosing the Gothic Transition. The quiet, restrained strength of the Romanesque married to the graceful curves and vaulting imagination of the Gothic makes a union nearer the ideal than is often allowed in marriage.[91]

Throughout the chapter Adams varied and elaborated on the metaphor of a style-marriage, the unification of two style-sexes: "What the Roman[esque] could not express, flowered into the

Gothic; what the masculine mind could not idealize in the warrior, it idealized in the woman; no architecture that ever grew on earth, except the Gothic, gave this effect of flinging its passion against the sky." Speaking of the *promenoir* in the *Merveille,* Adams called it an exceedingly beautiful hall, uniting the splendid calm and seriousness of the Romanesque with the exquisite lines of the Gothic.[92]

Adams' correlation of the visual-esthetic with the world of religious thought, as undertaken later in Chapter XV "The Mystics," constituted the finest formulation of the transitional style in the whole book:

> The Transition is the equilibrium between the love of God—which is faith—and the logic of God—which is reason; between the round arch and the pointed. One may not be sure which pleases most, but one need not be harsh towards people who think that the moment of balance is exquisite. The last and highest moment is seen at Chartres, where in 1200, the charm depends on the constant doubt, whether emotion or science is uppermost. At Amiens, doubt ceases; emotion is trained in school; Thomas Aquinas reigns.[93]

Chartres, or more specifically its western portal, is the apex in the triangle formed by what Adams calls, significantly, the "Trinity of Transition." The two other corners are represented by the *promenoir* of the Mount and the *crypt* of St. Denis. All three of these highpoints of the transitional style date from the years 1115-20. To that visual trinity of transition corresponds one of the spirit: "The Abbé Suger [of St. Denis], the Abbé Bernard [of Clairvaux, who laid the foundations of the monastery in 1115] and the Abbé Abélard are the three interesting men of the French transition."[94]

The rhythmical-triadic Hegelian bent of Adams' mind, its bias towards geometrical form, is obvious in the construction of such tripartite, triangular patterns of thought. This was the result of his esthetic sensitivity for relationships, which never failed him. He never viewed an object in isolation or entertained an isolated thought. His ideas were, so to speak, born in triplets, or at least in couplets. For instance, we have seen how the overtone of Chartres resounded when the lower note of the Mount was struck.

The fourth chapter "Normandy and the Ile de France" deals with the relation of the Mount to Chartres, that of the Norman to the French, the Romanesque to the Gothic. Yet, before Adams set out for his pilgrimage to Chartres and the Virgin, in the third chapter he took a last look at the Mount, to him a more perfect architectural symbol of unity than Chartres: "The whole Mount still kept the grand style; it expressed the unity of Church and State, God and Man, Peace and War, Life and Death, Good and Bad; it solved the whole problem of the universe."[95] And a final nod of departure in the direction of the Mount: "One looks back on it all as a picture; a symbol of unity; an assertion of God and Man in a bolder, stronger, closer union than ever was expressed by other art."[96]

It is in the fourth chapter that the hunting for *flèches* begins: "There is no livelier amusement for fine weather than in hunting them as though they were mushrooms, and no study in architecture nearly so delightful. No work of man has life like the flèche!"[97] The hunt, though entertaining for Adams, threatens often to efface the blueprint of constructive ideas and might annoy the reader because of the accumulation of rather dull information. The chapter loses its fire through the choking pressure of hardfact clinkers.

Adams is on his way to Chartres and the Virgin, but he takes his time; he saunters slowly along the roads of Normandy, visiting the churches of Coutances, Falaise, Lessay, Cérisy le Forêt, Bayeux, Caen, and some lesser ones, all still in Normandy, until at Mantes he crosses into the Ile de France, into Gothicland and the queendom of Nôtre Dame. He has Chartres, his goal, always before him, but it is as though some stronger power turns his head backward in the direction of the Mount. While he professes to look forward, he is found to look backward. The chapter is still a hymn to the Norman and the Romanesque.

This preference for the Norman made him stress its formative influence far beyond that of the other regional styles also responsible for Chartres; first in importance comes always that of Normandy, then that of Britanny, third that of the Ile de France and Paris, and fourth that of the Touraine and the valley of the Loire. Adams called the Norman "commonly the most practical, and sometimes the most dignified" of them. The country of Chartres, situated in the center, becomes "the fighting ground between them all."[98] With the exception of that of the Ile de France, the other regional styles are not mentioned later; it was on the Norman that he concentrated his interest.

Adams pushes Chartres closer to William the Conqueror's Romanesque in Caen than to that flower of the Gothic, Nôtre Dame in Paris, a procedure which he justifies chronologically as well as esthetically. Of the importance of the church of St. Denis he is as unaware as of that of St. Martin of Tours. The design and character of the Norman *clocher* and *flèche*, the manner by which the square shape of the *clocher* is led into the polygonal shape of the *flèche*, connects Norman Romanesque Caen with transitional Chartres. This evident influence of the Norman on the French school of architecture, especially as felt in the old spire of Chartres, had been noticed, as Adams acknowledged, by Viollet-le-Duc. Since the latter criticized the Normans for not having "that instinct of proportion which the architects of the Ile de France . . . possessed to a high degree,"[99] however, his discovery could not be so fully exploited, could not be made the focus of crystallization for the Gothic, as in Adams' treatment of the subject. This ingenious solution of bridging the square and the polygon made possible the ecstatic verticalism—"the flaming up of feminine grace"—of the Gothic.[100]

That excessive verticalism of the spire set the pace for all the other characteristics of the Gothic, the slender height of the nave, the broken arch, the wall consuming fenestration, in short for the Gothic revolution in dealing with space, light, and subsequently even with color. Before this step was definitely taken, the Romanesque gave birth—as a prelude to the Gothic, so to speak—to another solution of verticalism. But it was a solution developed strictly from its own structural and spiritual premises: the central tower or *clocher*. In the way it appears on the cathedral of Coutances, Adams called it "the most effective feature of any possible church."[101] He used words which recall his comments on the Mount: "Wherever the Norman central clocher stands, the Church Militant of the eleventh century survives."[102]

Thus we are carried back to where we started in the first chapter. How reluctantly Adams took leave of Normandy and the Romanesque style! Against Viollet-le-Duc's panegyric on French Gothic taste, he insisted that "the Norman language, to the English ear, expressed itself quite as clearly as the French, and sometimes seemed to have more to express."[103] He had to tear himself away from the

Norman Romanesque by an act of will: "Here we must take leave of Normandy; a small place, but one which, like Attica or Tuscany, has said a great deal to the world."[104]

In the fifth chapter we finally stand in front of the "Towers and Portals" of Chartres cathedral. In the first part of the chapter the theme of the *flèche*—reaching its most celebrated peak in the *old* spire of Chartres—is developed, but not without sounding again the theme of the Norman and that of the early Crusades. But in Chartres the flèche-theme is presented, according to Adams, with *adresse*, as Viollet-le-Duc put it. Adams translated the French term *adresse* as "cleverness, dexterity, adroitness or simple technical skill," and called it a word "one never caught one's self using . . . in Norman churches." The female Gothic announces itself, the returning crusader bends his knee *adroitely* before the image of the Queen of Heaven.

The same situation of the male knight worshiping the eternal female is met at the Chartres portals, enriched and complicated by the fact that the Northwest, the feudal, occidental, manly world, came to embrace in the Crusades the Oriental female, the great Mother Goddess of the Southeast: "At Chartres one can read the first crusade in the portal. . . . You can see the ideas they brought back with the relics and missals and enamels they bought in Byzantium."[105]

Adams was one of the few writers of his time to explain the sculptural elongation of the pipe-like figures at the west portal as Byzantine rather than Gothic. He spoke of "that peculiar Oriental dignity of style" when dealing with these figures and saw in them "an officer or official in attendance on the Empress or her Son" at the court of Byzantium.[106]

It was certainly Adams' acquaintance with the appreciation of archaic Greek art which enabled him to see values in sculpture which pre-expressionistic taste usually called stiff and lifeless and definitely inferior to the thirteenth century groups at the north and south portals of Chartres. Adams obviously directed a passage in *Chartres* against these prejudices: "These statues are the Eginetan marbles of French art; from them all modern French sculpture dates, or ought to date. They are singularly interesting; as naïf as the smile on the faces of the Greek warriors, but no more grotesque than they."[107] His ob-

servation of the parallelism in style between the Eginetan marbles
and the Chartres figures of the west portal antedated Elie Faure's
similar observations in his *Spirit of the Forms* by more than a decade.
In his own generation Adams found a fellow enthusiast in J. K. Huysmans, who called them in his *Cathédrale* (1898), "Beyond a doubt,
the most beautiful sculpture in the world," which Adams quoted in
Chartres.[108]

The sculpture at the north portal, a gift of the royal family of
France, is so much more developed in the direction of motion, life,
and realism that "people prefer [this] thirteenth century work and
think it equals the best [classical] Greek," but Adams himself pronounced it neither inferior nor superior to the twelfth century group
of the west portal and left the question open.[109] He noticed the
changes in the presentation of the Madonna theme at the two portals,
however; "A hundred years have converted the Byzantine Empress
into a French Queen," he wrote,[110] and stated more specifically some
pages later: "The Virgin of the thirteenth century is no longer an Empress; she is Queen Mother—an idealized Blanche of Castile."[111]

Such a fusion of the Virgin and the *grande dame*, such a secu-
larization of the Madonna theme should, according to his and his
brother's theory of decline, mean also an esthetic devaluation. But
Adams was sometimes evasive and inconsistent; he could enjoy a decadent situation, and obviously did so here. The question of the
Gothic church as an expression of the *Queen of Heaven* is definitely
settled in the interior of the church. There she reigns unchallenged,
as she shall reign in the interiors of all the French churches during
the twelfth and thirteenth centuries. For that reason Adams entitled
chapter six, dealing with the interior of Chartres, "The Virgin of
Chartres." In this chapter, in connection with a style which builds
inside-out, the term *Gothic* is discussed for the first time as the name
of a problematic style: "To most minds it casts too many shadows, it
wraps itself in mystery."[112] Yet here, for once Adams was anti-roman-
tic, anti-mystical. Chartres and the taste expressed by it, while certainly feminine, was to him "not in the least vague, dreamy or mystical in a modern sense."[113] The interior of Chartres "is a child's fancy;
a toyhouse to please the Queen of Heaven."[114] The childlike and
child loving character of the Virgin shapes the character of Her
house: "Whatever Chartres may be now, when young it was a smile."

The Virgin "liked both light and colour . . . she required space."[115] Thus the space, the light, the color, the rich decoration of the Gothic interior meant to Adams naïveté, youth, gaiety, riches, almost worldliness, all qualities and values of life on earth, rather than of the *beyond*.

This harmonizes with his interpretation of the Madonna as often taking sides with sinful man against Heaven and the Trinity. His whole conception of the Virgin was unorthodox, almost pagan, and he noted that after the West had again come in contact with the East through the Crusades, "She began to overshadow the Trinity itself."[116] It was St. Bernard of Clairvaux who became Her great lover, and "nearly every great church of the twelfth and thirteenth century belonged to Mary."[117]

Many times Adams repeated the statement that contrary to the traditional romantic idea—as held for example by Heinrich Heine[118]—the Gothic was not an expression of religious gloom, but stood first of all for light. The necessity for light and always for more light was the prime motor of the Gothic architect: "No doubt the first command of the Queen of Heaven was for light, but the second, at least as imperative, was for colour."[119] And he summed up Her needs: "The Virgin required chiefly these three things, or, if you like, these four: space, light, convenience; and colour decoration to unite and harmonize the whole."[120]

Light and color had become heightened to Adams the artist since he first discovered them in the South Seas, and that may be the deeper cause for his taking such a gay, positive attitude towards them when he finds them in the Gothic interior. He dedicated them as a precious adornment to the favorite deity of his old age, the Virgin, in the way in which a native of those happier isles might adorn his favorite idol with flowers, shells, and feathers. There is a connection between the love for light and color and the cult of the eternal female, of which Adams' love for the Virgin was the expression—no surprise in one who, being somewhat of an *homme à femme*, felt himself best understood by women.

"Roses and Apses" is the name of the seventh chapter, in which Adams interpreted these architectural features as though they were jewels of the Madonna, something like round and half-round

brooches or clasps in artful filigree and openwork, to hold together
and decorate the Madonna's mantle.

Even the weak points of Gothic vaulting, the flying buttresses,
though "probably cheap . . . were graceful," something like machine
made lace.[121] Adams saw very well the Romanesque character of the
rose window, which "needed a great deal of coaxing to feel at home
within the pointed arch."[122] In the same way he correctly traced the
origin of the half round apse to the Oriental and Byzantine half dome,
transmitted to the Gothic architect directly from his Romanesque
predecessor. Yet, in Chartres they are expressions of the same genius
who is ruled over by the woman's taste of pointed refinement.[123]

After such preparation one is not at all shocked to find Adams
explaining the apse of Chartres cathedral as the private room of the
Virgin, the *Queen's own apartment*, something like a religious bou-
doir. It was for that apse, he stated, that the whole interior of Chartres was built, "not for the people or the court, but for the Queen."[124]

"The Twelfth-Century Glass" is the title of the eighth chapter.
Adams saw the stained glass windows as *the crowning glory* of Chartres, the greatest revelation of glowing color, the final unification of
pure color and light.[125] Since this book is limited to Adams' ideas and
observations that differed from those of his contemporaries or anticipated modern opinions, reviews of his remarks on the technical process of making stained glass and his descriptions of the intricate
iconography of the Chartres windows are omitted. These subjects
fill the pages of this and the two subsequent chapters, "The Legendary Windows" (IX), thirteenth century glass, and "The Court of the
Queen of Heaven" (X), the stained glass in the north aisle. We conclude our discussion of the visual arts as dealt with in *Chartres* with
another of Adams' emphatic exclamations:

> These three twelfth-century windows, like their contemporary
> portal outside, and the flèche that goes with them, are the ideals
> of enthusiasts of mediaeval art; they are above the level of all
> known art, in religious form; they are inspired; they are
> divine![126]

From this passage in the eighth chapter one would conclude that
Adams definitely found the highpoint of medieval art in the twelfth
century transitional style and that his sympathy for the Virgin of

Chartres had helped him to arrive at that decision. But he pleaded with similar enthusiasm for the unparalleled excellence of the Romanesque, the style of the fighting archangel. An attempt was made above to resolve this obvious contradiction by observing that Adams esthetically favored the archangel while emotionally he favored the Virgin.

Taking the book as a whole, a clear decision in favor of one or the other of the two contesting powers is actually avoided or not even intended. Adams established two highpoints and so tried to encompass opposites. Is that why the title *Mont-Saint-Michel and Chartres* was chosen? The simple placing together of the names of these two great works of medieval architecture seems to indicate an even distribution of emphasis. They are architectural symbols of the two forces between which the unity of the Middle Ages realized itself.

SOURCES OF
MONT-SAINT-MICHEL AND CHARTRES

This list contains only titles mentioned by Adams in the text of the book. A more comprehensive list has been compiled by Max I. Baym ("Appendix 1: Philological Items," *The French Education of Henry Adams*, New York, Columbia University Press, 1951: 290-301). Baym enumerates books and pamphlets in Adams' library, "most of them containing his scorings," which could have been used.

Bulteau, Marcel Joseph, *Monographie de la cathédrale de Chartres*, 2nd ed., Chartres, 1887-1901, 3 vol.

Caumont, Arcisse de, *Histoire de l'art dans l'ouest de la France depuis les temps les plus reculés jusqu'au XVIIe siècle*, Paris, 1830-41, 6 vol. (*Moyen-âge: Architecture religieuse*, vol. 4).

Clerval, Jules Alexandre, *Guide Chartrain; Chartres, sa cathédrale, ses monuments*, Chartres [1896].

Corroyer, Edouard, *Description de l'Abbaye du Mont-Saint-Michel et de ses abords, précédée d'une notice historique*, Paris, 1877.

Du Sommerard, Alexandre, *Les Arts au moyen âge, en ce que concerne principalement le Palais romain de Paris, l'Hôtel de Cluny, issu de ses ruines, et les objets d'art de la collection classée dans cet hôtel*, Paris, 1838-46, 7 vol.

Du Sommerard, Edmond, *Musée des Thermes et de l'Hôtel de Cluny: Catalogue et description des objets d'art . . . exposés au musée*, Paris, 1881.

Enlart, Camille, *Manuel d'archéologie française depuis les temps mérovingiens jusqu'à la renaissance*, Paris, 1902-16, 3 vol.

France. Commission des monuments historiques. Photographs from its archives.

Huysmans, Joris Karl, *La Cathédrale*, Paris, 1898.

Labarte, Jules, *Histoire des arts industriels au moyen âge et à l'époque de la renaissance*, Paris, 1864-66, 4 vol. and 2 albums of plates.

Lacroix, Paul, *Le Moyen âge et la renaissance, histoire et description des moeurs et usages du commerce et de l'industrie, des sciences, des arts, des littérature et des beaux-arts en Europe*, Paris, 1848-51, 5 vol.

Lassus, Jean Baptiste Antoine, *Monographie de la cathédrale de Chartres* (publiée par les soins du Ministre de l'instruction publique), Paris, 1867. *Explication des planches par Paul Durand*, Paris, 1881.

Lasteyrie, Ferdinand de, *Histoire de la peinture sur verre, d'après ses monuments en France*, Paris, 1857-58, 2 vol.

Mâle, Emile, *L'Art religieux du XIIIe siècle en France; étude sur l'iconographie du moyen âge et sur ses sources d'inspiration* (nouv. éd.), Paris, 1902.

Martin, Arthur, and Charles Cahier, *Monographie de la cathédrale de Bourges; Première partie: Vitraux du XIIIe siècle*, Paris, 1841-44, 2 vol.

Michelet, Jules, *Histoire de France* (nouv. éd.), Paris, 1876-78, 19 vol.

Molinier, Emile, *Histoire générale des arts appliqués à l'industrie du Ve à la fin du XVIIIe siècle*, Paris [189-?], 4 vol.

Ottin, L., *Le Vitrail; son histoire, ses manifestations à travers les âges et les peuples*, Paris, 1896.

Renan, Ernest, *Averroes et l'averroisme; essai historique*, Paris, 1852.

Rohault de Fleury, Charles, *La Sainte-Vierge: Etudes archéologiques et iconographiques*, Paris, 1878-79, 2 vol.

Viollet-Le-Duc, Eugene Emmanuel, *Dictionnaire raisonné de l'architecture française du XIe au XVIe siècle*, Paris, 1858-68, 10 vol.

Viollet-Le-Duc, Eugene Emmanuel, *Dictionnaire raisonné du mobilier français, de l'époque carlovingienne à la renaissance*, Paris, 1858-75, 6 vol.

Westlake, N. H. J., *History of Design in Painted Glass*, London, 1881-94, 4 vol.

6. Other Art and Artists

(Early American Art;
Contemporary Art and Artists)

*F*rom Henry Adams' extraordinary understanding for the archaic as it appears in Greek and medieval art, from his stress on the spiritual element in the arts, one would expect sympathy with those trends in the art of his own time which led to a revolution in style in the last decades of the nineteenth century in the art of Gauguin, Cézanne and Van Gogh. But this is decidedly not the case. Adams had neither sympathy nor understanding of the progressive tendencies of the art of his own time, simply because he believed that there could be no upward trend in evolution, that all must be downward to decay and futility.

This decay started, according to Adams, with the work of Michelangelo, which was at the same time the beginning of modern art. Witness two letters of 1899 to his wife's niece Mabel Hooper, who had recently married the young painter Bancel La Farge, the son of Adams' friend.

> There is nothing worth knowing in Europe but the Greek and the Norman—and Michael Angelo, who was the first great anarchist. All the rest is fragmentary, individual, personal and owes its merit to its author. It is Titian or Velasquez or Rembrandt, not a race, or a structure. (Rome, 12 May.)[1] The modern world artistically begins with Michael Angelo, and I don't like it. There is no peace or protection or repose about it. (Paris, 5 Sept.)[2]

Adams was concerned about art as an interesting and puzzling phenomenon. Therefore he liked to associate with artists, to visit

125

studios and exhibitions, to buy occasionally, even to give commissions to some artists, but he did not believe in the art of his own time, in its function and future in society. The lack of faith, at least the doubt, was evident even in his relations to his three friends, Richardson, La Farge and Saint-Gaudens, who will be dealt with more fully in later chapters. Here we are dealing with art and artists in the outer circle around Adams, chiefly within the radius of his travels and his long stays in the art centers of Europe, Rome, London, and Paris. Artists and works of art appeared casually within this radius and were casually dealt with in his letters and *Education.*

Adams' general observations on contemporary art are expressed in his *Letters to a Niece*, to Mabel Hooper. She had taken up drawing and painting more or less as a hobby and turned to him for advice. It was not very encouraging:

> There is nothing new to say—at least not in our formulas. Everything has been said many-many-many times. The pleasure is in saying it over to ourselves in a whisper, so that nobody will hear, and so that neither vanity, nor money can get in as much as a lisp. I admit that this unfits one for one's time and life, but one must make some sort of running arrangement on every railroad and even in every school; and if you are to stop five minutes for refreshments at the Art Station, you must have those five minutes clear.[3]

Another letter dealt with the methods taught at professional art schools and the ways of the professional artist and the dilettante:

> I am glad you are interested in your art school, though the same danger lurks there. One learns just enough of professional methods to disgust one with one's own limitations. The professional artist is a fraud of the worst kind in that respect. He labors to root out amateurishness, and yet he is himself the most miserable of amateurs, or worse, when he undertakes seriously to rival real artists. Not one has a sense of color; almost none has a sense of line; never a picture or a figure is *felt*; and in both the Paris salons you may seek a whole season to find a work of art that is more than clever. The greatest artist's greatest art is to imitate naïveté, like Puvis, or to be super-habile like Sargent. A third-rate Rembrandt knocks the stuffing out of all the picture-exhibitions of Europe and America combined.
>
> Still, nothing matters much, and as you want only amuse-

ment, perhaps you will find as much of it in the art-school as out of it. Anyway, one's freshness must soon fade in our dry intellectual atmosphere, and faded freshness is a very stale thing. So I suppose we must cultivate what the world cultivates, and try to wear our tailor-made clothes as though they were imperial purple. Thanks to La Farge, you will hardly forget what color is, and when one's eye has once learned to see color and line, one does not easily lose that sense. Sometimes I feel even a feeble suspicion that the times are drifting us back towards a certain revival of our senses.[4]

It is interesting to note that Adams, who saw in medieval art manifestations of the most profound thoughts and feelings and generally seemed to believe in art in his search for the meaning of life, should use so often such words as *amusement* and *amusing* in his relation to the art of his own time. His observations of trends in modern art which might lead to a revival of the senses also seem to be in tune with that basically sensuous approach. This contradictory situation is another manifestation of Adams' polarity of character, taste and beliefs. In commenting on a sketch sent by his niece, Adams expressed his ideas about professional art education:

Your study for "Dancing" certainly has not the freshness of the open air; but that is not your fault. It smells of the studio and the lamp; but that is why it exists . . . Nothing absolutely annoys me in the sketch, and although of course the school always begins by abolishing color—that being the only essential element in paint, and thereby deprives you of your chief natural advantage, still you have instinctively struggled to recover what you could of your paralysed strength by using light and shade as boldly as you dared. . . .

If you were to be professional, I should highly approve your working close down to the conventional school standard, which probably represents the nearest practicable compromise between art and existing society. . . . After all, from the point of view of true imagination and pure art, I do not know that Titian and Rembrandt are less mercantile than Sargent and Carolus. I find no real peace short of the windows at Chartres and the mosaics at Torcello and Murano.[5]

From these excerpts it appears that Adams' main criticisms of the art of his time were that the artist had nothing new to say because there was nothing new to say, that painting lacked color, the lifeblood of the art, and that it was hopelessly soulless and mercantile. Although this was certainly true for most of the academic or *professional artists,* as Adams called them, he completely overlooked those art movements which were born as protests against these tendencies. Even as an eyewitness of the Impressionist movement, one of the great outbursts of colorism and luminism, Adams still exclaimed in the *Chartres* chapter on twelfth century glass, "No school of color exists in our world today, while the Middle Ages had a dozen."[6] In this connection he mentioned Delacroix's losing battle for color and noted that society in the nineteenth century agreed rather with Ingres, the champion of line, than with the romantic colorist.

Lack of color, mercantilism, soullessness were all, according to Adams, symptoms of decline. During the nineties he was especially aware of decay, describing the *fin-de-siècle* in his *Education:*

> Drifting in the dead-water of the fin-de-siècle—and during this last decade every one talked and seemed to feel fin-de-siècle— where not a breath stirred the idle air of education or fretted the mental torpor of self-content, one lived alone.[7]

What he observed about the literary arts—"the symbolic poets, or Verlaine's expiring gnashing of rotten teeth," were the "refuse of a literary art" which had "nothing left to study but the subjective reflection of its own decay"[8]—he also applied to the visual arts, as we shall see in the case of Rodin. And from these observations he concluded that "artists, of course, disappeared long ago as social forces."[9]

The inability of the contemporary artist to function as an active force in the society of his time seems to be the main reason for Adams' doubts about the work of the best artists of his time and even about that of his friends. He criticized them more on sociological and ethical than on esthetic grounds. Certainly he was not altogether a reactionary in his taste, someone who insisted on photographic realism in painting. Through the mouth of Wharton (La Farge) in *Esther* he said that "the merit of a painting was not so much in what it explained as in what it suggested,"[10] a statement which would make him fit to understand the art of Whistler.

There was little appreciation of painting and sculpture in the Adams family until Henry Adams became interested in the arts. His father collected coins, but paintings other than portraits were in gen-

8. "A View of Rhenen," by Aelbert Cuyp. Wash Drawing.
The Fogg Art Museum, Harvard University, Cambridge,
Massachusetts. Gift of John S. Newberry. Date of Henry
Adams' purchase, 1867, is on the back in his own hand.
Courtesy of the Fogg Art Museum.

9. "Nebuchadnezzar Eating Grass," by William Blake.
Color Monotype. The Museum of Fine Arts, Boston,
Massachusetts. Gift of Mrs. Robert Homans. Formerly
owned by Henry Adams. Courtesy of the Museum of Fine
Arts.

10. Henry Hobson Richardson. Photographed in 1880. The Bettmann Archive.

11. "Henry Hobson Richardson in his Studio," by Hubert von Herkomer. Wash Drawing, about 1885. Location Unknown. The Bettmann Archive.

eral looked upon as luxuries. It was different with the Hooper family which, closely related to the Sturgises, was traditionally interested in art and supported Boston artists and the Boston Museum of Fine Arts, to which they had donated Washington Allston's "Elijah." Mrs. Henry Adams (Marian Hooper) corresponded with her father about Allston, who had been a friend of the Sturgis family. A Salvator Rosa landscape from the Robert Gilmor collection in Baltimore was recommended by her for purchase:

> It is weird enough to suit Vedder, reminds me strongly of Allston's Elijah in character, is about five feet long by two or more high—a storm-bent tree in left foreground, a high bank on the right, a brilliant blue sky with one great hot white cloud cummulus rolling over it, a flock of far-off birds and a group of figures in robes watching them. It tempts me very much. I hate Salvator's molasses pictures as a rule; we both went to scoff and remained, if not to pray, at least to respect and like.[11]

Allston was mentioned again in Marian's correspondence in reference to a plan to found an art school in Charleston, South Carolina, and to collect money for its construction: "We must help educate and cultivate a vanquished foe. Allston and Richardson show that there is seed worth forcing in that barren land."[12]

Adams too was convinced of the important position of Washington Allston in the culture of America's formative years, connecting not only the South and the North, but also young America with old Europe. In his *History of the United States during the Administrations of Jefferson and Madison* he considered Allston to be the most representative American figure in the field of the arts.[13] In the chapter on literature and art he arranged the whole of American art life during the years 1800-17 around Allston. This is Adams' only significant attempt at a history of early American painting:

> While Bryant published *Thanatopsis* and Irving made his studies for the *Sketch Book*, another American of genius perhaps superior to theirs—Washington Allston—was painting in London, before returning to pass the remainder of his life in the neighborhood of Boston and Harvard College. Between thirty and forty years of age, Allston was then in the prime of his powers; and even in a circle of artists which included Turner, Wilkie, Mulready, Constable, Calcott, Crome, Cotman and a swarm of others

equally famous, Allston was distinguished. Other Americans took rank in the same society. Leslie and Stuart Newton were adopted into it, and Copley died only in 1815, while Trumbull painted in London till 1816; but remarkable though they were for the quality of their art, they belonged to a British School and could be claimed as American only by blood. Allston stood in a relation somewhat different. In part, his apparent Americanism was due to his later return and to his identification with American society; but the return itself was probably caused by a peculiar bent of character. His mind was not wholly English.

Allston's art and his originality were not such as might have been expected from an American or such as Americans were likely to admire; and the same might be said of Leslie and Stuart Newton. Perhaps the strongest instance of all was Edward Malbone, whose grace of execution was not more remarkable than his talent for elevating the subject of his exquisite work. So far from sharing the imagination of Shawanee Indians or even of Democrats, these men instinctively reverted to the most refined and elevated schools of art. Not only did Allston show from the beginning of his career a passion for the nobler standards of his profession, but also for technical quality—a taste less usual.

Alston was also singular in the liberality of his sympathies. "I am by nature, as it respects the arts, a wide liker," he said. In Rome he became acquainted with Coleridge; and the remark of Coleridge which seemed to make most impression on him in their walks "under the pines of the Villa Borghese" was evidently agreeable because it expressed his own feelings. "It was there he taught me this golden rule; never to judge of any work of art by its defects." His admiration for the classics did not prevent him from admiring his contemporaries; his journey through Switzerland not only showed him a new world of Nature, but also "the truth of Turner's Swiss scenes—the poetic truth—which none before or since have given."[14]

Only the Philadelphia painters of about a generation earlier could compare with Allston and his circle when measured against European standards:

Gilbert Stuart, the best painter in the country, came to Philadelphia, and there painted portraits equal to the best that England or France could produce—for Reynolds and Gainsborough were dead, and Sir Thomas Lawrence ruled the fashion of the time. If Franklin and Rittenhouse no longer lived to give scientific fame to Philadelphia, their liberal and scientific spirit survived. The reputation of the city was not confined to America, and the accident that made a Philadelphian, Benjamin West, President of the Royal Academy in succession to Sir Joshua Reynolds, was a tacit compliment, not undeserved, to the character of the American metropolis.[15]

Although Adams found fine words of appreciation for early American painting, he was not interested in the field as a collector. Neither portraits, nor historical paintings, nor still-lifes appealed to his taste. He left this interest, like that in English eighteenth century portraiture, to Marian's more traditional taste, which embraced the whole of eighteenth and early nineteenth century American art. Her interest in American art was the main motive for her recommending the purchase of an Audubon oil for the Boston Museum when she wrote to her father:

> As to America, there is a curious picture at Barlow's on the Avenue sent for sale from Mississippi (don't count the s's if you love me) signed by Audubon; an oil painting about twenty inches square or more, of dead birds, some in an overturned basket, some on the ground, a spray of purple convolvulus on the left background—painted in oils with great delicacy and accuracy rather as one would paint who was more used to the handling of water colours; three hundred dollars is the price asked. Neither of us cares for "still life" in any shape—on canvas or off—but the Art Museum might do very well to buy what is on internal evidence a good and unusual specimen of Audubon. It was left as a legacy to the sergeant of the Senate by a Mississippi relative, so Barlow says. The signature may be forged of course, but if any artist in America could paint birds as well as that, except Audubon, he ought to be spottable and a bird savant could easily identify the birds.[16]

Adams lacked the intimate ties with American art his wife brought to collecting as part of her family background and upbringing. He also almost completely lacked interest in early American architecture in his writings, though the gambrelled Adams family manse in Quincy, Massachusetts, is a good example of an eighteenth century American clapboard house. Furthermore, since his childhood Adams was familiar with the most distinguished examples of classicist architecture in and around Boston and Washington, yet he dealt only once in his *Education* with the family houses in Boston and Quincy. They hardly received detailed architectural descriptions but rather quick sketches of the difference between the Boston town house, where the family lived during the winter, and the Quincy country house, where they spent the summer. Although not particularly sympathetic to the Quincy house, he apparently preferred it architecturally to the Boston house:

> It smacked of colonial age, but not of Boston style or plush curtains. To the end of his life he never quite overcame the prejudice thus drawn in with his childish breath. He never could compel himself to care for nineteenth-century style. He was never able to adopt it, any more than his father or grandfather or great-grandfather had done. Not that he felt it as particularly hostile, for he reconciled himself to much that was worse; but because, for some remote reason, he was born an eighteenth-century child. The old house at Quincy was eighteenth century. What style it had was in its Queen Anne mahogany panels and its Louis Seize chairs and sofas. The panels belonged to an old colonial Vassall who built the house; the furniture had been brought back from Paris in 1789 or 1801 or 1817, along with porcelain and books and much else of old diplomatic remnants. . . . The dark mahogany had been painted white to suit daily life in winter gloom.[17]

The Quincy house fared worse in his letters. Adams spent his first two summers there after his return from England in 1868, and wrote to his friend Charles M. Gaskell that "the house had been made habitable . . . and the Lord knows the house needed it. Also they are building or to build a fire-proof affair for the library and the family papers, but what species of thing, I know not."[18] In spite of these efforts toward remodeling and modernizing, Adams developed no particular appreciation for the homestead of his ancestors. He wrote to Gaskell in 1869:

> I find my family unchanged and looking very well and contented. They are trying to make their house habitable, but Wenlock is a joke to it in this particular. I never was in such a wretched old trap, for it hasn't even the merit of being well-built. In fact I am not enthusiastic about the homes of my ancestors, and only wish their taste had been better.[19]

He was even more outspoken in a letter to the same friend two years later: "My family has emigrated again to Quincy, where they live merrily or at least soberly in their pig-stye, and I go over once or twice to see them."[20] Adams remained on the visitor's footing in his relation to the house during his Harvard teaching years.

Adams' niece Abigail Adams Homans, daughter of his brother John Quincy, wrote that "the family house on Adams street has survived almost intact, complete with some of the family pictures, most of the china, and all of the furniture, a curious jumble of federal and diplomatic debris." John Adams had called it Peacefield. It started as a small farmhouse on the estate of a gentleman called Vassall. John Adams bought it in London in 1787 from a Vassall heir. A later addition to the eastern side accommodated a parlor with French furniture for Abigail Adams, and a study was built for her husband. West of the house is a delightful formal garden, still beautifully taken care of. Charles Francis Adams built the freestanding stone library for the family books and papers.[21]

In his *History* Adams only very briefly dealt with the subject of American architecture, often in a somewhat flippant and deprecating way. He said of domestic architecture around 1800: "Fifty or a hundred miles inland more than half the houses were log cabins, which might or might not enjoy the luxury of a glass window. Throughout the South and West houses showed little attempt at luxury; but even in New England the ordinary farmhouse was hardly so well built, so spacious, or so warm as that of a well-to-do contemporary of Charlemagne."[22] And his judgment on public architecture was even more acrimonious:

> The Capitol at Washington was designed, in rivalry with a French architect, by Doctor William Thornton, an English physician, who in the course of two weeks' study at the Philadelphia Library gained enough knowledge of architecture to draw incorrectly an exterior elevation. When Thornton was forced to look for someone to help him over his difficulties, Jefferson could find no competent native American, and sent for Latrobe. Jefferson considered himself a better architect than either of them, and had he been a professor of materia medica at Columbia College, the public would have accepted his claim as reasonable.[23]

As to Adams' association with contemporary American artists, William Morris Hunt was the first one about whom there is any information. He painted Adams' father's portrait in Paris around 1865. The episode is mentioned in the *Education*:

> The only American who came by, capable of teaching, was William Hunt, who stopped to paint the portrait of the Minister which now completes the family series at Harvard College. Hunt talked constantly, and was, or afterwards became, a famous teacher, but Henry Adams did not know enough, to learn. Perhaps, too, he had inherited or acquired a stock of tastes, as young men must, which he was slow to outgrow. Hunt had no time to sweep out the rubbish of Adams' mind. The portrait finished, he went.[24]

But the portrait made a much greater impression on Adams than one would conclude from this passage. "It is in the severest and truest style," he wrote to his brother Charles, and continued, "You know by this time my canons of art pretty well, and you know that what pleases the crowd, would have a poor chance of pleasing me. Whoever is right, the majority is wrong."[25] An echo of this impression is found in the portrait by the eponymous Esther of Adams' novel of her father, which "was admitted to have merits even by Wharton, though he said that its unusual and rather masculine firmness of handling was due to the subject and could never be repeated."[26]

It is to be regretted that Adams did not say more about this picturesque teacher and artist. Hunt's tragic death in September 1879 caused Marian to remark in a letter to her father: "We were shocked to hear last night that William Hunt has put an end to his wild, restless, unhappy life. Perhaps it has saved him years of insanity, which his temperament pointed to."[27] Having received his art education in France, Hunt had switched from the camp of the idealists to that of the realist Millet, and became his chief champion in the United States. Hunt had taught John La Farge, as well as William and Henry James, and thus was very close to several men in Adams' circle. Henry James penned a fine portrait of him in his *Notes of a Son and Brother*.

During his stays in Rome, Adams used to visit, the first time in 1859, another Bostonian, William Wetmore Story, a sculptor who was very much overrated in his own day. He saw very soon that Story "could not touch the secret of Michael Angelo,"[28] and his letters about

him were already critical.[29] Adams took Marian to Story's studio
in 1873. She wrote to her father in a gossipy manner about the bohe-
mian environment and bluntly expressed her dislike of "how [he
does] spoil nice blocks of white marble. Nothing but Sibyls on all
sides, sitting, standing, legs crossed, legs uncrossed and all with the
same expression as if they smelt something wrong. Call him a genius!
I don't see it."[30] They also visited Elihu Vedder; in a letter to her
father, Marian's reactions were similar:

> We went to Vedders' studio and he was away, but Mrs. Vedder
> received us and showed us about. She is an ordinary little girl
> and won't push him up to anything great. We were not impressed
> with his work; he seems to me to be losing ground fast; has got
> a mania for painting stuffs and accessories in his pictures and
> forgets they ought to be secondary. I wouldn't have given ten
> dollars for anything in his studio. He came back before we left
> and came to see me. He's grown fat and quite common; was
> much excited by our Cairo photographs of street scenes, shops,
> etc. I urged him to go to the East and told him it was his place,
> but he says he longs to and can't. He asked particularly for you
> and spoke of our pleasant day in Paris together seven years
> ago.[31]

In 1866 the Adamses bought a picture by Vedder, which Marian was
only too glad to dispose of in 1873, as she wrote to her father from
Oxford, England, on 1 June: "I was so glad that my Vedder sold for
five hundred and fifty dollars—more even than I was fool enough to
pay for it seven years ago. It's pleasant to think that someone else is
a bigger one than I was."[32]

To round off the tour through the then fashionable artists' studios
in Rome, they visited the Spanish painter and etcher Mariano Fortuny
who "is quite the rage now"; but here too Marian saw through the
glamour of a merely temporary fame: "I don't see any *soul* . . . in his
pictures."[33] At the same time her husband noted in one of his letters
that "the pictures were not exactly [my] notion of good painting."[34]
Yet notwithstanding this sound judgment, Marian bought a Fortuny
watercolor for her father in Paris in 1873.[35] While traveling in Spain
and Spanish Africa in 1879 they were "several times sure" they saw
"the very place where Fortuny took [the] sketch" Marian had

bought for her father and "found that he had been twice in Tetuan—
first in 1863, then in 1873."[36]

To return to American art and W. W. Story, after Adams had
read Henry James' *William Wetmore Story and his Friends* (1903),
he wrote to the author:

> It all spreads itself out as though I had written it. . . . The painful
> truth is that all of my New England generation, counting the
> half century, 1820-1870, were in actual fact only one mind and
> nature. . . . Harvard College and Unitarianism kept us all shal-
> low. . . . One cannot exaggerate the profundity of ignorance of
> Story in becoming a sculptor. . . . Story and Sumner, Emerson
> and Alcott, Lowell and Longfellow, Hillard, Winthrop, Motley,
> Prescott and all the rest, were of the same mind,—and so, poor
> worm!—was I! Type bourgeois-bostonien![37]

Other famous American artists the prominent American traveler
abroad could not help running into were Sargent and Whistler.
Adams' opinion of the *superhabile* Sargent and his mercantilism has
been noted. But Adams was not always negative in his judgment of
Sargent's art, as a letter to Mabel La Farge from London in 1897
shows:

> But just now we all go to the Royal Academy to see Sargent's
> portrait of Mrs. Mayer and her two children. . . . Decidedly this
> time, Sargent has done it. The art of portrait-painting of Jewesses
> and their children may be varied but cannot be further perfected.
> Nothing better ever was done, or can be done. Yet he has also
> a little girl in black—Laura Lister—which is in one respect even
> finer, at least to me, because it seems almost felt; a quality in
> painting and generally in art which not only has ceased to exist,
> but has ceased to be missed in the universal solvent of money
> valuations. These two works put Sargent quite by himself. I am
> really pleased for once to admire without qualification and to
> say so as loudly as I can.[38]

Sargent was cited for the last time in the Adams correspondence on
the occasion of an exhibition in Washington in 1908. Among the
younger artists he was definitely *vieux jeux*: "We have rather a good
American Artist Show here at the Gallery. The things rather gen'ly
echo their inspiration—except Sargent, who swashes all over the place
as he likes—but there is much that is respectable and American. We

are timid and conventional, all of us, except T. R. and he has no mind."[39]

Adams wrote about Sargent's portraits of his friends Theodore Roosevelt and John Hay in his letters. The one of the President showed "a young intellectual idealist with a taste for athletics, which I take to be Theodore's idea of himself."[40] "His Hay is good, but, as I tell Hay, it will take a few years to show me just what meanness I hadn't, in forty years intimacy, fully recognized in him. . . . All the same, Sargent is stodgy! . . . The generation of Harry James and John Sargent is already as fossil as the buffalo."[41] Marian also mentioned a Sargent portrait in her letters, but that was about twenty years earlier. He was then not yet the celebrated painter of international society, but a "promising Philadelphia artist whom we fell in with at Seville in 1879." The portrait was of a Miss Burckhardt which "made a sensation in last year's salon."[42]

Whistler appeared in Adams' writings as an eccentric rather than as an important artist. He used him as a dark foil to show off the personalities of his artist friends La Farge and Saint-Gaudens. There was Whistler's "frank vulgarity of self-advertisement" to which La Farge "rarely or never resorted."[43] Observing both artists at a dinner conversation, he remarked on the silence of La Farge and the vehemence and eccentricity of Whistler. The latter discussed political topics of the day with "a willingness to seem eccentric, where no real eccentricity, unless perhaps of temper, existed." Yet Adams seemed to have appreciated Whistler's "nuance and tone far beyond any point reached by La Farge," who "lavished this vehemence, which Whistler never betrayed in his painting, on his glass." The Plutarchian comparison between Whistler and Saint-Gaudens was the former's emotionalism, "brutalized . . . by the brutalities of his world," and the latter's control.[44] Marian also disliked Whistler as a personality and painter but appreciated him very much as an etcher. The Adamses saw the portrait of his mother when it was exhibited in London in 1872 and found it "interesting but affected."[45]

While visiting the Grosvenor Gallery in 1879 Marian remarked that the portrait of the dancer Connie Gilchrist "is all that Ruskin could ask to justify his charge that it was 'flinging a paint pot in the face of the public.'"[46] Whistler was introduced to her the same summer. She wrote that he was "even more mad away from his paint pots than near them. His etchings are so charming, it is a pity he should leave that to woo a muse whom he can't win."[47]

To turn to the contemporary European art world, Marian became acquainted with Whistler's brother-in-law, the surgeon and etcher Seymour Haden, when he was brought to the house in Washington in 1883 "to see the drawings and water colours, which seemed to delight him. He could at sight put the name to every drawing and knew the collector's initials and all."[48] Haden's graphic work must have had no less appeal to the Adamses than his connoisseurship and his personality. Of the other graphic artists then fashionable, Adams noticed Jean François Raffaelli and Anders Zorn. He bought Raffaelli's facile yet rather empty work. A color print of *Les Deux petits Anes* was purchased in Paris "because the two small donkeys are wonderfully like me and my brother Brooks."[49] Adams probably knew Zorn through Saint-Gaudens, whose portrait Zorn etched. On his Scandinavian trip Adams was apprehensive of meeting him, "lest he should expect me to eat and drink; for they all drink like Vikings."[50] Yet he could not avoid seeing "a few thousand Zorns."[51]

Adams' association with contemporary English artists during his secretaryship to his father in London has already been discussed. The sculptor Woolner was the only Pre-Raphaelite he knew personally. Yet he saw the works of the Pre-Raphaelites with his wife in the Grosvenor Gallery in 1879, if not earlier. The gallery had been opened as a refuge for them two years before. A painting there by Walter Crane, a follower of the Pre-Raphaelites of the younger generation, best known as a designer and teacher, was hilariously described by Marian as "three females in diaphanous rainbow nightgowns dancing a double shuffle on a beach; they look all three like pensive soap bubbles."[52]

The Adamses also looked for examples of Morris' and Rossetti's craftwork in the shops, but they got tired of it.[53] A year later, after visiting his shop Marian wrote, "Morris rather bores me; is getting affected in style." The description of the visit is amusing: "I said 'arsenic,' and the salesman cooly replied, 'If you wish them without arsenic you must pay more for them.' I've asked Bumstead [owner of a

wallpaper shop in Boston], who is here, to blow up the poet."[54] Louis
Comfort Tiffany's related designs were much appreciated by the
Adamses. Marian wrote from England: "We got an enchanting little
red-bronze cream pitcher at Tiffany's . . . some of the work which took
the first prize at the French Exposition and for which queens and
duchesses wept."[55]

Although the Adamses were critical of progressive art in England,
they must have found the conservative official aspect of English art,
the exhibitions at the Royal Academy, even less rewarding. During
his early years in London, Adams had already called the exhibitions
there "rather a chaos."[56] "The continuous life in England made
French art worst of all," but "it did not prove that English art in 1866
was good."[57] The artists of the school of Barbizon, "the painter's
Mecca" as Adams called it,[58] had already made a name for themselves, and Manet and the other Impressionists had exhibited with
the *Indépendents,* so his views on French art certainly appear to be
prejudiced. However, Adams summed up his reaction to art in France
in 1891 in a letter to John Hay: "As yet, the painting and the sculpture have made me only sea-sick; with all the good-will in the world
I have not been able to face the terrors of French Art, but I will still
try, mon ami—I will try."[59] After the turn of the century the work of
the Barbizon painters seemed in retrospect to gain in significance.
Adams wrote to Mabel Hooper La Farge:

> The most ambitious work is the first to go, and yet we are all here
> discussing now the Angelus, to find out whether in truth it is the
> Angelus that has gone to pieces, or the generation. The Angelus
> affected simplicity above all things. It is simpler now than ever
> before, and yet is generally treated as a wreck. By the bye, I
> think the same darkening process applies to all the Millets, but
> to none of the Corots. Yet the Corots are, if possible, less es-
> teemed now than the Millets.[60]

But later, when Adams became an almost yearly summer resi-
dent in Paris and kept up with the exhibitions, he did not materially
change his judgment about the works of art seen in them. In regard
to the Paris Exposition of 1900 he mentioned "the futilities of Saint-
Gaudens, Rodin and Besnard."[61] The combination of those three
names with Adams' favorite term *futility* was not meant, however,

in an altogether negative sense. He wrote to Mabel about the exhibition:

> The young painters are now puffing Besnard to the skies. Oh Lord! one has seen so many such puffs! St. Gaudens has a swan goose or two. A few youths still hang to MacMonnies. The pictures in the Exhibition are the best and most serious part of it —better than the automobiles; but the last word of art is that skunk Boldini's portrait of Whistler.[62]

Eleven years later Adams referred to Besnard's *plafond* for the Théâtre Français.[63] The bright, sparkling colorism of the decoration seems to have delighted him. At another time he spoke of the same painter as being absent from the exhibition of 1908, one of the salons which, "as usual [are] growing worse and worse every year, according to Mme de Ganay. I told her that I began with that understanding just fifty years ago and that as far as I could see, the worseness varied only in its quantity."[64]

The artists Adams specifically mentioned, either as absent or present at the 1908 salon, must have meant something to him—Paul Albert Besnard (1849-1934), Léopold Joseph Flameng (1831-1911), Jean Béraud (1849-1936), a pupil of Léon Bonnat, and Giovanni Boldini (1845-1931). Today they are ranked as second rate or forgotten, as are such other then successful portraitists his friends employed as Jacques Emile Blanche and Paul César Helleu.[65]

The work of Bancel La Farge should not be overlooked. His "La Pluie," a tempera in the style of the later idealists, was his first picture to be accepted in the Paris Salon (1909). Adams mentioned it in a letter to his young friend Bay Lodge[66] and wrote a letter of thanks to Bancel for a reproduction. The latter is especially important because of Adams' criticism of the art of the salons and his comments on the neglect of religious art:

> Many thanks for the reproduction of your charming picture which has just arrived. A work of so much refinement and delicacy should be seen by itself, not in contact with the violence of our Salons, which are intentionally made to stimulate coarse effects. . . . Unfortunately our artists do not now produce enough refinement to fill one small room. . . . I note too, as a curious sign of our artistic movement, that religious motives have disappeared. Scarcely one or two religious pictures are shown in the

Salons, and even these are more or less travesties. The result is curious. I find it amusing and instructive, but not as art.[67]

Of all the French artists of his time, Adams seems to have been most interested in Auguste Rodin because of his originality. But here too, the relation was one of repulsion as well as attraction. The sensuality of Rodin attracted him, but he tried to hide his mingled feelings of pleasure and guilt behind the damning word *decadence*. How Adams came to know Rodin is not certain; probably it was through Saint-Gaudens. They first met in 1895, as he wrote to Elizabeth Cameron: "I am going, as a last resort, to call on Rodin, and try to buy one of his small bronze figures. They are mostly so sensually suggestive, that I shall have to lock them up when any girls are about, which is awkward; but Rodin is the only degenerated artist I know of, whose work is original."[68] And he wrote later:

> I have passed an hour with Rodin in his studio looking at his marbles, and especially at a Venus and dead Adonis which he is sending to some exhibition in Philadelphia, and which is quite too too utter and decadent, but like all his things hardly made for "jeunes personnes" like me and my breakfast-table company. Why can we decadents never take the comfort and satisfaction of our decadence. Surely the meanest life on earth is that of an age, that has not a standard left on any form of morality or art, except the British sovereign. I prefer Rodin's decadent sensualities, but I must not have them, and though rotten with decadence, I have not enough vitality left, to be sensual. Victoria and I and our age are about equally genuine. We are beyond even vice.[69]

Adams managed, however, to buy Rodin's "Ceres" for Henry Higginson.

It was mostly due to an accident that the chaste Saint-Gaudens, who was not free of prejudices and faulty judgments concerning the art of Rodin, should be mentioned along with the French master. His "Sherman Monument" and Rodin's "Eve" were both exhibited in the salon of 1899. Adams wrote about this to John Hay: "We have all been to the Salon, to see the Sherman and Rodin's Eve, and to discuss them afterwards—great things both."[70] He also mentioned these two works in a letter to Gaskell.[71] Adams tried to secure some bronzes by Rodin for Helen Hay and wrote to her husband: "Please

tell Helen that I've quite failed to get any answer at all from Rodin
about her bronzes. He refuses to say anything."[72] Is this characteristic of Rodin's handling of business affairs, or was the failure the
fault of the American?

It is a pity Adams was so secretive about his contacts with the
French sculptor and did not give us a description of the man. His
interest in Rodin's art marks the most advanced point in his appreciation of contemporary art. But we wonder if he would have seen
qualities in that part of Rodin's work which pointed beyond the nineteenth century and *fin-de-siècle* to the twentieth: Rodin's nearly abstract handling of form in his "Balzac" (1892-97), and his stress upon
spiritual beauty, his avoidance of prettiness and pseudo-heroic trappings in the "Burghers of Calais" (1884-86).

As has been noted, the Adamses did not associate with the Post-
Impressionists, or even with the Impressionists. This is affirmed by
the description of a visit they paid to the Goupil Galleries in Paris in
the fall of 1875. Through their establishment in Paris and their
branches in the art centers of Western Europe, they almost completely controlled the traffic in modern art. Today the name Goupil
has survived chiefly because the galleries employed Vincent and
Theo van Gogh. The works of the Impressionists and the unsalable
paintings by Vincent van Gogh were kept, like dynamite or forbidden
literature, in the small *entresol* of their spacious quarters on the
Boulevard Montmartre. Distinguished visitors—Julius Meier-Graefe
specifically mentions Americans[73]—saw none of the radical works.
As a concession to modern fashion, they were shown Barbizon and
pseudo-romantic pictures, which went so well with dark wainscot
and oriental rugs. Marian appreciated the Barbizons Millet, Troyon,
and Daubigny.[74] To her Decamps and Fromentin ranked highest
among the pseudo-romantics. The latter was also admired as the
writer of *Les Maîtres d'Autrefois*.[75] The Adamses wanted to buy a
Fromentin watercolor of "a group of two or three mounted figures,"
but had found it too expensive.[76] They especially liked Decamps.
Marian wrote enthusiastically from Paris in 1879:

> Tell [brother] Ned the Decamps at the Louvre seem to our grop-
> ing souls to take the lead of all the modern French paintings and
> do hold their own with any; and charming as they are, I think

his would hold its own with the best. One picture of Decamps, a line of camels in a burning desert throwing up a golden dust as they tramp, is enchanting.[77]

Marian had mentioned other successful artists of the day in 1875:

We explored Goupil's further shop one afternoon lately and saw some charming pictures; a Troyon, not large, for 25,000 francs, the most fascinating one I ever saw; a superb Decamps, and a small Fortuny of an eastern turbaned creature cleaning a sabre —very delightful! But Goupil's prices are very steep.[78]

There is only one document relative to Adams' interest in Gauguin. La Farge wrote to him, apparently in reply to a lost inquiry about the puzzling Frenchman:

I say "wild Frenchman"—I should say stupid Frenchman. I mean Gauguin. No, I think that he went there just as we arrived in Paris in 1891. His pictures were on show with Whistler's portrait of his mother. I was then told that our Frenchman was going to our Islands and then Tati told me about him. Very little to me; perhaps more to you. After that accidentally I came across some letters of his . . . written from Tahiti. They were meant to be expressive of a return of the over-civilized to Nature. They were very foolish and probably very much affected but also naïve and, I think, truthful . . . He described his meeting some of our ladies . . . All that seemed natural enough; stupid enough; and yet there was something of the man who has found something . . . I mean that they are driven to do something to attract attention. Even their own attention.[79]

What a strange mixture of disbelief and understanding, of malice and fairness, such a letter is! Were the pioneers of the modern movement, in whose front rank we find Gauguin, merely driven to do something to attract attention? Are we not reminded of the arguments brought forward by detractors of contemporary art in our time? It was just that drive towards the new and unknown which Henry Adams and his friends failed to understand since they did not believe in its sincerity, since fundamentally they had no faith in the forces of the new century and in the future of man.

III
The Artists of
the Inner Circle

7. The Architect, the Painter, and the Sculptor

*T*he artist-members of Henry Adams' *Inner Circle*, Henry Hobson Richardson, John La Farge, and Augustus Saint-Gaudens, are counted not only among the most important but also among the most representative figures of American art during the last quarter of the nineteenth century. They were highly esteemed by many of their contemporaries and were looked upon as leaders in their respective fields of architecture, painting and sculpture. They shaped the American artscene not only through their own creative work but also through their teaching and their general influence upon the artists of the next generation.

From Richardson stems much of America's public, domestic, and industrial architecture, both good and bad. Here was started an evolutionary process which, through the works of Sullivan and Adler, connects him with Frank Lloyd Wright. John La Farge, though his reputation as an artist has been challenged of late,[1] is certainly with Winslow Homer an important link in the tradition of American watercolor. Most of all he is one of the outstanding figures in American mural painting and the founder of the American stained glass industry. Augustus Saint-Gaudens is the first great figure in the history of modern American sculpture, holding a position similar to that of Rodin in France.

The three men cooperated, albeit their contributions were of varying degrees in importance, on the Boston Trinity Church built during the years 1875 to 1877, to bring about the realization of that exalted goal of the later idealistic art movements, the fusion of the fine arts. While engaged in that endeavor they were observed by their friend Adams, whose interest and belief in the importance of this particular church is reflected in his novel *Esther*. Trinity Church and some of the men involved in its construction were used by him as material for this work of fiction.

The seventies of the nineteenth century were in more than one respect years of destiny for American art. Largely through the efforts of La Farge and Saint-Gaudens, an American school of art was created. This did much to establish the United States, through work, teaching, artists' organizations and exhibitions, on the European art stage, centered at that time in Paris. Also, by their previous long sojourns in Paris and their apprenticeships in the famous art schools and studios there, La Farge and Saint-Gaudens helped to make the endeavors of their countrymen fashionable.

Adams became friends with the three artists rather early in their artistic careers, before they had achieved national fame. He saw them reach maturity and international reputation, but was not particularly the literary interpreter of their work as would have befitted his ability. The references to it in his writings are not too copious. Even of La Farge, with whom he spent much time and whom he therefore knew most intimately, he wrote that he "preferred to talk little about him, in despair of making either him or his art intelligible to Americans."[2]

As a patron—Adams would have hated the very sound of the word—he certainly did not shower his friends with commissions. The Hay-Adams House in Washington (1884-85), since torn down, was one of the least successful examples of Richardson's domestic architecture, and the Adams' section was the less important, more modest part of it.[3] La Farge did not receive any direct commissions from Adams to decorate it with murals or stained glass; it was Hay who secured La Farge windows for his part.[4] There is not even a portrait of Henry Adams by La Farge. The reason for this singular fact might be that Adams "disliked very much the thought of having himself painted or even photographed."[5] To us it seems that abstaining from commissions to La Farge was the appropriate result and best proof of their great intimacy. It was a sign of pride on both sides, and a way of keeping the integrity of their friendship intact.

Augustus Saint-Gaudens was the least intimate among the intimate artist friends. He did not belong to their generation, being a decade younger. Besides he was, relatively speaking, a latecomer to the circle, and was described by Adams as reticent and inarticulate in an exuberant group of men. But it was Saint-Gaudens who was the creator of the work which was the most perfect realization of the group's spirit, connecting the Adams name most closely with it: the Adams Monument in Rock Creek Cemetery in Washington. This work, its genesis and criticism, as well as the Hay-Adams House built by Richardson, will occupy us later. They represent the direct results of Adams' contacts with his artist friends. Beside such concrete proof there is more intangible evidence, namely the influence of Adams' ideas on those of his inner circle friends, especially on La Farge.

As in the field of politics, Adams played the role of the hidden power in his relations to La Farge and Saint-Gaudens, gently guiding them through the brilliancy and originality of his conversation. His influence might be likened to that of the great ladies of eighteenth century France who organized salons, or to that emanating from the courts of the Renaissance. In his *John Hay,* Thayer compared the Adams' *breakfast-table* in Washington "to the Renaissance coteries of Florence and Ferrara."[6] We shall therefore emphasize the philosophy of art and life shared by Adams with these two artist friends. Richardson was long dead when the Washington breakfast table flourished, and had never been under the influence of Adams' mind.

The next point of importance in our investigation into Adams' relationship to his artist friends are their formative years, during which they shared with Adams the problems of an American young man adjusting himself to Europe. We shall study their active participation in the European art movements and their direct contact with European artists, as well as their more theoretical attitude towards European art and artists as expressed in their writings. We shall be particularly concerned with their position in the struggle of the two late nineteenth century movements of idealism and realism, in which as artists and to a lesser degree as thinkers they all took part.

The factual-biographical side of the relationship of Adams to the three artists will not be neglected, but we despair of catching all the elaborate cross-relationships among the three artists themselves. This task becomes even more difficult when we are forced to add to the circle the more peripheral figures of the two Hunts, the two Jameses, and Richardson's two disciples, Stanford White and Charles F. McKim. We review the three artists chiefly from the vantage point of Adams' life and writings. Our central star is and remains Adams, and we aim at something like completeness only in regard to Adams' relations to the three inner circle artists. His *Education* and his letters, therefore, remain our main source of information. Beyond this we rely for the work and lives of Richardson, La Farge, and Saint-Gaudens chiefly on standard works: for Richardson, Henry-Russell Hitchcock's study; for La Farge, Royal Cortissoz's book, which contains the artist's fragmentary autobiography or "Reminiscences"; and for Saint-Gaudens, *The Reminiscences of Augustus Saint-Gaudens*, published, edited, and commented upon by his son Homer.[7]

8. Henry Hobson Richardson
(Architecture)

*H*enry Hobson Richardson was an exact contemporary of Henry Adams (both were born in 1838) and his oldest friend among the three artists. He was in the same class with Adams at Harvard, the class of '58. Always conscious of belonging to a generation, Adams had this to say about the distinguished names listed in the college catalog for the years 1854-61: "Alexander Agassiz and Phillips Brooks led it; H. H. Richardson and O. W. Holmes helped to close it."[1] Yet he insisted his later attachment to the architect had little to do with the fact that they belonged to the same class at Harvard:

> A student like H. H. Richardson, who came from far away New Orleans, and had his career before him to chase rather than to guide, might make valuable friendships at college. Certainly Adams made no acquaintance there that he valued in after life so much as Richardson, but still more certainly the college relation had little to do with the later friendship. Life is a narrow valley and the roads run close together. Adams would have attached himself to Richardson in any case, as he attached himself to John La Farge or Augustus St. Gaudens or Clarence King or John Hay, none of them were at Harvard College.[2]

After their college years Adams and Richardson met again in Paris during the Civil War, but their meetings seem to have been more devoted to the pleasures of youth than to very serious discussions on architecture:

As often as he could, Adams ran over [from London] to Paris, for sunshine, and there always sought out Richardson in his attic in the Rue Du Bac, or wherever he lived, and they went off to dine at the Palais Royal, and talk of whatever interested the students of the Beaux Arts. Richardson, too, had much to say, but had not yet seized his style. Adams caught very little of what lay in his mind, and the less, because to Adams, everything French was bad except the restaurants, while the continuous life in England made French art seem worst of all.[3]

Richardson was then steeped in the taste of the Beaux-Arts.[4] Nothing seemed to have been more natural for him than to take up the study of architecture in Paris. His youth, spent in Louisiana, predestined and prepared him for France. He was born on Priestley Plantation, in the parish of St. James, at a time when Louisiana was far more a French cultural province than it is today. He had started to draw as a boy of ten in New Orleans and spoke French since early childhood. Thus he was only in a slightly lesser degree French orientated than La Farge or Saint-Gaudens, who were both second generation French-Americans.

The fact that Richardson was a southerner was forcefully brought to his attention in Paris when the outbreak of the Civil War cut him off from home and his allowance. Adams referred to Richardson in a letter from London, dated 10 September 1863, as "politically on the fence."[5] But this did not exactly agree with the facts, as we shall see. Richardson had probably hidden his real feelings from his friend, the son of the "Yankee Minister," as "his unwillingness to take the oath of allegiance to the Northern States"[6] during his brief stay in Boston in 1862 shows. This refusal was also responsible for his return to Paris and an insecure living in the same year.

Adams' letter quoted above refers to him as *Fez Richardson*, but it is not known what this means. Presumably the architect earned it from his habit of wearing a fez, a headgear which might have gone well with his Pasha-like, rotund appearance, and his love for food and drink acquired in Paris.[7]

Since so little is known of the private life of Richardson and his appearance, the descriptions of the Adamses, John La Farge, and Augustus Saint-Gaudens are valuable. They might also help to explain Richardson's penchant for the heavy and vigorous in architecture as conditioned by his mighty physique. Adams compared him several times to Chief Tati Salmon of Tahiti, son of a Jewish father and a Polynesian princess, "whom he markedly resembled."[8] Tati fascinated Adams, just because he owned that "sort of overflow of life that made Richardson so irresistible."[9] The chief's sister Marau "has the same big, Richardsonian ways that her brother Tati has."[10] Marian Adams appreciated Richardson as a dinner companion and conversationalist, "most entertaining and full of talk,"[11] "gay and full of life."[12] "He can say truly 'I am my own music' for he carries off any dinner more or less gaily."[13]

John La Farge too observed the similarity and wrote about it in his *Reminiscences of the South Seas:* "It was pleasant to be with Tati again and hear him laugh, something like Richardson, whom he resembles in size as well as in many little matters."[14] This picture is rounded off in Saint-Gaudens' *Reminiscences:* "Richardson was an extraordinary man, and it would require a Rabelais to do justice to his unusual power and character. He had an enormous girth, and a halt in his speech, which made the words that followed come out like a series of explosions. . . . Richardson wore a brilliant yellow waistcoat, and his appetite was in full harmony with his proportions."[15] Thus Richardson himself was Romanesque in appearance.

It is not our intention, however, to oversimplify the investigation into the origin of Richardson's Romanesque by starting it with a comparison of the architect's mighty girth to the roundness, heaviness and solidity of the Romanesque arch. Though there might have been an inclination towards it caused by character, temperament and stature, the preference of Richardson for the Romanesque is chiefly the result of education and outside influences. One is at first reminded of a similarity of Richardson's mature buildings to those of the Romanesque style in Germany. But the German Romanesque was a possible influence only during his years at Harvard. He entirely lost this interest in the style later on. During his European trip in 1882 he did not even travel in Germany to study the very significant examples of that style there, for he was then predominantly interested in the Spanish and Italian Romanesque.

But to return to Richardson's Harvard years. Then he was subject to the same Germanophile influences of taste and philosophy as Adams.[16] Hitchcock made it appear very probable that what is today called Romanesque—the term for it then was Byzantine—first became known to Richardson in nineteenth century German adaptions, such as the pre-Civil War buildings by Leopold Eidlitz, for instance his City Hall in Springfield, Massachusetts (1854-55).[17] Of the same character were the buildings Paul Schulze, another German, had erected on the Harvard campus, Appleton Chapel and Boylston Hall, both built while Richardson was an undergraduate. Hitchcock calls the Appleton Chapel "Richardson's own first illustration of the [Romanesque] style."[18] But it should not be overlooked that this too was secondhand German Romanesque and did not inspire him later to any intensive study of the original in Germany.[19]

One of the strongest factors contributing to Richardson's Romanesque seems to us to be early Syrian church architecture, specifically the so-called Syrian arch. This type of arch with a particularly wide span rising from the ground became known in France through De Vogüé's *Syrie Centrale.* Richardson might have come across the illustrations in this work as early as 1865, the year the first volume was published, his last year in France. But since he made no use of the Syrian arch before 1877, the years of Richardson's French apprenticeship (1859-65) are hardly any more directly responsible for his Romanesque than his impressions of the secondhand German Romanesque at Harvard.[20]

Adams is certainly correct in saying that when he saw him in Paris in the early sixties, Richardson had not yet found his own style. This is best demonstrated by Richardson's most important work in France, the Hospice d'Ivry for the Incurables. Since 1862 he had been in the employ of Théodore Labrouste, brother of the more famous Henry. "The Hospice certainly represents the form in which Richardson absorbed most completely the French official tradition," Hitchcock wrote.[21] It shows little of the later Richardsonian Romanesque; only the lavish use of the round arch might be construed as an early symptom. But in this too Richardson was, as Hitchock points out, merely following a general French tendency of that time which preferred the round arch to the pointed one.

The Gothic Revival definitely did not appeal to the student at the Beaux-Arts. We conclude this from Richardson's negative attitude towards Viollet-le-Duc, the chief promoter of this style in France. Richardson appreciated him as an archeologist and an authority on restoration, and owned his *Dictionnaire*, but when Napoleon III tried to force him upon the students and faculty of the Ecole des Beaux-Arts as a professor, Richardson protested with the others and spent a short time in jail, from which he was released due to the lucky accident of sharing a cell with Théophile Gautier. La Farge mentioned this demonstration in his "Reminiscences": Richardson "had been a militant, joining the young men who hissed away Viollet-le-Duc from his lectures, from a mixture of anti-Gothic and anti-Napoleon the Third opinions."[22]

This opposition to the Gothic or rather neo-Gothic was not final. When Richardson began to build in the United States he employed that style occasionally. The Church of the Unity in Springfield, Massachusetts (1866-69), his first important church after his return to the States, shows it, though not as a result of Viollet-le-Duc's influence, but of English Victorian Gothic.

The greatest gain of Richardson's years in France was not in acquiring command of any particular style vernacular,[23] but in such general achievements as being able to plan on a large scale and with clear distribution—"the chief virtue of the French tradition."[24] Monumentality and clarity of form are certainly also the qualities of the French idealistic school of painting. But in comparing styles of architecture to those of painting, we come up against terminological difficulties. Our specific problem is the classification of Richardson's style, retaining such terms as *idealism* and *realism*, coined originally by the historians and critics of painting. To apply to architecture, the two terms must undergo some modifications in their definitions.

Idealism in architecture might stand for form expressed in the clearly mathematical treatment of layout and elevation, as well as for the use of such parts as columns of the classical orders, classical pediments, and sculptural decoration employed symbolically to convey such values as the loftiness and dignity of antiquity. While Richardson owed much to the classical school of French architecture in the sense of form, that is, clear layout and well proportioned elevation, the superficial, purely traditional use of columns and pediments was always anathema to him.

What, on the other hand, is generally the meaning of realism in architecture? It is stress on use and function, rather than on symbol or meaning, and certainly a disdain for the conventional trappings of classicism. Form in architectural realism would then be the result of practical planning and function, and would not, as in classicism, be identical with preconceived geometrical shapes. But pure realism in the sense of modern functionalism is extremely rare in the second half of the nineteenth century. Even as advanced an architect as Richardson, in sympathy with realism as we have defined it, did not entirely refrain from the use of falsely decorative details such as turrets, dormers, and Gothic tracery. Even the Syrian arch, which in Richardson's architecture approached functional use, might become a merely decorative hallmark of his style. There was, then, in Richardson's buildings a certain degree of impurity and inconsistency which is even more apparent in the work of La Farge and Saint-Gaudens.

We find the artists of the inner circle, their European *Wanderjahre* behind them, for the first time united in that prime example of the American artist's aspiration towards a new and original style, Trinity Church in Boston. Richardson won the competition for it in 1872, against such public favorites as the Beaux-Arts architect Richard M. Hunt, and by this victory suddenly achieved national fame and prominence.

The three artists and Adams moved closer to each other. Then assistant professor of history at Harvard (1870-77), Adams lived in Boston at 91 Marlborough Street or in Beverly Farms, Massachusetts. Richardson moved to Brookline near Boston in 1874. Though they kept their studios in New York, La Farge and Saint-Gaudens were often employed around Boston and spent considerable time there during the seventies. A web of friendly relationships was there woven among these men. Adams' previous contacts with Richardson have been noted; they renewed their friendship now.

La Farge had met Richardson in the office of the architect George B. Post; he had known Post and his partner Gambrill in New York since 1859. The actual date of the first meeting of La Farge and Richardson is not quite certain, but it must have been around 1867 when, replacing Post, Richardson became Gambrill's partner. In his

"Reminiscences" La Farge said he knew Richardson some few years before the work on Trinity Church, and continued: "George [Post] introduced him as a clever man who would make his mark. He was then designing something of his own, a Gothic church based upon a rather strict view of Gothic principles."[25] Since this obviously alludes to Unity Church in Springfield, Massachusetts (1866-69), it corroborates the date given by Cecilia Waern for the first meeting of La Farge and Richardson, 1867.[26]

Adams "had sat at [La Farge's] feet since 1872," the year of the Trinity Church competition.[27] According to Cater it was Edward William Hooper, Harvard treasurer, art collector, and Adams' brother-in-law, who brought them together.[28] La Farge had been a tutor at Harvard in 1871.[29]

Saint-Gaudens did not become associated with the other members of the group before 1875, after he had returned from his second trip to Italy. He came to know Richardson through Stanford White and Charles F. McKim, both of whom he met more or less by accident in the German Savings Bank Building in New York, where he had rented a studio. At about the same time Saint-Gaudens cemented a lasting friendship with La Farge. The first work he executed after La Farge's design was, according to his *Reminiscences*, the King Monument for the cemetery at Newport, Rhode Island. As a result of this association he helped La Farge to do the paintings in Trinity Church after the latter had taken charge of the whole decorative scheme late in 1876. Saint-Gaudens painted some of the angels in the lantern.[30]

It is probable that Adams, who must have visited the church very often while work was in progress, met Saint-Gaudens there.[31] Unfortunately, Saint-Gaudens and Adams both reveal nothing about it. Mrs. Adams visited Saint-Gaudens' studio in New York at the time of the Shaw Monument, first in 1883; Adams' letters first mention Saint-Gaudens in June 1886. Adams was then on his way to San Francisco to embark for Japan; he spent "a delightful day with King, Saint-Gaudens, etc." in New York.[32]

Since Adams here mentioned Saint-Gaudens without any comment and in conjunction with his close friend King, it is safe to conclude the sculptor must have been on terms of growing intimacy

since the years of Trinity Church. However that may be, the artists'
circle around Adams was complete in 1876, with Trinity Church as
their common meeting ground. Yet it seems that the most decisive exchange of ideas concerning the architecture and decoration of the
church went on between the architect and the painter, rather than
between the architect and the historian. This is supported by the
fact that it was not the first association of the kind between them. In
a lecture delivered before a society of young architects in 1892, La
Farge said: "Mr. Richardson desired for the Brattle Street Church in
Boston an interior with painted decoration as important at least as
the sculptured work of the large exterior bands of bas-reliefs. In this
painting Mr. George Butler was to assist me but the scheme fell
through."[33] The date given by La Farge for this project was 1872.
The bas-reliefs referred to were by the French sculptor Frédéric
Bartholdi. Besides the famous angels blowing trumpets, they contained some portraits, including Richardson and La Farge.[34] La Farge
was also responsible for the meeting of the French sculptor and
Richardson, which took place in the painter's studio, where Bartholdi
had found temporary shelter when he had come to the United States
in 1872, after the Franco-Prussian War. It was in La Farge's studio
that he created the model of the Statue of Liberty.

Brattle Street Church was the first Romanesque building by
Richardson and the direct forerunner of Trinity Church. The 1872
project for the latter showed a certain resemblance to the former.[35]
La Farge was chiefly responsible for the great changes in design,
which to a certain extent effaced this resemblance. A passage in La
Farge's "Reminiscences" proves his decisive share in the final design
of Trinity Church, and with it in the evolution of Richardson's style:

> When [Richardson] competed in the most courageous way with
> Dick Hunt, among others, for Trinity Church, and won, he had,
> as yet, not taken hold seriously of the Romanesque problem. He
> designed a building which was intelligent but not what could be
> done and especially wanting in any historical character. Grad-
> ually he felt it. We spent many hours together. He was then in
> Staten Island, a married man, and glad to give me long day and
> night hospitality. . . . I was able to propose to Richardson to
> change entirely the character of this building so far at least as

externals, which in this case would not be separated from the
great basis of plan, etc. I brought him photographs of the Spanish Romanesque churches, Avila, and so forth, of which I had a
special collection, made for Queen Victoria during her visit.
Meanwhile, Richardson built the Brattle Street Church.[36]

It is known, however, that finally it was not the Avila churches,
such as San Vincente and St. Peter, but the old cathedral of Salamanca, specifically the lantern with its dormers and octagonal tiled
roof, which Richardson's associate Stanford White, following La
Farge's photographs and advice, adapted in his execution of the design to fit the older scheme of Trinity Church. Certainly the proportions and unity of the building profited by the reduction of the excessive verticalism of the central tower, reminding one in the earlier
design of a giraffe's neck, to its present squatty, compressed sturdi-
ness. It is interesting to observe that the building owes so much of its
success and fame to Richardson's exposure to the *historical style* of
the Spanish Romanesque, brought about by La Farge and White.

The new detail of the interior, especially the elaborate poly-
chromatic scheme in the style of the Auvergnat Romanesque, the
Romanesque of southern France, might have derived, as Hitchcock suggests, from the reproductions in Revoil's *Architecture Ro-
mane du Midi de la France*, published just at that time in 1873.[37] It is
tempting to see there, too, not only the influence of the historically
trained, elaborate taste of Stanford White, tending to Victorian pic-
turesqueness, but also that of the always color-conscious painter
La Farge, who took care of the interior of Richardson's *color church*.

About La Farge's great share in the decoration of the interior—
the first large-scale attempt in the history of American architecture
and actually the beginning of the American mural on a large scale—
we are well informed by his "Lecture to the Young Architects" and
a lengthy passage in his "Reminiscences." Both accounts stress the
extremely short time allowed for the completion of the interior, since
funds for the decoration became available only a few months before
the consecration. Work on it began late in 1876, while the absolute
deadline was the date set for the consecration of the church, 9 February 1877. They further mention the lack of money for suitable scaffolding and the difficult circumstances under which the work had to

proceed in winter, with the enormous windows not filled until very late in the season. All this meant hardships, even risks of life and limb, for the people carrying on the work.

La Farge emphasized the fact that he had to create the technical conditions for American mural painting from scratch, though he neglected to mention that William Morris Hunt was faced at about the same time with a similar situation when he painted the ceiling decorations in the Senate Chamber of the New York Capitol at Albany. La Farge said he had to fight "hand to hand with commerce," and continued: "Good materials were difficult to purchase, methods of applying them had to be devised on the spot . . . At the end we had to work both night and day, and were only able to guess at what might be the result when the scaffolding should come down."[38] One is reminded of the tribulations of Michaelangelo while painting the Sistine Chapel ceiling and the technical troubles of the German Nazarenes when they revived mural painting in Rome in the Casa Bartholdi.

These truly dramatic circumstances are of special interest to us here because they were used by Adams for his novel *Esther*, published in 1884 under the pseudonym of Frances Snow Compton. Robert E. Spiller, editor of a reprint, noted in his introduction some of the parallels between the setting and the persons in the novel and the building of Trinity Church and its artists. According to him, the church in the novel, St. John's, Fifth Avenue, New York, is Trinity Church, Boston, and Wharton is La Farge. He further showed that besides Trinity Church, Adams drew certain features also from St. Thomas' Church, Fifth Avenue, New York, the decoration of which "La Farge had recently completed."[39]

The many co-workers employed by La Farge at Trinity Church to bring the work to a rapid conclusion are in the novel reduced to one assistant, Esther Dudley, a member of New York society and an amateur painter. She creates a mural of St. Cecelia under Wharton's supervision. Spiller observed, "There is, of course, no St. Cecelia at Trinity, but there is a window in the North Transept representing St. John's vision of the Holy City," and continued, "Adams in his story has moved it from the western to the eastern wall so that the October morning sunlight may shine through it, and he has consecrated his

12. Self-Portrait by John La Farge (detail). Oil Painting, dated October 26.27.1859. The Metropolitan Museum of Art, New York. Courtesy of the Metropolitan Museum of Art.

13. Portrait of John La Farge by Wilton Lockwood, 1902. Oil Painting. Private Collection. Reproduced from the Collections of the Library of Congress.

14. "Scene at Tahiti," by John La Farge. Watercolor. The Fogg Art Museum, Harvard University, Cambridge, Massachusetts. Courtesy of the Fogg Art Museum.

15. Augustus Saint-Gaudens. Commemorative Bronze Plaque by Frederick W. MacMonnies. Inscribed *Augustus Saint-Gaudens Statuaire. Aetatis LVI.* Collection of Dr. and Mrs. Ernst Scheyer, Detroit, Michigan. Photographed by Joseph Klima, Jr.

16. The Adams Memorial, Rock Creek Cemetery, Washington, D.C. Bronze Sculpture by Augustus Saint-Gaudens. Reproduced from the Collections of the Library of Congress.

church to it." One might add here that the opening situation of the novel was obviously inspired by the aforementioned consecration service at Trinity Church.

Spiller further observed, "There may also be a connection between Wharton's 'four great figures of the evangelists' and La Farge's Angelesque figures of St. Peter, St. Paul, David, Moses, Isaiah and Jeremiah on the upper walls of the tower of Trinity." And finally he noted that the unconventional terms under which Esther did her painting and the haste and casual character of the work are clearly suggested in La Farge's own report as reprinted by Cortissoz. The fact that the role of the leading artist is assumed by the painter, while neither architect nor sculptor is mentioned in the novel, makes it probable that Adams relied chiefly on La Farge. He also must have used his own observations on the spot and what the minister of Trinity Church, his cousin Phillips Brooks, might have told him. As previously mentioned, the fictitious Stephen Hazard, minister of St. John's, was a fusion of Brooks and Adams.

In addition to Spiller's observations, there are a few other parallels between historical truth and novelistic fiction, between Richardson's Trinity and Adams' St. John's. In the first chapter "unfinished frescoes" and an "unfinished transept" are mentioned, alluding to the speed with which the work had to be carried out at Trinity.[40] In Chapter IV, "The north transept, high up towards the vault of the roof, was still occupied by a wide scaffold which shut in the painters and shut out the curious, and ran the whole length of its three sides, being open towards the body of the church."[41] This reminds us of the unsatisfactory scaffold and the dangers described by La Farge. Then there is a "John of Patmos," a mural "next to that which Esther was to paint."[42] A "St. John of Patmos" had actually been painted by La Farge in 1862-63 for the altar of a Catholic church.[43]

"The first effect" of the interior of St. John's, which "was as impressive as though she were in the Church of St. Mark's," is an allusion to the rich and colorful interior of Trinity with its dull terra cotta, gold and blue green.[44] The remark by Strong (King) at the beginning of the story, "Wharton's window is too high-toned," and Esther's reply, "You all said, it would be like Aladdin's,"[45] parallels Hitchcock's observation that at Trinity "the La Farge windows in the façade are magnificent in colour and scale once the eye is adjusted to the key of their rich tones. They imitate no earlier glass and yet rival the best of the past in their quality of low burning intensity."[46]

Although the architect of Trinity does not appear in the novel, his library—"an elaborate collection of illustrated works on art, Egyptian, Greek, Roman, Mediaeval, Mexican, Japanese, Indian"—seems to be described. However, its contents reflect Adams' taste as well. A further passage in the novel referring to the library—"It happened that Hazard's knowledge and his library were often drawn upon by Wharton and his workmen . . . his collection of books was the best in New York, and his library touched the church wall,"[47]—reminds one of Richardson's excellent library in Brookline, which was housed next to his office and living quarters, and was used by his associates White and McKim, and probably also by Adams. Adams may have consulted Richardson's "illustrated works" on the Middle Ages while lecturing on that subject at Harvard. Adams had not then been to Spain—he went there in 1879—and he had not yet come to appreciate French Romanesque architecture during his travels. The inspiration, then casually transmitted, came to a full blossoming much later.

In 1882, a few years after the completion of Trinity Church, Richardson made a trip to Europe. Traveling in France, Spain, and Italy, he came finally face-to-face with the original works he had known so far only from the reproductions in his library. Yet too much should not be made of that. As Hitchcock remarks, his "style was too completely matured to be much affected by external influences."[48]

Richardson's trip was undertaken with Phillips Brooks and led first to London and England.[49] What interested him in that country were chiefly contemporary art and architecture, while no special study was made of medieval buildings. He found the architecture of the Gothicists William Burges and George Street disappointing, and did not meet personally the progressive English architects Philip Webb and Norman Shaw. However, he purchased photographs of the interiors of Shaw's Chelsea houses. The greatest gain of his stay in England seems to have been from a visit to Merton Abbey, where he spent a short time with William Morris and other members of his circle, among them most probably Burne-Jones.

In France Richardson neglected the Gothic but studied the Romanesque with great enthusiasm, for instance Nôtre-Dame-du-Port at Clermont-Ferrand. Since he had already shown an interest in the southern French Romanesque while building Trinity Church, naturally he visited Arles, where he especially admired St. Trophime. He found St. Gilles less attractive. Then came Italy; to him Pisa was the finest thing he saw in Europe. In Florence he was impressed by the Bargello. Ravenna, especially the Tomb of Theodoric with the granite helmet of its cupola, must have struck a familiar note in Richardson; its wide arches came closest to the Syrian. St. Appollinare in Classe's round campanile, so much like an American silo, must have fascinated him.

But the country "with whose Romanesque architecture he felt most at home," as Hitchcock said, was Spain. The world of the library of illustrated books and photographs sprang into reality. He stood in front of Avila's churches; he saw Salamanca Cathedral, whose influence transmitted through photographs had helped so much to establish his fame. Richardson returned via France; he stopped in Poitiers, where he studied Nôtre Dame la Grande, and ended his trip in Paris, which he had not seen since 1865. There he looked up his friends, the architects Guadet and Gerhardt, both good practitioners of the Beaux-Arts vernacular.

Certainly the most important meeting with European artists during the trip was the one with William Morris and his friends. Hitchcock remarks further that "Richardson and Morris had perhaps more similarity of temperament than either shared with his ordinary associates."[50] Indeed the two men were amazingly alike in many respects. There was their exuberant joy in life, food, and drink, their sensuous pleasure in materials, their patriarchal attitude towards family and associates. They shared the conviction of the interrelationship and unity of the arts, and both found means for its realization.

Richardson certainly had read some of the writings of Morris, since his attitude towards the crafts and their function in architecture was so obviously guided by the Englishman's ideas. There is a marked similarity to the designs of William Morris in the carving of Richardson's fireplaces, such as the one of 1878 in the Ames Memorial Library, North Easton, Massachusetts, with its pomegranate tree pattern, and even more so in the leaf pattern of the 1882 fireplace in Austin Hall, Harvard, reminding one of the marginal decorations in Morris' *Kelmscott Chaucer*.[51] Finally, Richardson resembled Morris in the use of stained glass for many of his buildings, for which he had in La Farge such an able collaborator.

All the members of the inner circle shared an interest in the Pre-Raphaelite movement, amalgamating it with that in Japanese art, or more correctly, *Japonism*. *Japonism* was, however, less pronounced in Richardson's work than in La Farge's. The architect was as averse to Oriental exoticism as he was to classical colonnaded and pedimented porches. The only direct traces of *Japonism* to be found in Richardson's work were the great Japanese symbols penciled on the orange plaster wall of the Payne house in Waltham, Massachusetts.[52] In such qualities in Richardson's domestic work as sensibility to materials, feeling for the site, preference for low lines, however, we observe a certain congruence with the principles of Japanese architecture. It is significant that La Farge became aware of this not too obvious connection. While contemplating the beauty of the wooden shrines and temples of Nikko in Japan and noting their superiority to Western stone buildings, he observed:

> Indeed I have always felt that perhaps in the case of poor Richardson just dead, we may begin to see the shape of an exception, and can realize what can be accomplished through what we called deficiencies. He was obliged in the first place, to throw overboard in dealing with new problems all his educational recipes learned in other countries.[53]

One would assume that the double house Richardson built for Henry Adams and John Hay at 1603 H Street and Lafayette Square was among the finest of the architect's domestic buildings in Washington, yet according to Hitchcock it was inferior.[54] Ernest Samuels noted that Hay, "a millionaire since the recent death of his father-in-law, bought the entire corner tract, conveying the west 44 feet to Adams on January 14, 1884. Squarely opposite the White House, it was indeed as Adams crowed 'a swell piece of land.' "[55] Since the house has been torn down and the Hay-Adams Hotel erected on its site, we must rely on Hitchcock's judgment, having only the designs and photographs in his book and in Thayer's *John Hay* to go by. Hitchcock's chief criticism is that the complex mass, originally to be built in rockfaced yellow sandstone with brownstone trim, suffered by its transfer to red brick. Especially the turrets then appeared as purely decorative, "arbitrary and out of scale," and "the windows mere holes in the wall surface." "The Syrian entrance arch of the house seems merely to have been repeated from the Trinity Rectory." "The redeeming feature" of the house "is in the interior," especially the great hall in Hay's part.[56] This was finer than the Payne hall in composition and superior in luxury of tone and texture to the Albany Senate Chamber. In this, Richardson's powers were shown to the full. These great halls, with monumental fireplaces and great staircases pouring "down into the room like a mountain cataract," are most characteristic of the interiors of the later Richardson houses.[57] These aspects were especially dealt with in Adams' letters to John Hay.

The commission was given in January 1884 when Mrs. Adams was still alive, and she took great interest in the project.[58] The house was finished in 1886, shortly after her tragic death on 6 December 1885. In June 1886 Adams left it, as though in sudden flight, for his trip to Japan. The house was built under ill stars; its only mention in the *Education* is fraught with melancholia: "In 1884 Adams joined [John Hay] in employing Richardson to build them adjoining houses on La Fayette Square. As far as Adams had a home this was it. To the house on La Fayette Square he must turn, for he had no other status—no position in the world."[59]

The melancholia certainly did not pervade Hay's part of the building. There exists a poem by John Hay in which it is called "The House Beautiful," full of art, music, love and children.[60] Adams' letters in 1884, that is before the catastrophe, breathe happy expectancy. He merely assumes the role of the reluctant grouchy miser whom the irresistible spendthrift Richardson persuades to spend money lavishly against his will. The first letter dealing with the house under construction is dated Washington, 26 October 1884, and addressed to Hay:

I owe you infinite amusement. Ten times a day I drop my work and rush out to see the men lay bricks or stone in your house. Mine is still where it was when you were here; but yours is getting on. The dining room wall is up to the next floor; the parlor and the whole front is up to the sills of the parlor windows. At this rate, your next floor will soon go in. The brick-work is beautiful. I am now devoured by interest in your door-arch which must soon be begun.

Richardson put back into my contract every extravagance I had struck out, and then made me sign it. After this piece of work he went off to seek other victims. He is an ogre. He devours men crude and shows the effects of inevitable indigestion in his size. . . . By the way, I was much amused by my brother John who was here last Wednesday, and who has just built a house in Boston. We took him over Anderson's house, and his disgust for his own became alarming. He swore horribly that Anderson's house was the cheapest thing he had ever heard of, and far handsomer than that of Fred Ames which cost a million or two. Judge Gray has bought the opposite corner to Paine's lot; my old family house; 1601 I Street.[61]

The *door-arch* referred to in the letter is the Syrian arch discussed above. The Fred Ames house must be the mansion in North Easton, Massachusetts, which John A. Mitchell had enlarged for the family in the seventies and for which Richardson built a gatehouse in 1880-81. The Anderson house, commissioned in 1881, is the closest relative to the Hay-Adams house in style, though a more satisfactory example of Richardson's architecture. Its successful execution was probably the immediate cause for the selection of Richardson as an architect, for Mrs. Adams wrote to her father on 22 April 1883 that they "went over Anderson's new house. It does Richardson great credit; if we had thirty thousand a year it would suit us to a T." Nicholas Longworth Anderson was a Harvard classmate and intimate friend of Henry Adams.[62] Adams wrote the next letters dealing with their house to his wife on 21 March and 10 April 1885:

[Richardson] is pleased as a monkey with his houses, especially with the cornices; and gloats over the few bits of ornament he has let go in, as though he had invented all the decoration of St. Ouen and stuck it on our caves. After kiting about the houses, he came back here and had a talk with Edmundson [the builder or contractor].

If you can reconcile yourself to it, please have a sea-green onyx fire-place. Should you see Richardson, ask him about this, and if he approves, as he will, let us have a Mexican onyx fire-place. . . .

The house does get on, no doubt, but the work done is no longer so easily noted from day to day. Hay's last chimney was finished yesterday, and the rest of his roof is getting astride of his dining room. So far, so good. To get the roof on at all is a triumph.[63]

The designs for the fireplaces were also mentioned in a later letter to John Hay, 20 April 1885:

I saw Richardson in Boston and lectured him with my usual severity. So far as I could see, I met with my usual success. He seemed much delighted by an equally severe letter from you, and showed me ravishing designs for your fireplaces which economy itself could not resist. Indeed I have given up resistance either on your behalf or my own. You don't back me up, and I don't support myself loyally. I shall get out of it by telling lies to Nick Anderson. When I saw the houses building in Boston, ours seemed like cottages and I became ashamed of them. As cottages they are thoroughly satisfactory, but as houses they make no kind of show except in an out of the way place like this.[64]

Adams removed himself from the scene of the building by taking up summer residence in Beverly Farms, leaving Theodore Frelinghuysen Dwight, librarian at the White House who became his companion and secretary after his wife's death, as observer in his old quarters in Washington. Dwight sent him regular reports about the progress of the house. On 26 July 1885 Adams wrote him somewhat alarmed:

Keep your eye on our house-front, and if you see the workmen carving a Christian emblem, remonstrate with them like a father. As yet I am myself uninformed as to their intentions. I wanted a peacock. The artist wanted a lion. Perhaps you can suggest a compromise;—say a figure of Mr. Blaine, Conkling or Bayard.[65]

[And about four weeks later:] Your account of the carvings fills me with terror. I can only hope that John Hay and you will receive the discredit of them, and divide it between you. . . . We have no news here, and watch the autumn approach with dread at the idea of taking up our architectural furnishing.[66]

As the summer declined, still at Beverly Farms, Adams wrote to Dwight, 13 September 1885: "I am relieved to hear that the stable is going up, and the paint going on. Pray tell me whether any mantle-pieces are finished; whether the kitchen range is in; whether the lift is under way; and whether any sign of completion in bathrooms, etc. is visible."[67] On 19 September 1885 he wrote to John Hay:

> The man-mountain Richardson (I suppose you include him among your purchased mountains) told us of your sudden ap-pearance and disappearance after our return. Richardson told me too some tedious tale about our houses being done. I know nothing to the contrary except its impossibility—besides which it is on its face a Richelaisian jest. Big as he is, he turned pale and trembled, when he told me he was going on to see what he had done; and should take the next train to the west! You can imag-ine, if the thought of seeing my house-front makes his brazen front blanch, what my delicate sensibilities are suffering. What will you give me for my night-mare as it stands?[68]

This probably referred to the trouble with the carvings, since a letter to Dwight a week later said specifically: "Your account of the cross and carving fills my heart with sadness, and steeps my lips in cocaine. I can neither revolt nor complain, though the whole thing seems to me bad art and bad taste. I have protested in vain, and must henceforth hold my tongue."[69]

In his last letter from Beverly Farms to Dwight, 2 October 1885, Adams noted that Richardson was to inspect the house after some changes had been made in the carvings: "Richardson will be in Wash-ington, I suppose next week, and give the house its final approval or disapproval, as the case may be. John Hay expects to go on with him."[70] After his return to Washington, he wrote to Dwight about changes in the carving of the arches, 4 November 1885:

> Many thanks for the drawing which shall rank in my new study if I ever get into it. As for the house, Richardson has toned down the worst carvings, and although I cannot pretend that I think them all appropriate, I say as little as possible on the subject. The arches have stood revealed for a week or more. I know not what the public says, and have heard of no newspaper criticisms. Omi-nous silence prevails within my range of hearing.[71]

Adams wrote the same day to John Hay from Washington, but did not discuss the arches; his interest was concentrated on the fireplaces. With this letter the correspondence concerning the house ends.[72] (Richardson had been seriously ill during the fall of 1885 and was to die half a year later.) About a month later, on 6 December 1885 Marian Adams committed suicide. She had not seen the new house completed and had never lived in it. Adams' first letter bearing the new Washington address, 1603 H Street, is dated Tuesday, 22 March 1886.[73]

The letter to John Hay of 4 November 1885 breathed an ominous air: "Your house is calm as the Pyramids, but your hall ceiling is up, and very handsome. Evans is still at work on the columns. My hall fireplace is finished. I feel sure it is yours, and that Klaber gave it to me to quiet me, and is making another for you; but I can't prove it. Klaber's man is constructing an awful onyx tombstone in my library."[72] Evans was regularly employed by Richardson for the carving of architectural details. The Romanesque columns and the base of the columns of the Hay fireplace can be seen in a photograph in Hitchcock's book.[74] Klaber apparently built fireplaces after Richardson's designs. The term "onyx tombstone," tragic and prophetic in view of Marian Adams' subsequent death, described well the heaviness of Richardson's late interior style.

Yet in spite of a certain heaviness inside and out, the house was described by Van Wyck Brooks as having sunny rooms, and he observed also a similarity to Sever Hall, Harvard, which, however, is very general.[75] The next style-relatives to the Adams house in Richardson's own oeuvre are the Trinity Rectory in Boston, the Anderson house in Washington, and for the interior, the Payne house in Waltham, Massachusetts. As to historical influences, Cater said that "an old French house in the Troyes region was Richardson's inspiration."[76]

In his article "At Mr. Adams's," James Truslow Adams observed: "This house built for him by his friend H. H. Richardson, was an odd home for such a fastidious man as Mr. Adams. The leather chairs, which abounded, were all so low that they seemed to have been made for the host's own use. . . . To the eye it was a very Bostonian house, though Mr. Adams did not care to have you think so."[77] George Santayana, who visited in the house as a young man, called it luxurious and remarked, "I got the impression that, if most things are illusions, having money and spending money, were great realities."[78] The most detailed description of the Hay-Adams House was patiently pieced together from conversations with relatives and friends of Adams by H. D. Cater. It reads in part:

> Facing south on Lafayette Square, directly across from the White House, it was a four-storied, red-brick structure, fronting directly on the edge of the sidewalk. It had little about it that was pretentious and much that was practical. There were two broad arches on the street floor which formed bays, one of which was covered by an iron grill, and the other formed the main entrance to the house. Since the house was built in the European manner; the main living-rooms were on the floor above, and a flood of light came into them from six large south windows across the front; three were for the library and three were for Adams's study. The two top stories were used for sleeping; the lower one of the two had a recessed balcony overlooking the Square. The front stairs, designed to make climbing almost effortless, led from the street level to a hall, which in turn opened into the large library. The latter served also as a drawing-room. In this room there was a fireplace of sea-green Mexican onyx shot with red. Off the library and to the rear, was the dining-room, which had an unusual fireplace in light stone carved with wild roses. These two rooms and Adams's study opened into each other by folding doors. In all these rooms there was a sense of color and light, but a definitely masculine atmosphere.[79]

Mrs. Homans' description of the living-dining room has been noted above. She noted further that the study was "furnished with a huge mahogany table, which took up most of the room."[80] The Adams-Hay House was completed in 1886, the year of Richardson's death (27 April). Adams' letters do not mention this event which, following so closely his own wife's death, must have shaken him. He embarked two months later for Japan, accompanied by La Farge. Later there were only occasional references to Richardson when Chief Tati's bulk and hearty laughter brought back memories of the "man-mountain."

It was not until Adams became passionately interested in the Romanesque style himself that he made his finest tribute to the architect, which was quoted above from a letter written while he was

working on *Mont-Saint-Michel and Chartres*: "I am now all eleventh
and twelfth century. . . . I caught the disease from dear old Richardson who was the only really big man I ever knew."[81] This undoubtedly refers not merely to his physical but also to his mental stature.

There is, as we have seen, occasional notice in Adams' writings
of the Richardson associates Charles F. McKim and Stanford White.
Two of their projects were related to the art of Richardson, and
Adams made comments about them: the Boston Public Library and
the Chicago World's Fair of 1893. The Boston Public Library,
started by McKim, Mead and White in 1887, a year after Richardson's death, and finished in 1895, was located opposite Trinity
Church. It is, in the words of Hitchcock, "the best and in all funda-
mentals the most Richardsonian of their works."[82] But the substitu-
tion of Renaissance for Romanesque was definitely in the direction of
the refinement, not to say the dilution of Richardson's style. Saint-
Gaudens planned sculpture for it and recommended La Farge for
murals. Yet the works which made the library the main shrine of
the Late Idealistic Movement in America were Puvis de Chavannes'
murals of 1895-99 on the stairway. They were highly admired by
Adams and his artist friends. He voiced the sentiment of the group
when he called the "Puvis paintings for the Library . . . the greatest
things ever painted."[83] They were the swan song of the movement;
the Chicago World's Fair was its perversion and defeat. Hitchcock
expresses the idea that the fair's effect might not have been so cata-
strophic had Richardson been alive and had Burnham sought "direction from him and not from the pompous Hunt and the brash Mc-
Kim."[84] In a letter to John Hay, Adams very frankly criticized the
fair:

> I want to talk . . . about the architecture, and discuss the true re-
> lation between Burnham, Attwood, McKim, White . . . and the
> world. Do you remember Sargent's portrait of Mrs. Hamersly in
> London this summer? Was it a defiance or an insult to our society,
> or a rendering in good faith of our civilization, or a conscious
> snub to French and English art, or an unconscious revelation of
> the artist's despair of reconciliation with the female of the gold-
> bug? . . . Well! the Chicago architecture is precisely an architec-

tural Mrs. Hamersly. I like to look at it as an appeal to the human animal, the superstitious and ignorant savage within us, that has instinct and no reason, against the world as money has made it.[85]

Even when he tried to defend the work of the architects individually, Adams found for the defense words of criticism regarding the social function of the fair's architecture as a whole: "All trader's taste smelt of bric-à-brac; Chicago tried at least to give her taste a look of unity."[86] And he wrote further in his *Education* about the artists and architects who "talked as though they worked only for themselves; as though art, to the Western people, was a stage decoration; a diamond shirt stud; a paper collar . . . a sort of industrial speculative growth and product of the Beaux Arts artistically induced to pass the summer on the shores of Lake Michigan."[87]

The Chicago fair was thus to Adams another example of the "gold-bug" taste, the unity was faked or forced and discordant features showed, disrupting the unity of the White City like wide cracks in the walls of marble veneer, in spite of the metal braces which a country grown rich and powerful could put behind them to hold the architecture together. The Chicago World's Fair was the tragic result of the struggle between idealism and realism. There could be no unity, only the desire, and in Chicago the brutal will towards unity.

9. John La Farge
(Painting; Stained Glass;
Theory of Art)

*J*ohn La Farge's art shows similar symptoms of
disharmony and unevenness, and is in this respect an even more typical product of the latter part of the nineteenth century than Richardson's. Yet on the other hand, none of the artists of the inner circle
had the critical faculty, the penetrating insight into the secrets of art,
past, present and future, as La Farge. La Farge was a connoisseur
of art, and only in the second place a creator of paintings.[1]

Henry Adams appreciated him most as a *causeur* on the arts.
The two men knew each other's minds inside out; they were practi-
cally of one mind in spite of certain individual differences brought
about by dissimilarity of temperament and background, which
Adams loved to exaggerate. Both have acknowledged their mutual
interdependence of thought. La Farge did it in the preface to *An
Artist's Letters from Japan*; Adams in the following passage in his
Education:

Of all the men who had deeply affected their friends since 1850
John La Farge was certainly the foremost, and for Henry Adams
who had sat at his feet since 1872, the question how much he
owed to La Farge could be answered only by admitting that he
had no standard to measure it by. Of all his friends La Farge
alone owned a mind complex enough to contrast against the com-
monplaces of American uniformity, and in the process had vastly
perplexed most Americans who came in contact with it. . . . His
approach was quiet and indirect; he moved round an object and
never separated it from its surroundings; he prided himself on

faithfulness to tradition and convention. . . . One was never quite sure of his whole meaning until too late to respond, for he had no difficulty in carrying different shades of contradiction in his mind . . . for even a contradiction was to him only a shade of difference, a complementary color.[2]

Thus, in describing his friend's mind, Adams described his own, and we are therefore justified in treating La Farge's ideas on art as an extension and professional elaboration of those of Adams. Especially on art theory and on contemporary art, where Adams' writings offer only limited information, La Farge's copious and brilliantly formulated observations are a most welcome supplement to those of his friend.

In their old age the two men grew inwardly and outwardly more and more alike.[3] Kindness was hidden behind sternness, tolerance behind self-assertion. "Personally La Farge proved a bit crotchety and very self assured," wrote Homer Saint-Gaudens.[4] Adams has given a sympathetic portrait of La Farge in the years of his maturity as the Wharton of his novel *Esther*. Though treated with poetic license in some minor details, it is essentially correct in description of La Farge's physical features, though less in that of his character:

> He was a man of their own age, so quiet and subdued in manner and so delicate in feature, that he would have been unnoticed in any ordinary group, and shoved aside into a corner. He seemed to face life with an effort; his light-brown eyes had an uneasy look as though they wanted to rest on something that should be less hard and real than what they saw. He was not handsome; his mouth was a little sensual. . . . He was apt to be silent until his shyness wore off, when he became a rapid, nervous talker, full of theories and schemes, which he changed from one day to another, but which were always quite complete and convincing for the moment.[5]

It is interesting to note that here, as in the description of La Farge's character in the *Education*, the changeableness and contradictoriness of his theories, as well as their completeness *for the moment*, are stressed—qualities La Farge shared in so high a degree with Adams himself.

Family background, racial, cultural and religious, was in the case of La Farge as determining a factor as in the case of Adams. Yet they were highly contrasting: La Farge, French, aristocratic, Catholic; Adams, New England, democratic, Protestant-Puritan. La Farge was French on both his mother's and his father's side, and remained French to such a degree that Focillon, reviewing the La Farge exhibition at the Metropolitan Museum of Art in 1936, could write: "To the French traveller . . . it seemed almost as if one caught the whisperings of a dual language, that of America and that of his own country."[6]

John La Farge's father, Jean-Frédéric de la Farge, ensign in the French navy, came to this country in 1806, a refugee from the massacre of San Domingo. He subsequently owned a plantation in Louisiana and property in New York State, and settled finally as a successful realtor in New York, where his son was born in 1835. John was thus three years the senior of Adams and Richardson.

The home in which John La Farge grew up was very elegantly furnished in the empire style; on the walls hung a seapiece by Vernet, pictures by Lemoyne, Salvator Rosa, Sebastiano del Piombo, and many Dutch paintings, among them a beautiful Salomon van Ruysdael. His artistic education was taken care of by his maternal grandfather Binsse de Saint-Victor, who had been a rich planter in San Domingo, lost his fortune in the uprising, and became a miniaturist and art teacher in New York. This grandfather started him "at six years old in the traditions of the eighteenth century."[7] His own early drawings of the fifties, La Farge wrote, "were largely based on line and construction."[8] Watercolor was taken up when he was in Columbia Grammar School. His teacher was an Englishman who gave *thoroughly English lessons.*[9]

La Farge attended St. John's College, now part of Fordham University, New York, and Mount St. Mary's College, Emmitsburg, Maryland, from which he graduated in 1853. At college a "professor in English took [him] into the literary and historical side of art."[10] This teacher was an Oxonian who had joined the first Oxford movement. Through him he first heard of Ruskin, whose ardent follower the professor was, and learned "how wrong all sorts of things in art were which did not agree with the mediaeval."[11] This seemed for a while to counterbalance the French eighteenth century. "The Ruskinian explanation connected with Turner was a large factor in my training and amusement," La Farge wrote. When he first went to Europe in 1856, La Farge studied the romantic movement in France and England, the two countries for which background and education had best prepared him, and where "the romantic leaven acted both in literature and in the other arts, even in the art of music."[12]

In Paris, La Farge had an introduction to the great men of art and letters as few American art students before him. His grand-uncle, the older Saint-Victor, "had been a writer upon art, a collector of fine paintings, and acquainted with many famous artists of his prime." He spoke to him of David and Guérin as young students and was somewhat critical of Ingres, "as a person a little too much tinged with sentiment, as a master *not sufficiently strict*" to suit his eighteenth century taste.[13]

But his son Paul de Saint-Victor was very sympathetic towards the young romantic generation. This cousin of La Farge was one of the most celebrated French writers of his time, author of many books and articles on literature, art, and the theater. Having been secretary to Lamartine, he belonged to a circle which counted Gautier, Baudelaire, Flaubert, and the Goncourts among its members. In 1870 he became inspector of the fine arts, but this was merely the official stamp on a long career devoted to the arts. Gérôme and Chassériau were acquaintances, and he introduced La Farge to them and their work. For a short time La Farge attended the atelier of the academic classicist Thomas Couture and then turned more strongly to realism by becoming a student of the Millet disciple William Morris Hunt.

Théodore Chassériau, who was to die young in the year La Farge came to know him, impressed the young man as did probably no other artist. He later wrote about him and his work in his "Reminiscences":

> These paintings are to me of extraordinary importance as reconciling the schools which he valued and as making the future of a person at that time quite unknown, and, in fact, not yet a character in arts; that is Puvis de Chavannes, who succeeded to a great deal of Chassériau's ideas and training and in fact, to more than that, to the drawings and studies and the personal friendships of this man whom I used to go and see. Another person who I think was influenced, was Moreau.[14]

And further: "At Chassériau's the war raged all the time. At once one was asked what one held in regard to M. Ingres and M. Delacroix." La Farge never did meet Delacroix, though he admired him very much.

La Farge was perhaps the first outside France to appreciate the importance of Chassériau, and certainly the first to introduce him to the American public in his lectures inaugurating the Scammon course at the Art Institute of Chicago, which appeared in book form in New York in 1908 under the title *The Higher Life in Art.* This is the finest work on the history and criticism of modern French art written by an American at the beginning of the century; it deserves to be given a prominent position in our concern with La Farge as a writer on European art. It is chiefly devoted to the artists of the Barbizon school, the so-called realists, but gives also in its first chapters an excellent survey of the preceding schools of classicism and romanticism. Chassériau is seen in true perspective as the man who reconciled the two schools. La Farge had a special liking and understanding for Chassériau. He was reminded of his own position and his own *fate*, as being "thrown in both camps (academic and intransigeant)," and wrote:

> A debate concerning these two names [Ingres and Delacroix] was centred in one man [Chassériau]. This man was to appear for a moment in the character of a student and a follower of both sides, was to bloom for a short moment, to be a mere promise, to represent the past, a good deal of the future which he might be thought not to be dreaming of, and then to die suddenly, and to be almost forgotten. . . . In a tendency to some simplification one can see the future Puvis de Chavannes and something also of the Millet who was to come. . . . Puvis kept to his death in his consultation case, as we might say, a certain number of drawings and studies of the Chassériau whom we knew, and who was the coming man, when Puvis hesitated yet as to what he should do.[15]

The experience of Chassériau's work bore fruit in La Farge's own paintings. We discover it especially in "Anadyomene," a theme treated also by Chassériau.[16] It is a work rich in pigment, reminding one of Gustave Moreau. Then there is La Farge's "Three Kings" in the Boston Museum of Fine Arts, which in the elegance of the slender figures and horses shows likewise traces of Chassériau, or perhaps of

Delacroix through Chassériau.[17] The influence of Chassériau's disciple Puvis de Chavannes is felt throughout the mural paintings by La Farge in composition, spacing and poses.

When, as a young man of twenty-one, La Farge entered the studio of Couture, he merely followed a fashionable trend:

> My American acquaintances were then very much inclined to the painter Couture, who had quite a number of Americans in his studio and had been the master of several of them, well known in Paris and having quite a position of their own. One of these, Edward May, took me to the master one day and I explained to him what I wished, which was to get a practical knowledge of painting, as practised by him. I also made him understand that I was doing this as a study of art in general and had no intention of becoming a painter.[18]

Since La Farge was not interested in becoming a little Couture like most of the others in the studio, he worked on his own, copying old master drawings in the Louvre and only occasionally returning to the studio. "On the whole," he said, "I did not stay there more than a couple of weeks." Into the time spent in Couture's atelier falls La Farge's personal contact with Puvis, who "came in one day, wanting a model" and chose the young American. "Perhaps . . . it was something in my face. I don't know what I posed for. Some study, perhaps."[19] After his brief stay in Couture's studio, La Farge traveled in Europe, studied in the museums, copied old master drawings in Munich and Dresden, Rembrandt in Copenhagen, and showed a special interest in Rubens and his school while in Belgium. Returning to Paris he did not rejoin Couture's studio.

> I do not know what I should have done had I remained in Europe and in Paris. But I did not admire his work or his views of art and he annoyed me, notwithstanding his friendliness, by his constant running down of other artists greater than himself. Delacroix and Rousseau were special objects of insult or depreciation. He never referred to Millet, for whom some of his best pupils, among others, William Hunt, had left him—a fact which he never forgave, as I learned later.[20]

La Farge observed in *The Higher Life* that "Couture was one of our teachers, occupying a place of his own but rather an uncertain one, as far as doctrine went; he was an executant, he was not an exponent of law."[21] He certainly had Couture and his followers in mind when he wrote about the *pseudo-classical* school, comparing their paintings to the theater and remarking that "the nineteenth century has given us bad habits of mechanical work."[22] Though written almost half a century after La Farge had been in Couture's studio, these words show an amazing independence of judgment for the beginning of the twentieth century.

Couture, whose "Romans of the Decadence" had been a world success in the Salon of 1847 and brought him scores of pupils from the rest of Europe—Anselm Feuerbach for example in 1852-53—and America, was then still considered one of the greatest figures in the history of French painting. To indicate his powerful and central position in European and American art, as well as La Farge's own place in the struggle between the classicists and romanticists, and the succeeding movements of later idealism and realism-impressionism, we have designed Chart II.

It is of interest to note, as our chart shows, that the Americans Hunt and La Farge both left the camp of academic classicism, or *pseudo-classicism* as La Farge called it more adequately, for the cause of the two progressive or *intransigeant* movements, romanticism and realism. The comment that he resented Couture's "constant running down of other artists greater than himself [such as] Delacroix and Rousseau" shows clearly where La Farge's sympathies were, at least in theory. In some of his later murals, however, he could be as pseudo-classical and academic as Couture.

To what degree the two American Couture students Hunt and La Farge identified themselves with the school of Barbizon, especially with Millet and Rousseau, is recorded by La Farge in his *Higher Life*, as spoken to him by Hunt after the International Exposition of 1868 in Paris, "Well our men have won."[23] This understanding attitude makes La Farge the best historian in English the Barbizon school has had. He was the first to see the connection between romanticism and realism, by stressing the relation between Delacroix and Millet. La Farge called "that great movement [romanticism and realism] a wave of the history of the world—the stormy

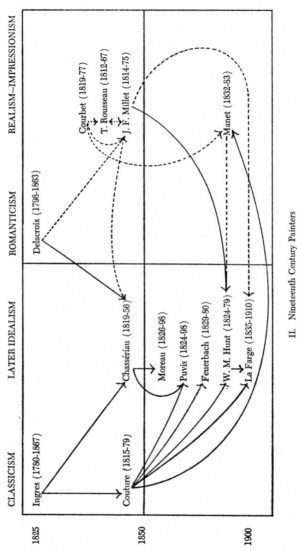

II. Nineteenth Century Painters

Solid lines indicate strong, direct influence
Broken lines indicate weaker, indirect influence

settling of the waters after the French Revolution and the spread of its effects through the wars of Napoleon."[24] That this movement, which he interpreted as the natural release of the powers of freedom and democracy, should strike his contempories as so extravagant, exaggerated and chaotic, was explained thus by La Farge:

> The story of this romantic and emotional and realistic school is associated with *this* difficulty. They met not a helping but a tyrannical formalisation of art, meant for the good of a general public but which to their independence was disastrous. Their forced opposition to the great school, the great government school, is the constant thread that unites all these men together.[25]

La Farge saw the *gloom* of the Barbizon landscapes, their lack of optimism, as a recoiling of the artist from an unsympathetic society. "The melancholy born of failure in fitting the issues of the world to one's own desires turns naturally into contemplation of that over which we have no control—that nature which continues undisturbed by the vicissitudes of man."[26] To La Farge, Delacroix was "the first call of a new era," while Millet was "a vision of emotional art fit to balance the record of Delacroix."[27] "Delacroix was Millet's first and only admiration among modern painters. In the work of Delacroix, Millet could see the proper dramatic expression belonging to the art of painting."[28]

But La Farge saw also the connection of Millet's figural compositions with the French classical tradition. We have noted La Farge's remark that in Chassériau's tendency towards simplicity "one can see the future Puvis de Chavannes and something also of the Millet who was to come." He pointed to specific sources of inspiration: "Virgil and the Bible are the books of [Millet's] great pictures, if we see them right."[29] In the way in which Virgil and the Bible create everlasting monumental types, so Millet's work for that very same reason "tended to a form of technique which resembles the idea of sculpture."[30] In other words, Millet's figures had sculptural form. "In these works of Millet remains the feeling which marks the great works of the Middle Ages in which the soul of old France established a form as important as the Greeks."[31] But he denied any trace of social criticism or even social consciousness in the sense of militant and political class-consciousness in Millet's work, as Millet himself had vigorously protested against such a false interpretation: "The critics saw social protest in what was really the expression of duty and resignation to the common fate of most men."[32] He ended the chapter by pointing out that Millet had his first great success with Americans and in America, since "the very seriousness which troubled the French mind was rather an appeal here than a difficulty."[33]

Millet was the hero of La Farge's book. The other members of the Barbizon school were treated no less understandingly but more briefly. He explained Corot's landscapes in a new manner, his "view of Nature [is] constantly steeped in that peculiar influence inseparable from the love of the human form. . . . That is to say, he is a composer, a builder of proportions, even though the apparent record is only that of landscape at a given time of day."[34]

In Théodore Rousseau's landscapes La Farge stressed an aspect very rarely noticed, his connection with the Japanese print, from which he learned "extreme luminosity by a few flat clear colours." But he noted also the "over-conscientiousness in Rousseau's work," meaning its photographic character.[35] He dealt with photography several times in the book, since its invention made realism problematic, and he predicted: "It might be some day that the vision of Nature would be still nearer if the photograph—the machine—should be able to give a little accurate colour. Then perhaps that line will be cut off and some great revolt of feeling might come."[36] Does that not sound like prophecy? Indeed the liberation of feeling and imagination from the burden of visual recording, now taken over by the camera, was one of the causes of expressionist as well as of abstract art.

La Farge stressed correctly the connection of Jules Dupré's work with the English school of landscape painting, by pointing to Dupré's relation to the French landscapist Paul Huet and his stay in England in 1836. But he had observed that influence so important for the evolution of French realistic and impressionist landscape painting already in Delacroix's paintings and watercolors. He further noted that Delacroix not only took lessons in the English method of watercolor from Copley Fielding, with whom he lodged, but that Delacroix was also the first "by half a century to praise before an unbelieving continental audience"—the Pre-Raphaelites.[37]

The knowledge of the work of the Pre-Raphaelites was the other great impression and gain which La Farge brought from Europe to America. He had been prepared for it by the enthusiasm of his English professor for Ruskin, but when in England for the first time he did not use a letter of introduction to the English writer. Like Henry Adams, he became more and more critical of Ruskin in later years. La Farge wrote that though he retained the liking for the Pre-Raphaelites, "Ruskin's writings had become stumbling blocks rather than helps to [his] likings and [his] judgment."[38]

While in Japan meditating on the role of the decorative artist and the position of so-called decorative art, so different in the East from that in the West, he was even more outspoken in his criticism:

> Many years ago I used to read Mr. Ruskin when "my sight was bad, and I lived within the points of the compass" and also the works of other men, who laid down the exact geography and the due distances, north and south, of a certain department or land of art which they called "Decoration."[39]

Another point of contact with the art of the Pre-Raphaelites was La Farge's interest in the Middle Ages, though this interest was originally directed towards literature and archeology, and only later towards the arts. While traveling in France he saw the originals of some of the medieval buildings about which he had read at home. He met Viollet-le-Duc shortly before he left for America, but he was critical of the archeologist's work. On a tour through Belgium he saw "some of the paintings which we may call mediaeval and [with] which begins modern art," he wrote, and he "was steeped in admiration."

> All this led me to a desire to understand the mechanical methods of the early painters, especially those who invented the modern art of painting in oils, and by some chance of good fortune I made the acquaintance, in Brussels, of Henry Le Strange, who you know decorated Ely cathedral. He was interested in me and in what he had to tell me practically about manners of painting. I learned from him about painting in wax, for instance, and was led to read various documents of information with regard to that question, of the early ways of painting.[40]

This knowledge of the old methods of painting prepared him not only for the art of the Pre-Raphaelites, who at that time revived in

England the forgotten art of mural painting and stained glass decoration, but for his own endeavors in these two fields as well.

In the fall of 1857 La Farge spent some time in England, but he did not yet meet the members of the Pre-Raphaelite Brotherhood, "because almost every one for whom I had letters was away from London."[41] In 1873, however, when he spent half the year in England, he made the acquaintance of Ford Madox Brown, the brothers Rossetti, their sister Christina, and Edward Burne-Jones.[42] He knew Christina Rossetti best; of her brother Dante Gabriel he remarked, "he made you feel that whether his painting or poetry 'came off' or not, it was the real thing." He was more critical towards Burne-Jones, whom he thought "interesting, but there were queer blank walls in his make-up that you bumped your head against." For Ford Madox Brown, the mural painter, he "preserved a special fondness," and "Brown was peculiarly friendly to the American down to the end of his life."[43] La Farge's biographer Cortissoz wrote, "Recalling his Pre-Raphaelite intimacies, he told me that he immensely liked Christina Rossetti . . . they used to talk together about religion."[44]

But to return to La Farge's first stay in England in 1857. It was then that he first studied the work of the Pre-Raphaelites, in Manchester at the first of the special exhibitions of paintings brought together from public and private collections. "But besides the miles of old masters, there were some of the quite new; the pre-Raphaelites, whom I knew of by reading and by some prints but whom now I could see carefully. They made a very great and important impression upon me, which later influenced me in my first work when I began to paint. But of that I had no warning."[45] As quoted by Cecilia Waern, he was more specific:

A visit to the Manchester Exhibition and a short stay in England determined for many years certain admirations, and confirmed me in the direction of my ideas of colour. The few pre-Raphaelite paintings that I saw, and the drawings of some of the leaders in that movement, appealed strongly to me. Nor did they seem disconnected from the charm of Sir Joshua and of Gainsborough, or from the genius of Turner, which yet offended me by its contradiction of the urbanity and sincerity of the great masters whom I cared for most. But the Pre-Raphaelites, as seen through my eyes—Millais and Hunt, and Rossetti and Ford Madox

Brown—Sir Edward Burne Jones had not yet appeared within
my horizon—seemed to me to be willing to meet many of the
great problems of colour and my youthful energies sympathised
with the stress and intensity of their dramatic programme.

These likings I retained later when I began to think again
of painting. . . . I find the trace of these influences pleasantly
lingering in some of the drawings which I made even ten years
later, and some few words of praise accidentally dropped by Millais or Rossetti in favour of some trifle of mind which had found
its way to England pleased me as establishing a relation to them
that my general tendencies of work and study could not imply to
many of my friends.[46]

The second part of the quotation refers to the time, after La Farge's
return to America in 1858, when he took a room in the Studio Building on Tenth Street and began to visit the ateliers of painters and
architects: "I only touched the merest corners of what was being
done. I did not know of our Pre-Raphaelites here, as a body, though
I spent some time with [William J.] Stillman, who was one of their
prophets."[47] La Farge's own work first came to the attention of the
Pre-Raphaelites in 1868, the trifles just mentioned. We read in the
"Rossetti Papers": "Showed Gabriel the photographs sent me by
Scudder after designs (Piper of Hamlin, etc.) by La Farge; he was
much pleased with them and took them off to show to Brown."[48]

Horace Scudder was the editor of the *Riverside Magazine,* a
periodical for the young, for which during a prolonged illness La
Farge had done drawings which were engraved by Henry Marsh.
Their titles—Bishop Hatto, The Giant and the Travellers, The Fisher-
man and the Genie, The Wolf Charmer (later made into the oil at
the City Art Museum of St. Louis)—show they pertained to folklore
and fairy tales. Their style quite resembled the flowing lines of the
artists of the brotherhood. La Farge shared with Scudder and Adams
an enthusiasm for William Blake, the rediscovery of Dante Gabriel
Rossetti. There was a project for La Farge to do a series of illustrations in Blake's spirit for the *Riverside Magazine,* which were not
executed, however.[49]

Not only La Farge's drawings, but also his early paintings, especially his landscapes, showed some influence of the Pre-Raphaelites in their minute observation of nature, their *veracity* (Ruskin),

combined with certain compositional features of the Japanese print. In his still-lifes too, for instance "Wild Roses and Water Lily," we come across that intermingling of Pre-Raphaelitism and *Japonism.*[50] Already there was a tendency to combine these two *isms*; Whistler's early paintings, for example "The Princess from the Land of Porcelain," are the best-known examples.

La Farge's interest in East Asian art followed the same curve of development as that of his friend Adams; from the Japanese print it rose to old Buddhist art. We are well informed about this education towards the true values of East Asian art through La Farge's writings. On the occasion of the auction of part of his collection (chiefly East Asian) in 1908, he wrote to James Huneker:

> It is just fifty years ago, that I bought my first Hokusai book— imagine the joy of first discovery. So I lit off and I have had my likings for Japan. In fact I know of no artists before me. My French people laughed at me for "Les amours exotiques." But here people thought moral ill of a lover of Jap art—as for the lover of Blake or Goya.[51]

This establishes La Farge as one of the earliest American *Japonists*, certainly as one of the earliest collectors of Ukiyo-e prints in this country.[52]

After he had come in contact in 1859 with William Morris Hunt, who also was an eager collector of Japanese prints,[53] La Farge took up their study in connection with his scientific interest in the theories of color and light.

> [John] Bancroft and myself were very much interested in Japanese color prints and I imported a great many in the early sixties for us both, through A. A. Low. I think it was in 1863. We had to risk our purchases entirely and got few things as we should have chosen them, as we had at that time no persons interested in such things. We had nobody over there in Japan to buy for us with any discretion. The point that interested us both has not yet, I think, been studied out. . . . The very serious point to me was the display in certain of these color prints, of landscape relations in color. . . . In the Japanese prints and in some of their paintings it is more obvious [than in Western art] because it is less covered up.[54]

La Farge had the most important teacher in the arts of the East in Okakura Kakuzo who, like all upper-class educated Japanese, had only contempt for the art of the Ukiyo-e and must have led La Farge gradually to the great art of the early periods. However, he supplied La Farge with Japanese and Chinese prints to instruct him in the techniques of East Asian art. La Farge became so adept in it that he could say: "I defy a Chinaman to deny that I have used correctly his basis."[55]

But La Farge owed to Okakura Kakuzo more than advice in technical matters; he became his teacher in the philosophy of East Asian art. La Farge expressed his gratitude to him in the second dedication of *An Artist's Letters from Japan* (the first was to Adams): "For a time you were Japan to me. I hope, too, that some thoughts of yours will be detected in what I write, as a stream runs through grass —hidden perhaps but always there." Okakura in turn dedicated his *Book of Tea* to La Farge, who represented to him *the* Westerner with a sympathetic understanding for the artistic culture of Japan.

More will be said about La Farge's interpretation of the great Buddhist art of Japan in our review of *An Artist's Letters from Japan*. Here we quote in conclusion La Farge's farewell to his earlier interest in Japanese bric-a-brac: "From all this poor stuff exhales the faded scent of a greater art and refinement, which is now invisible, or destroyed, or subsisting only in fragments, difficult of access, or which are far away."[56] Later in his life La Farge devoted a masterly essay to his first love in East Asian art, Hokusai, in his *Great Masters*. In the introduction to this book he wrote:

> There is no possible comparison between the elegant but somewhat superficial beauties of the Japanese artists whom we know best (Ukiyo-é) because we have them in printed form, and the deep sentiment, the serenity or spiritual uplifting of the Buddhist art of Japan—or again the synthetic view of all nature which belongs to the artists of an earlier date.[57]

The interest in the Japanese print, with its resulting studies of light and color, is part of the complex of *scientific realism* in La Farge's oeuvre. It was carried on during his stay in the studio of William Morris Hunt in Newport, Rhode Island. La Farge knew Hunt through his brother the architect and was also attracted by the great reputation the painter had gained in Couture's studio. La Farge went to him in 1859 with the specific intention to continue the studies he had interrupted in Couture's atelier in Paris. This was a natural step to take, since Hunt had been "a favorite and brilliant pupil of Couture's," as La Farge wrote.[58] "But a disappointment was in store for me, and it was this,—that Hunt had abandoned the practice of Couture, which was what I wished to continue."[59]

Certainly, as far as artistic influences were concerned, Hunt had one of the most checkered careers of any American artist. He first studied at the Academy of Düsseldorf, where a sentimental genre was taught, which attracted many American artists during the first part of the nineteenth century. While later a pupil of Couture in Paris he championed nevertheless the cause of the romantic Géricault, whom he called one of the greatest of modern painters. He had been invited to Delacroix's studio after he exhibited his "Marguérite" in the salon of 1852. But under the influence of Millet he foreswore all historical painting.

"I like joy in my studies and I don't like literary indigestions," Hunt wrote in his *Talks on Art*.[60] Another famous anti-academic sarcasm of his was: "Draw fearlessly, avoid that kind of finish that rats give to cheese." Van Wyck Brooks has given the best description of Hunt's picturesque personality which intrigued the Bostonians. Though he chided them, and though they laughed about his extravagances, they flocked to his lectures. "Why didn't you like Cambridge?" he was once asked, and Hunt answered, "Because I love art. Cambridge is like Kaulbach's pictures. It is all literature."[61]

When La Farge entered the Newport studio Hunt was in his most enthusiastic Millet phase. He owned many oils by the Frenchman, among them the famous "Sower," and many drawings. Some of these as well as his considerable collection of the French romantic-realistic sculptor Barye came later into the possession of the Boston Museum. But La Farge did not fall immediately for the Millet cult. "It was not what I had come to get," he wrote.

> Though I even copied a Millet or two, I was firmly resolved against following him either with or without Hunt, in the methods which were especially developed by the great Frenchman. His previous methods which one sees more distinctly in some of

his landscapes, and, of course, in his early work, were nearer what I had been looking for.[62]

What La Farge wanted to apply "were principles of light and color of which I learned a little." He had started this pursuit even earlier under the influence of Chevreul's writings and said that his reading on the optical views of color "determined, I suppose, more than anything else the direction which my painting took."[63] It is interesting to note that Chevreul's works influenced not only the French Impressionists but also American painters such as La Farge and Winslow Homer.

The first distinctive paintings that show the result of these studies were landscapes done in the winter of 1859-60, all of them studies taken from the window. One of these, "Old House in Snow Storm, Newport, Rhode Island," was painted in a soft and dreamy manner in spite of the starkness of the old clapboard house.[64] It reminds one technically much less of Millet than of Hunt's landscapes, such as "Ballplayers" in the Detroit Institute of Arts. Others were done, quite in contrast to that poetic softness, with emphasis on geological structure, as in the background of Millais' portrait of Ruskin. Still others, for instance "The Hill Top" in the Boston Museum, remind us, especially the passage with two women resting under a pine tree, of the earliest landscapes with figures by French Impressionists such as Frédéric Bazille. Of course we do not hint at any direct influence; the successful fusion of realistic and classical elements lends them a certain similarity. Durand-Ruel, the art dealer of the Barbizonists and the Impressionists, must have early become aware of these qualities of La Farge's landscapes. One of the Newport studies, "The Lost Valley," hung in his galleries in London in the seventies between a Rousseau and a Delacroix. But his hopes to establish La Farge in Europe did not come about.

"Refinement of tone and color" was La Farge's alleged aim in these landscapes.[65] Yet in his endeavor to achieve an all-over tonality, his pictures often became too soft and look wooly and boneless, like those by George Inness during his vague last phase. In front of La Farge's most important landscape, "Paradise Valley," painted in 1866/68 after his stay with Hunt, one is also reminded of Inness, but the Inness of the Medfield years (1859-64). Cortissoz was right in calling "Paradise Valley" a significant painting in the history of American art. In its candid sincerity it antedated Impressionism, but it is more subdued in color, having been painted on a cloudy day. La Farge himself liked it and was sure of its importance. He painted it from a little hut which he had built among the rocks.

> I undertook a combination of a large variety of problems which were not in the line of my fellow artist here, nor did I know of anyone in Europe, who at that time undertook them. . . . My programme was to paint from nature a portrait, and yet to make distinctly a work of art which should remain as a type of the sort of subject I undertook, a subject both novel and absolutely "everydayish." . . . Nature, meaning in this case, the landscape we look at, looks as if it had done itself and had not been done by an artist.[66]

Although it is an excellent picture, La Farge's claim of the uniqueness of this type of landscape painting in Europe and America at that time was not quite correct. From the first part of the nineteenth century there are a number of such *pre-impressionist* paintings which look as though they had done themselves, though most of them were considered to be mere sketches by their makers: Constable in England, Dahl in Norway, Corot in France, Blechen, Wasman and the young Menzel in Germany. In America landscapes by William S. Mount, for instance "The Artist and his Wife Sketching," and by the early Inness, such as "On the Juniata" of 1856, compare well with the best of the European *pre-impressionist* group.

Both William and Henry James, who were fellow students with La Farge in Hunt's atelier, were enthusiastic about his Newport landscapes. William James joined La Farge on his sketching trips to the Newport Glen,[67] while Henry James devoted several pages to La Farge's Newport landscapes, especially to the "View of the Paradise Rocks over against Newport," as he called it. "We knew already, we knew then, that no such range of airs would ever again be played for us on but two or three silver strings."[68] La Farge's influence on his fellow students was great and his advice often changed their lives. He urged Stanford White, who had come to him with his plan to become a painter, to choose architecture. He advised Henry James to turn writer, though he had the *painter's eye*. A portrait of Henry

James by La Farge, exhibited in New York in the summer of 1858, is a document of this friendship. William James, however, became a philosopher on his own account, though this was a great loss to painting. He drew beautifully and some of his paintings, for instance the wonderful portrait of Miss Katherine Temple of 1861 (who was also painted by La Farge), according to Henry James' sensitive observation, had "much the air of a characteristic Manet."[69]

To Henry James we owe the best description of Hunt's workshop around 1860, as well as a long and penetrating analysis of La Farge's character. In *The Notes of a Son and Brother* James called La Farge "quite the most interesting person we knew . . . a character above all, if there ever was one."[70] His *foreignness* impressed both brothers. "La Farge was of the type—the 'European,' and this gave him an authority for me that it verily took the length of years to undermine."[71]

> It was as a man of the world, that, for all his youth, La Farge rose, or still better, bowed, before us, his inclinations of obeisance, his considerations of address being such as we had never seen and now are almost publicly celebrated.[72]
> The wealth of his cultivation, the variety of his intentions the inveteracy of his forms, the degree of his empressement made him with those elements of the dandy and the cavalier, to which he struck us as so picturesquely sacrificing, a cluster of bright promises, a rare original . . . an embodiment of the gospel of esthetics.[73]

But La Farge was also their guide to literature. Browning, Balzac, and Mérimée were introduced by La Farge, who was "unexhaustibly bookish," said Henry James, and he continued, "The artist's serenity by this conception, was an intellectual and spiritual capital that must never brook defeat."[74]

The Civil War ended the period of the early La Farge, the European La Farge, the La Farge of the James brothers. In the seventies the artist emerged as the master of great projects: world traveling, mural painting, stained glass designing, and writing on art. It was the time of his intimacy with Henry Adams.

The circumstances under which La Farge and Adams met were not recorded by either of them. Cater states that Adams' brother-in-law Dr. Edward William Hooper brought them together.[75] They probably first came in closest contact with each other during the building of Trinity Church in Boston (from 1872), as we have noted above. In 1886 they embarked together for Japan. Adams wrote about their friendship to John Hay from San Francisco: "Adventures we discard, for we are old and no longer vain; but La Farge makes a delicate humor glimmer about our path."[76] And similarly he wrote to his English *intimus* Gaskell: "I took with me a well-known New York artist, John La Farge, an old acquaintance, and a very unusual man, who stands far away at the head of American art, but who interests me more as a companion than as a painter, for he kept me always amused and active."[77] Thus it was not the painter but the man La Farge that Adams *took* on the trip to Japan. His letters described the entertaining character of his fellow traveler; he wrote to Hay:

> [La Farge] continues to be the most agreeable of companions, always cheerful, equable, sweet-tempered, and quite insensible to ideas of time, space, money or railway trains. To see him flying through the streets of Tokio on a jinrickshaw is a most genial vision. He peers out through his spectacles as though he felt the absurdity as well as the necessity of looking at the show as though it were real, but he enjoys it enormously, especially the smell, which quite fascinates him. He keeps me in perpetual good humor. . . . I am lost in wonder, how he ever does work; but he can be energetic, and his charm is that whether energetic or lazy, he has the neatest human, the nicest observation, and the evenest temper you can imagine. When he loses the trains, I rather enjoy it. After all, who cares?[78]

In the last letter from Japan to John Hay, Adams summed up the results of the Japanese trip for them:

> We will turn out a new Japan of our own. La Farge has bought materials enough—vast mounds of rubbish—to construct a world of decoration, paint forests of pictures, and exhaust the windows of Christianity. . . . I will tell you all about it when we meet; but La Farge is so much more amusing about it than I can be, that you had better wait till our book comes out, in which he will write the story, and I draw the pictures.[79]

In spite of the bantering tone of these letters, which stress the good comradeship between the two men, it must have been a difficult and delicate assignment for La Farge to be the always amusing traveling companion to a man like Adams, especially after the tragedy of his wife's death. On top of all that, Adams paid the bills! Yet there is only frank admission of the situation in the dedication of *An Artist's Letters from Japan* to Adams: "Without you I should not have seen the place." It said the book was indeed theirs, their common brain child. In a certain sense they both wrote it. La Farge acknowledged this not only in the dedication but also in the text; for example:

> My dreams of making an analysis of these architectural treasures of Japan were started . . . by the talk of my companion, his analysis of the theme of their architecture and my feeling a sort of desire to rival him on a ground for fair competition. But I do not think that I could grasp a subject in such a clear and dispassionate and masterly way, with such natural reference to the past and its implied comparisons, for A[dams]'s historic sense amounts to poetry, and his deductions and remarks always set my mind sailing into new channels.[80]

Yet as the book unfolds, the strong personality of Adams recedes from the pages, though his mind remains present. Subjects Adams neglected in his letters were taken up by La Farge, for instance the Japanese interior. La Farge was impressed by it and saw not merely "the toy, the nursery" in it, like Adams, but also: "The domestic architecture is as simple, as transitory, as if it symbolized the life of man."[81] And further: "It is possible that when I return I shall feel still more distaste for the barbarous accumulations in our houses, and recall the far more civilized emptiness persisted in by the more esthetic race."[82] This was written before Lafcadio Hearn and Pierre Loti voiced similar ideas and educated the West to understand Japan. The lesson was certainly lost on Adams!

To Nara, which Adams barely mentioned, La Farge devoted extremely fine observations, in which he is farthest from *Japonism*, bric-a-brac, and the "vast mounds of rubbish" Adams accused him of acquiring. La Farge wrote about the painting and sculpture of the Golden Hall of Horyu-ji, that wonderful relic of Chinese Buddhist T'ang civilization in Japan:

> Their placid elegance, the refinement of their lines, their breath of religious peace, explained those claims to a solemn and glorious past for Japan which look like a conventional exaggeration

in a today that is delicate and small and dry. . . . The recall of
Greek perfection was not forced, and while still vaguely unwill-
ing to confuse one excellence by referring to another I could not
help again thinking of the Greeks and of Tanagra images.[83]

While in the East, La Farge could never free himself from the
fascination Western antiquity had for him, "the one beauty which is
to outlast all that is alive."[84] While dealing with Adams' stay in the
South Seas, we noted it was precisely this belief which kept him as
well as La Farge from seeing landscape and especially figures with
new eyes, and from dealing with them on their own native terms. The
Polynesians on Tahiti *had* to be the Greeks of the Homeric Age and
Tahiti a Pacific Arcadia. This Hellenisation of the Pacific is especially evident in the more labored *finished* paintings done by La
Farge in the South Seas.

This second trip to the Orient, undertaken in 1890, four years
after the first, was again financed by Adams, who extended an invitation to La Farge to join him. The wound caused by Adams' wife's
death had not yet healed. La Farge was again the understanding and
entertaining companion, the physician of the soul that he took along.
Adams described to Elizabeth Cameron how he had to drag La
Farge to the boat, away from his New York activities of "three pictures to paint" and "two windows to lead." "He was very gay and
impecunious as ever, and is going to take his Japanese boy with him.
To my constant amusement he always ends with the same grave
serenity that he shall do this at his own expense."[85]

We have already dealt with Adams' attempts to draw and paint
in watercolor under La Farge's guidance; his greatest gain from this
trip was his discovery of color. To achieve this, the friends had aided
each other: one contributed his technical ability, the other his keen
observation. La Farge's landscapes, especially those in watercolor,
belong to the best of his whole work. The volcanoes on Hawaii,
the peaks and mountain ridges of Tahiti covered with clouds, the
waves of the Pacific, and especially the sketches of mountain huts on
Fiji,[86] might be compared in quality to the best of Winslow Homer's
watercolors from the Bahamas. His brush was wielded with the same
courage and looseness. The colors, however, only occasionally
reached Winslow Homer's brilliancy; they remind one mostly of
Whistler's subtlety.

Adams, who thought very little of his own attempts at water-color, highly praised the work of his friend. "Naturally all my paint-ing was childish, but I hope, I induced La Farge to catch something worth keeping," he wrote to Elizabeth Cameron, and described in the same letter the colors of the Polynesian world as La Farge taught it to him: "Sky, sea and land, are all judicious watercolors, toned with one general purplish wash with the most exquisitely delicate grada-tions, but never running into violent contrasts. Even the whites have an infinite gradation of violets, when contrasted with the dead white of a ship or a house."[87] Adams wrote about La Farge's facility with watercolor:

> He has a wonderful faculty for getting light into his color. I study in vain to find out how he does it, though I see all his proc-esses. . . . He splashes in deep purples on deep greens till the paper is soaked with a shapeless daub, yet the next day, with a few touches it comes out a brilliant mass of color and light. Of course it is not an exact rendering of the actual things he paints though often it is near enough to surprise me by its faithfulness; but whether exact or not, it always suggests the emotions of the moment.[88]

Other passages in Adams' letters from the South Seas regarding La Farge dealt with his friend's native name *La-Fa-ele* (which he liked because it happened to be identical with *Ra-fa-ele*—Raphael) upon his adoption into the same clan of Teva, of which Adams and Mrs. Robert Louis Stevenson were also made members, and finally with La Farge's mania to collect photographs, which Adams disliked.

La Farge's letters from the South Seas appeared in book form under the title *Reminiscences of the South Seas*. They were published in 1912, after his death.[89] Henry Adams disclaimed all literary am-bitions to add some notes to his friend's book: "I can imagine few things more incongruous than my poor Bostonian, Harvard College, matter of fact Ego, jammed between the South Seas and John La Farge."[90] But Adams' own letters to his friends and La Farge's, mostly to his son, were not at all incongruous; on the contrary, they were very much alike in their references to Homer and the Greeks, their interest in the dances, in the stories of the Teva clan, even in the search for Nirvana. The "Epilogue" in La Farge's book reads as though directly inspired by Adams, not only in content but also in form: "In such a repose of nature we passed our days as if preparing for the final close."[91]

It was chiefly in the description of art objects that La Farge, as in the book on Japan, was more specific and often more understanding, witness his appreciation of Samoan art:

> The fitness and close relation of all I have seen makes a something like what we strive to get through art.—These people make little; the house, the elementary patches upon their bark cloth, the choice of a fine form for tombs, is all the art, that is exterior of themselves and of their movements, into which last they have put the feeling of completeness and relation, that makes the love of art.[92]

"Completeness and relation, that makes the love of art." In these words La Farge revealed his own aspirations. It is strange that the art of mural painting, by which La Farge impressed his contemporaries most profoundly, is to us today farthest from this goal. Idealism and realism do not complement each other to a synthesis but remain in a state of dichotomy.

It does not seem to us accidental that Adams refrained from practically any specific reference to his friend's mural paintings in his writings. Though he generally stated that La Farge interested him more as a companion than as a painter, he devoted lines of fine understanding to his watercolors from the South Seas and was very interested in his experiments and activities in the field of stained glass. Thus, the neglect of La Farge's murals must have its deeper reason in a somewhat critical attitude on Adams' part. Only in his letters to Mabel Hooper La Farge were her father-in-law's murals briefly mentioned, and then he expressed respect for the physical vigour of the old painter more than interest in the work. He wrote to her from Washington on 6 April 1897: "La Farge is now with me, a rival wreck but grandly purposing to paint his 70-foot canvas as though he had still legs and a stomach."[93] This refers to La Farge's "Ascension" for the chancel wall of Stanford White's Church of the Ascension at Fifth Avenue and Tenth Street in New York, which was completed in 1899. Our critical analysis of La Farge's murals will be

limited to this one and those in the Minnesota State Capitol, since
they show best his virtues and faults in the medium.

The "Ascension" is La Farge's most successful mural, though the
elements in it are of a very heterogeneous nature.[94] The idea for the
grouping of the figures can be traced back to a sketch La Farge did
in the fifties, shortly after his return from Europe. The composition
with its hexagonal pattern and its careful spacing of figures looks as
though a Venetian of the sixteenth century had gone to study with
Puvis de Chavannes in Paris. Frank J. Mather pointed out that "the
composition is merely a grandiose amplification of Palma Vecchio's
'Assumption' in the Venice Academy . . . the soaring Christ . . . is a
Venetian enlargement of an Umbrian conception; the color has taken
much from Titian and more from Delacroix."[95] The landscape is
similar in line to works of the Japanese Kano school. Indeed, La
Farge found the inspiration for it in Japan, for he wrote:

> The landscape I wished to have extremely natural, because I de-
> pended on it to make my figures also look natural and to account
> for the floating of some twenty figures or more in the air. . . . At
> that moment I was asked to go to Japan by my friend Henry
> Adams, and I went there in 1886. I had a vague belief that I
> might find there certain conditions of line in the mountains
> which might help me . . . and on one given day I saw before me
> a space of mountain and cloud and flat land which seemed to me
> to be what was needed. I gave up my other work and made there-
> upon a rapid but very careful study, so complete that the big
> picture is only part of the amount of work put into the study of
> that afternoon.

And he concluded: "I had one objection, brought up by a friend, a
lady, who was troubled by certain news she had heard. That was that
I had made these studies of clouds in a pagan country, while a true
Episcopalian would make them, I suppose in England."[96]

It is characteristic of what we call the dichotomy of idealism and
realism that La Farge should seek in Japan a realistic setting of a
Christian scene of such a miraculous nature. That he wanted to bring
out this aspect of the scene is shown in a passage from *An Artist's
Letters from Japan*: "For I had proposed to make my studies serve
for the picture of the 'Ascension' . . . in an atmosphere not inimical, as

ours is, to what we call the miraculous."[97] While the work was in
progress, he conversed a great deal with Okakura Kakuzo, who had
just come from Japan with the Imperial Commission to Study Western Art. La Farge described the hours spent listening to the Japanese
scholar's instructions:

> During that summer my friend Okakura spent a great deal of his
> time with me and I could paint, and then, in the intervals, we
> could talk about spiritual manifestations and all that beautiful
> wonderland, which they have; that is to say, the Buddhists, where
> the spiritual bodies take form and disappear again and the edges
> of the real and the imaginary melt.[98]

But notwithstanding his occupation with the spiritual which
one could identify with the nonrealistic, he made sure that his Christ
and angels, "by a combination of the clouds and figures," might have
"the look of what the mystic people call levitation." And in order to
achieve that natural look of the unnatural, he studied what he could
"of the people who are swung in ropes and other arrangements across
theatres and circuses."[99] A strange assortment of the most incongruous elements indeed! La Farge combined the Renaissance tradition,
the mathematics of Puvis, the color of Delacroix or Chassériau, Japan
and Buddhism, and finally the realism of a Degas or Toulouse-Lau-
trec in observing trapeze artists.

East and West, idealism and realism, meet in La Farge's murals
in the Supreme Court Room of the Minnesota State Capitol, St. Paul.
The building was erected in the pompous classicism of Cass Gilbert.
La Farge received the commission to paint four large lunettes. For
the theme, the Law, he selected scenes from four civilizations to il-
lustrate its eternal and international character. In the first mural,
"Moral and Divine Law," he showed Moses on Mount Sinai, and
figures of Aaron and Joshua. For the second, "The Relation of the
Individual to the State and the Interdependence of Men," the scene
was chosen from the opening book of Plato's *Republic*, showing Socrates in the circle of Polemarchus.

The third, dealing with the China of Confucius, is called "The
Recording of Precedents." The fourth lunette, inspired by the Christian Middle Ages, specifically the first Crusade, is entitled "The Adjusting of Conflicting Interests." Count Raymond of Toulouse is

shown swearing the liberties of his city. In an explanatory leaflet La Farge said: "The intention has been to give to each separate work the sense of a special and different historical moment. Consequently of a very different attitude of mind in the actors of each drama. For this purpose, also, differing lights and colors for each picture."[100] The whole smacks of a literary program!

The first lunette is the finest because it is the least literary, the simplest in composition, and the most blended in its severe colors. According to his leaflet, La Farge intended to express "the forces of nature and of the human conscience." In the poses of the figure, especially that of Aaron, and in the noble folds may be detected Chassériau as well as Puvis—the French classical-idealistic tradition. The lines of the mountains and the clouds have a certain similarity to those in the "Ascension"; indeed, they too are of Eastern origin. According to Frank J. Mather, the Moses lunette's "magnificent volcanic landscape [is a] Hawaiian reminiscence," and the "landscape of the 'Confucius' was painted from sketches made in Japan."[101]

Adams mentioned both lunettes in letters to Mabel Hooper La Farge: "Also I saw your pa-law, who has done Moses and very fine and concentrated it is."[102] "In New York I saw . . . your papa-law, whose Confucius waited me. Uncommonly good it was, and he is altogether miraculous, for no gambler would have backed any man of his age and health to finish such a huge job as these four panels, but it is done, and there they are now in the wooly west!"[103]

The "Socrates" shows a great many figures and an elaborate architectural setting, and though in the leaflet La Farge tried to stave off any criticism that the murals were literary or realistic by pointing out that "there has been no strict intention of giving an adequate and therefore impossible historical representation of something which may never have happened," one is only too willing to believe Cortissoz's statement: "The incident . . . is photographed for us as with a modern camera."[104] While the "Socrates" was dedicated to Greek philosophy, the "Confucius," to whose practical-moral philosophy La Farge had been introduced by Okakura Kakuzo, was meant to be an homage to the wisdom of the East.[105] Okakura had helped La Farge to inscribe on the scroll Confucius is reading, in Chinese characters, "First the white and then the color on top," one of the sage's sayings.

This was also chosen as a token of gratitude for the instruction on the philosophy and painting of the East which La Farge had received from Okakura. The Count Raymond mural has nothing special to recommend it.

La Farge's stained glass presents a similar conglomerate of styles and civilizations. It shows the influence of Gothic and Renaissance ornament, of East Asia cloisonné and Pre-Raphaelite line. Though it brought La Farge the highest honors during his lifetime, it seems to us a perfect symbol of the Gilded Age and the era of eclecticism in its opaline scintillation. To Adams it was this side of his friend's activity which was of most lasting influence on his own creation. The instruction in watercolor and the discovery of color, which he owed to La Farge while in the South Seas, were merely preparatory steps for it. La Farge's work in stained glass and his general interest in the Middle Ages were important factors in the writing of *Mont-Saint-Michel and Chartres*, which Adams acknowledged in a letter to Osborn Taylor: "It was really La Farge and his glass that led me astray. . . . To clamber across the gap [between Anglo-Saxon law and medieval art] has needed many years of La Farge's closest instruction to me, on the use of eyes not to say feet."[106] The inordinate space devoted to stained glass in Adams' *Chartres* is proof enough, and also the following passage in his *Education*:

> With the relative value of La Farge's glass in the history of glass-decoration, Adams was too ignorant to meddle, and as a rule artists were if possible more ignorant than he; but whatever it was, it led him back to the twelfth century and to Chartres where La Farge not only felt at home, but felt a sort of ownership. No other American had a right there, unless he too was a member of the Church and worked in glass. Adams himself was an interloper, but long habit led La Farge to resign himself to Adams as one who meant well, though deplorably Bostonian; while Adams, though near sixty years old before he knew anything either of glass or of Chartres, asked no better than to learn, and only La Farge could help him, for he knew enough at least to see that La Farge alone could use glass like a thirteenth-century artist. In Europe the art had been dead for centuries, and modern glass was pitiable. Even La Farge felt the early glass rather as a document than as a historical emotion, and in hundreds of

windows in Chartres and Bourges and Paris, Adams knew barely
one or two that were meant to hold their own against a color-
scheme so strong as his. In conversation La Farge's mind was
opaline with infinite shades and refractions of light, and with
color toned down to the finest gradations. In glass it was insub-
ordinate; it was renaissance; it asserted his personal force with
depth and vehemence of tone never before seen. He seemed bent
on crushing rivalry.[107]

The great historian of medieval art Henry Focillon, concurring
with Adams in praise of La Farge's glass, called it a "tapestry of sunlight, as of jewels collaborated with heavenly fire to create an undis-
covered universe" and a "treasure at the bottom of a deep vault lit up
by the lamp of an Arabian magician."[108] The first quotation reads
like a description of the windows of Chartres while the second points
to Oriental inspiration, and indeed the Middle Ages and the Orient
were the two most important sources for La Farge's interest in glass.
He developed a liking for it during his first stay in France and wrote:

> The churches brought me to the knowledge of ancient glass and
> I was able to use, for understanding it, what I had read in the
> writings of the illustrious Chevreul. He had explained more es-
> pecially, years before, the paints of ancient work in glass and
> then he had written . . . on the optical views of color. . . . Much
> later I was to use these principles and these theories when I took
> to working in glass.[109]

This was during the years after the Civil War when his pictures did
not sell well and his friend the architect Van Brunt proposed he do
one of the windows for Memorial Hall at Harvard. La Farge destroyed the first window, since it did not satisfy him, but after he had
invented opaline glass with the help of a Luxembourg glass maker,
he did it over again.

The subsequent windows are too numerous to list completely.
In 1873 La Farge visited England for the second time and associated
with the Pre-Raphaelites. Burne-Jones and William Morris had made
stained glass windows for the Boston Trinity Church; it is not impossible that La Farge had something to do with it. But a report compiled twenty years later by Samuel Bing (a famous *Japonist* and
founder of L'Art Nouveau shop in Paris) contains a contribution by
La Farge criticizing the Pre-Raphaelites:

I thought that I had noticed in the works of the English artists in stained glass that they had come to the end of their rope, and that their work in glass had ceased improving, and it seemed to me that the cause of this was mainly because the designer had become separated from the man who made the actual window. . . . Moreover they made designs for the drawing and not for the result; beautiful drawings—bad result![110]

La Farge's windows were especially appreciated in France. He received the Legion of Honor for his Watson Memorial window exhibited at the Paris Exposition of 1889. The official citation said: "He has created in all its details an art unknown before, an entirely new industry, and in a country without tradition."[111] Today one sees the relationship of La Farge's windows to Tiffany's opalescent glass and of both to the soap-bubble wealth of the era much more clearly.

The architects of the period were not unaware of these connections between opaline windows and the wealth of their clients. McKim employed La Farge for a window in his house for Dr. R. H. Derby in Maine. The design was taken from a *Hypnerotomachia Polyphili* borrowed from the library of Charles E. Norton, which contains the magnificent early Venetian Renaissance woodcuts William Morris was so fond of.

In Richard M. Hunt's Cornelius Vanderbilt house in New York, built in strict Francis I French Renaissance, La Farge also did windows which, of course, had to be in the style of the period, to which he added an admixture of Japanese cloisonné. In the decoration of the interior La Farge cooperated with Saint-Gaudens, who did the wood carvings. A window for the Frederick L. Ames house in Boston used the East Asia peacock. It and the windows with the same motif in the Worcester Art Museum remind one of Whistler's Peacock Room, made for Frederick Leyland in London (1877) and now in the Freer Gallery of Art, Washington, D.C., where likewise Japanese art and Pre-Raphaelitism were blended.

To us it seems highly significant that the work the German Emperor William II admired most in Alma-Tadema's lavishly decorated studio in London, and which he would have liked to take with him, was a window by La Farge.[112] The Kaiser was certainly a representative of the taste of the period with its showy ostentation and false glitter. Into that cultural framework fits a fantastic scheme

Clarence King recounted in his *Recollections* as the common brain child of himself and La Farge. They planned to have the cupola of the projected tomb of U. S. Grant "filled . . . with the richest and deepest of figured glass . . . a pharos, a light-house, to be seen from afar by night."[113]

Adams himself was probably never nearer to La Farge and never felt more indebted to him than when the painter unexpectedly showed up in France in 1898. At that time Adams had started on the preparatory work for *Chartres*. He wrote in his *Education*: "His solitude was broken in November by the chance arrival of John La Farge. At that moment, contact with La Farge had a new value."[114] La Farge's spiritual share in *Chartres* is certainly considerable, though chiefly limited to the three chapters which deal with medieval stained glass (VIII-X). The copy of *Chartres* Adams sent to La Farge (Henry E. Huntington Library) is inscribed "To John La Farge, his pupil H. A."[115] The relations between Adams and La Farge remained close until La Farge's death in 1910.

A letter of 22 April 1901, from Adams to Elizabeth Cameron, described well the cordiality of a meeting of the circle in his Washington house. Saint-Gaudens and his wife were also present; the sculptor remained "gloomy even in a paradise of smiling cherubs" and was "always singularly inarticulate." Adams jokingly used Saint-Gaudens as the somber background for a description of the scintillating La Farge:

> With these has come our own La Farge, younger, gayer, more entertaining than ever; full of work, interest, feeling and variety; the most extraordinary of men. I can never get the range of his curiosity and observation. His faculty for wasting time and energy is a downright fraud on me, because it ends in doing more work in a year than ever I did in a lifetime. He hangs about, reads a little, sleeps much, chats occasionally, and delights me always. And you remember how solemnly I attended his funerals only fifteen months ago. We buried him every day for two months with all the rites of the holy church, and now I am reading him my Miracles of the Virgin! He is the biggest miracle the Virgin ever struck.[116]

For both friends this was an Indian Summer of the creative faculties. Adams, now 63 years old, read from the manuscript one of the most poetic chapters of *Chartres* to his friend, 66 years of age, who after a severe illness shortly resumed a new project with the Minnesota murals.

Nine years later the circle's convivial gatherings had terminated with the death of most of its members. Adams, the lone survivor, wrote from Paris to his oldest English friend Gaskell on 14 December 1910: "My friends die daily. John La Farge dropped out, the other day. William James preceded him a week or two. Alex Agassiz passed first in the summer. I am far from easy about Henry James, and as for my other invalids, I pass my time in holding their hands."[117] The finest characterization of John La Farge is found in Adams' correspondence with Royal Cortissoz concerning material for his book on La Farge, started in the year immediately after the painter's death. But first, La Farge's ideas about the Impressionists and Post-Impressionists, and art in general as expressed in his *Considerations on Painting* will be considered.[118]

As to the art of the Impressionists and Post-Impressionists, La Farge made no specific statement about individual artists in his *Considerations*. But from the letter about the "stupid Frenchman" Gauguin one must conclude that his attitude in general was negative, though inclined to be occasionally more tolerant than Adams, who saw nothing but frantic striving for originality at all costs in the work of the younger artists. This is demonstrated in a passage in his *Education* which deals with the Paris exhibits of 1892:

> At the galleries and exhibitions, he was racked by the effort of art to be original, and when one day, after much reflection, John La Farge asked whether there might not still be room for something simple in art, Adams shook his head. As he saw the world, it was no longer simple and could not express itself simply. It should express what it was; and this was something that neither Adams nor La Farge understood.[119]

Fifteen years earlier, when the Impressionists were struggling for recognition, La Farge too had struck out against *French ambitions* and "this curse of modern art, this little assemblage of all sorts of pieces" in a letter to Saint-Gaudens.[120] Yet the theories on art expressed in his *Considerations* are amazingly advanced, even prophetic for their time. They were originally delivered in 1893 as a series of lectures to young art students at the Metropolitan Museum of Art in

New York and are almost forgotten today, though the discriminating Frank J. Mather paid a fine tribute to them:

"Considerations on Painting" lacks the firm contour of the classics of art criticism, but in compensation it is perhaps the honestest book that was ever written on the subject, and its intimations (like the author's own painting) are not made in line and mass but in reverberations of colour. It is difficult reading, but hardly another book of modern times so irradiates the finest wisdom.[121]

La Farge's *Consideration* holds an important place in the history of American esthetics, somewhere between James Jackson Jarves' *Art Idea* (1864) and *Art Thoughts* (1869),[122] and the present writings of the expressionist wing in American esthetics. With Jarves the book shares the emphasis on art "as an expression of the inner life" (Jarves). Among La Farge's painter colleagues it was Inness who entertained similar ideas; he stressed "the force of emotion" as most essential in the arts.[123] But while Inness was a confused mystical thinker, La Farge's ideas are clear as well as profound.

Though not quoting any of the professional schools of esthetics and relying almost exclusively on his own experiences as a creative artist, La Farge used the most modern terminology; for instance, he spoke of art as a *language*[124] and called style "a living form which the life spirit wraps around itself,"[125] like Focillon in *La Vie des Formes.* Like Kallen and DeWitt Parker, La Farge also called art a "free world that . . . escapes the chances of the exterior world."[126]

La Farge anticipated the modern approach of teaching the Humanities on a comparative basis: "The different arts (Poetry, Painting, Music) have each, and in common, one property, which is Expression."[127] According to La Farge, art is expression but it is also *structure* and *abstract form.* La Farge used these two now so familiar terms, which recall Cézanne's pronouncements on art: "Everywhere all is enveloped in an order implied within the idea of structure. Gradually there is no form in nature which does not supply some suggestion of abstract form and is not told of in some settled form whose final establishment is a creation of man;[128] [and] Our way of looking at things is composition."[129] While here La Farge professed the mathematical bias of the modern artist, in another passage he embraced the creed of such artists as Brancusi in his belief in the artist as a child: "The artist can hope that in his fullest development he may become again as a child . . . it may seem impossible to discriminate between what is the ingenuous statement of ignorance and the consummate-synthesis of knowledge."[130]

La Farge plead for an integration of technic and meaning in the arts: "It is not that the methods, the workmanship, can be detached from thought, but that the methods are so intimately connected with it, are such a necessary instrument of it, that they make one thing."[131]

He too, like most of his contemporaries, was sold on the idea of evolution taking place in three phases. In the *progress* of an artist he put "instinct and inherited disposition" first, the "accumulated memories which give him a language of his sentiments" second, and the "tendency to translate the hand" (technic) third.[132] We are less in agreement with La Farge when he generally distinguished three style phases in an artist's career: "He learns; he masters; he repeats."[133] This recalls the Winckelmann-Goethe three styles of youth, maturity and decay of the arts, and the more recent *theory of the cycle*. It puts a premium of creativity on the artist's mature years and thinks of old age as the phase of necessary decay or stagnation. That thesis is certainly repudiated by the work of a Titian, El Greco, Rembrandt, Frans Halls, and many lesser artists, who did not repeat but invented in their *old age*, reaching a new peak of their creative powers.

Of special interest is La Farge's attitude towards the idealism versus realism controversy, of which his own art bears witness, and which he did treat as a historical phenomenon in *The Higher Life in Art*. In *Considerations* he dealt with the character of the two terms irrespective of specific art movements or artists, advanced a definition, and attempted a reconciliation between them. In the chapter "Personality and Choice" he said:

> At some moment or other you will have brought before you that most important conflict of realism and its opposite. I don't say idealism, because I don't so distinctly know what is meant by it; while realism has been in the market now for quite a time, and has served as a beautiful playground for various intellects.[134] [And he cut the Gordian knot with:] There is for you practically no such thing as realism. . . . You will always give to nature, that is to say, that [which] is outside of you, the character of the lens through which you see it—which is yourself.[135]

Compare Zola's "a corner of reality seen through a temperament." Nature to the artist was similarly expressed by La Farge. "Nature for us painters only assumes existence in ourselves—is merely the recall of innumerable memories of sight."[136] La Farge stressed the freedom of the artist and his right to select from nature what suits him—after all the artist's only choice—but he knew also that artistic freedom does not and cannot exist without self-imposed limitations: "Let there be no misunderstanding—Art is not a lawless game,"[137] but "rules exist for art, not art for rules."[138]

Against the excessive historicism of his time, a bastard child of both realism and idealism and the tendency to confuse art with literature, he warned, "Art begins, where language ceases!"[139] But here he criticized himself, for one asks, why then pamphlets with explanatory notes for his murals and long descriptions in exhibition catalogs? The man of literature conflicts here with the artist and yields to the temptation of the word.

Although his *Considerations* dealt chiefly with paintings, La Farge defended the "greatness of the smaller arts." Giving Japanese lacquer as an example, he said: "We can feel at ease in the spaces occupied by *all* the arts that appeal to the sight . . . all we can do is to assume that they all must fall within a universal geometry."[140] Refer in this connection to his remarks about the arts of the household in his travel books on Japan and the South Seas.

Towards the conclusion of the lectures La Farge proclaimed: "I confess to the extreme pleasure in thus bringing the East and the West together."[141] Thus in La Farge's philosophy of art there was again a striving for synthesis and unity, an attempt to resolve contradictions by thinking in contradictions. And weighing La Farge's thinking about art against his doing of art, we decide that he was more successful in achieving a synthesis in art theory than in art practice. In describing his friend's complex and contradictory mind in his *Education*, Adams struck the same keynote of unity and tolerance.[142] Adams' letters to Royal Cortissoz, a year after La Farge's death, merely elaborated on the two themes.

To Cortissoz' request for material about La Farge for his forthcoming book, Adams replied:

I have, I believe, nothing of La Farge's that would help you. . . .
When he wrote letters on subjects, he generally used them afterwards, as in Japan and the South Seas so that you have them in
his books. He wrote as he talked, so that you have his conversation almost exact in his writings.

In [expressions] he was, as you know, very abundant, and
his choice of words and figures very amusing, so as to put him
among the best talkers of the time, if not actually the first, as I
thought he was; but the charm of talk is evanescent and largely
in voice and manner. . . . I think his letters from Japan repeat his
table-talk much better than any memory could recall it.

I am such a matter-of-fact sort of person that I never could
try to approach La Farge from his own side. He had to come over
to mine. Yet he, like most considerable artists, worked so much
more instinctively than intellectually that he could not have
taught me much, had he tried; because I would work only intellectually. For that reason I could follow him best in his glass,
where his efforts were strong and broad. Although I thought him
quite the superior of any other artist I ever met,—and I have no
special reason for limiting the remark to artist alone,—he was so
"unAmerican"—so remote from me in time and mind—and above
all, so unintelligible to himself as well as to me, that I have preferred to talk little about him, in despair of making either him
or his art intelligible to Americans; but if I did try to do it, I
would rather try by putting some of his glass side by side with
that of other centuries back to the twelfth. Perhaps by that
means he might become intelligible.

He was a marvel to me in his contradictions. . . . He had one
of the most perfectly balanced judgements that could ever exist.
Towards me, he seemed always eventempered to an inconceiv-
able degree. I do not mean benevolent, or sentimental, or com-
monplace, but just *even*, and in his disapproval as well as in his
acceptance. Of course, he was often severe but his severity itself
was shaded and toned. Yet he was not easy to live with, thus con-
tradicting even his contradictions.

The task of painting him is so difficult as to scare any literary
artist out of his wits. The thing cannot be done. It is like the attempt of the nineteenth-century writers to describe a sunset in
colors. . . . Complexity cannot be handled in print to that degree. La Farge used to deride his own attempts to paint sea and
sky and shadow in the South Seas, and was rather fond of pointing out how, at a certain point of development, he always failed,
and spoiled the picture. At a certain point of development the

literary artist is bound to fail still more, because he has not even
color to help him, and mere words only call attention to the fact
that the attempt to give them color is a predestined failure. In the
portrait of La Farge, you must get not only color but also constant change and shifting of light, as in opals and moonstones
and star-sapphires, where the light is in the object. You need to
write as an artist, for artists, because the highest educated man
or woman in the world cannot comprehend you, if you qualify
and refine, as La Farge did, and then contradict your own refine-
ments by flinging great masses of pure force in your reader's
faces, as he did in his windows.

I wish you the utmost possible success, though I talk dis-
couragingly. It will be always a great work.[143]

The next letter from Adams to Cortissoz was written from Paris after
the book had been published:

Your volume arrived yesterday, and I read it at once. It gave me
great pleasure and great satisfaction on La Farge's account. I
am sure it would have pleased him, and it pleases me the more
because of that thought. He had a true artist's longing for appreciation. There is room for a very nice parallel between him and
Whistler on that line of artistic striving; for although he rarely or
never resorted to Whistler's frank vulgarity of self-advertisement,
he took even more trouble than Whistler did to gain a favorable
press, and was equally careful of his claims on posterity. . . . I
was always brutally telling him that he was living in illusion;
that he imagined a public and a posterity which did not exist;
that he was tearing himself to pieces for a society that had disappeared centuries ago, and would never appear again; and that
we are only a little knot of a few dozen people, who talked about
each other, and might as well burn up all we had done, when
we should take our departure;—he admitted the fact but sheltered
himself behind the screen of mice-catching for a living. This
was only his word-play. Really he worked only for the grade of
a great artist among the great artists of the world of the past. He
wanted to be coupled with Delacroix and Hokusai. On that point
I was wholly with him. We could both of us live in,—and for,—
the past with infinite satisfaction. Where we parted was in living
for the present. I really suffered to see him working to create an
audience in order that he might please it. The double task passes
any endurance.

Luckily the painter's world is relatively compact and organised, and within its limits will be probably worth living for. I

wish I could say as much for the literary artist's world; but I see no hope of organised self-defense there. La Farge, like Fromentin, aspired to both positions, and thanks at least in part to you, I trust he will take his place there soon and finally. He made a wonderful fight for it, and, without him, my generation in America would leave, except in a few scattered remnants, scarcely a trace worth leaving.

He was behind his profession, a gentleman, by birth and mind, and he never forgot it.[144]

The third and last letter to Cortissoz concerning his book on La Farge was apparently in reply to Cortissoz' response to the second letter:

Your letter of the 12th has just arrived, and although it needs no answer, I write this line merely to express my deep sympathy for you, if, as you say, you have been suffering from our common epidemic of neurasthenia. I take it, on the evidence of Albert Duerer, that human nature is always trying to become neurasthenic as its highest flight, and that it is the penalty that artists pay for attainment; but the attainment is hardly worth it.

La Farge seemed to me strongest in his energy which carried him against the current of neurasthenia. He never yielded to it. He seemed held up by an instinctive conviction that society had hidden qualities which he could appeal to. He had the instinct of a primitive cave-dweller, who painted hairy elephants, on a cave's stone roof. The God knew how good they were! I always broke down at the door. After middle-life—say fifty years of age—I was satisfied that our society contained no hidden qualities that artists could appeal to;—that it is really what appears on its surface. . . . La Farge always admitted this in talking; but in working, he always had the strength to rise above it. He never betrayed contempt for his audience. Of course he felt it, but he never once betrayed it in his work. As a matter of fact, he had no audience, and all his work was done for the little group of us who looked on. You can count them individually, within a narrow chance of error. Especially in his strongest field,—that of color—he had to deal with an atrophied social instinct which got worse in the mass of the world, every day of his life. He educated a few dozen of us, and that was all.[145]

It was almost a pathological trait in Adams that he denied not only to his own work but also to that of his friends any effect beyond the narrow confines of the circle. He despaired of their function in society, because he had no confidence in the society of his time. How amusing and how wrong are his remarks on the atrophied color-sense of his time, just when color started a grandiose comeback in the paintings of the Impressionists, and in the work of the Expressionists would outshine all that had been done before.

10. *Augustus Saint-Gaudens*

(Sculpture)

A dams' attitude towards the function of sculpture in his time was no less pessimistic than that towards painting. He presented sculpture as a lost art, for which the Adams Memorial by Augustus Saint-Gaudens was the final touchstone. Due to the more than often foolish remarks of the sightseers in front of it and because of their insistence on a rational explanation of the nameless statue, he wrote in his *Education*: "Indeed, the American people had no idea at all. . . . They had lost the sense of worship; for the idea that they worshipped money, seemed a delusion."[1] From then on he bore a personal grudge and his attitude towards the American public at large became even more contemptuous than before. And as for the artist Saint-Gaudens who created the touchstone?

Adams spoke of Saint-Gaudens as though he was suffering from delusions, as though he was almost a clinical case. He called Saint-Gaudens *neurasthenic*. On one of his visits to the sculptor's Paris studio he found him "scared, as usual, by grim monsters in the air of his perfectly infantile terrors." And this was Saint-Gaudens in the hour of triumph, after his "General Sherman" had been a big success at the Paris Exposition of 1899. On that occasion Adams treated his sculptor friend

> with the usual flippancy; told him, that [he] never felt any other way, and rather liked it; that Michael Angelo not only lived in it, but made his greatest work out of it, in the Penseroso and Medici tombs; that Albert Dürer made a picture of it ["Melencolia"]; and that it was really very good fun when you got used to it, and knew what a good fellow it was.[2]

Soon thereafter Adams wrote to Mabel Hooper: "St. Gaudens is drudging away, up on Mont-Parnasse, and every now and then I drag him out of his dreary den where he creates nothing but nightmares, and I bring him here for a change."[3]

Adams had the character of the egocentric; in calling his friends *neurasthenic* he made them accomplices to his own despair, converted to his own esthetic nihilism. The other phrase Adams used often in connection with Saint-Gaudens was *inarticulate*. But only in a relative sense could this be said about him, only in comparison to the brilliance of the other members of the circle, all great talkers. And it is by no means clear whether Adams thought Saint-Gaudens' alleged inarticulateness a fault or an asset. A passage in his *Education* might shed light on that:

> Of all the American artists who gave to American art whatever life it breathed in the seventies, St. Gaudens was perhaps the most sympathetic, but certainly the most inarticulate. . . . All the others—the Hunts, Richardson, John La Farge, Stanford White —were exuberant; only St. Gaudens could never discuss or dilate on an emotion, or suggest artistic arguments for giving to his work the forms that he felt. He never laid down the law, or affected the despot, or became brutalized like Whistler by the brutalities of his world. He required no incense, he was no egoist; his simplicity of thought was excessive; he could not imitate or give any form but his own to the creations of his hand. No one felt more strongly than he the strength of other men, but the idea that they could affect him never stirred an image in his mind.[4]

A similar picture of Saint-Gaudens' mind and character was painted by Adams in his letters. He loved to joke about the sculptor's complete lack of "knowledge of the actual world."[5] He saw in him a babe lost in the woods. He wrote to Mabel Hooper from Paris: "St. Gaudens is just unpacking to begin work. . . . He is a simple-minded babe, much younger than you . . . and I fear, that Paris will not do him much good. He can learn here only the réclame."[6]

These qualities of the sculptor increased, according to Adams, as he grew older. At the gathering together of the circle in Adams' Washington house during the Indian Summer of their lives, Adams found Saint-Gaudens, in comparison to La Farge, "singularly inarticulate," and continued: "He can say very little, he belongs to the French type of Rodins, and has even narrower range, so that he adds little to gaiety of a depressed crowd. He is 'journalier' or even 'hourlier,' and Langley's bolometer could hardly keep up with his changes of temperature."[7]

Yet in spite of all that chaffing criticism of the sculptor's character and mind, Adams counted Saint-Gaudens until the end of his life among his intimates,[8] and he certainly loved the striking appearance of the man, which he described in his *Education*: "Yet in mind and person St. Gaudens was a survival of the 1500; he bore the stamp of the Renaissance, and should have carried an image of the Virgin round his neck, or stuck in his hat, like Louis XI."[9] Thus Saint-Gaudens struck Adams as eminently French and eminently Early Renaissance. Both are true also of his art; one thinks of Michel Colombe and the artists of the *Détente*.

Saint-Gaudens was French on his father's side. The family name was that of a small place in the *arrondissements* of Haute-Garonne, five miles from which was Saint-Gaudens' father's birthplace, Aspet. On his mother's side he was Irish. His parents had met in Dublin, where Augustus was born in 1848, but he was brought to this country at the age of six months, and New York became the town of his childhood and adolescence. In both his paternal and maternal families there was a long line of solid artisans.

It was as an artisan rather than as an artist that Augustus Saint-Gaudens started on his career. At the age of twelve or thirteen he was apprenticed for two or three years in New York to Avet, a Savoyard, the first stone-cameo cutter to come to America. In his *Reminiscences* Saint-Gaudens said: "To this training . . . I attribute a habit of work."[10] This *habit of work* may mean not only unusual industry in the sense of keeping one's nose close to the grindstone, but also a certain economy of design, the habit of working on a very limited plane, which made Saint-Gaudens such an excellent medallist. While working for Avet he went to night school at Cooper Union in New York, to learn drawing.[11] But an Abraham S. Hewitt could teach him not much more than the beginnings of the technic.

His second master in New York was likewise French, Jules Le-Brethon, a shell-cameo cutter with whom he stayed three years. This early training stood him in good stead later, after he had chosen the career of a sculptor. While employed in Paris by the Italian Lupi, who lived near the top of Montmartre, or in Rome on his own account, he could always make a modest living with cameo cutting; it was the heyday of cameo brooches.

He sailed in 1867 for France as a youth of nineteen to see the Paris Exposition and to visit the land of his father. Although he had very little money, he managed to stay on until 1869. He applied for admission to the Ecole des Beaux-Arts, and filled the nine months of waiting for the registration by studying at the Petit Ecole. This was the name under which a school in the Rue de l'Ecole Médecine was known; it was especially intended for the education of artisans preparing for positions in the crafts and artistic industries. But the school had a good reputation. Lecoq de Boisbaudran had taught there in the fifties, creating a novel way of teaching drawing by training the memory. Many famous men had been his pupils: the painter Fantin-Latour, the engraver Legros, the sculptor Dalou, the medallist Chaplain, and most famous of all, Rodin (around 1855). Saint-Gaudens' later medals show a certain similarity to the work of Chaplain who, with Ponscarme, revived the art of the medal at the time Saint-Gaudens entered the school. Three years before, Rodin had created his *Homme au nez crasé*, stirring the stagnant waters of official French sculpture.

But none of the men who had taught in Rodin's time at the Little School were among Saint-Gaudens' teachers in 1867-68, though it must be assumed Boisbaudran's teaching methods were still practiced. Saint-Gaudens mentioned among his teachers there a certain Jacquot, a fictitious name he admitted, and Laemelin, but recorded only studio anecdotes about them. More important is the fact that Saint-Gaudens met there Albert Dammouse, later one of the leading ceramists of France. It was on Dammouse's recommendation that he selected the studio of Pradier's pupil Jouffroy when he was finally admitted to the Beaux-Arts. One of the chief reasons for choosing Jouffroy was the fact that the students in his atelier carried off most of the prizes.

Jouffroy was, like his teacher Pradier, the typical Napoleon III academician. His work, technically dazzling but spiritually false or empty, was slick and superficial. Saint-Gaudens mentioned his "large decorative groups . . . at the entrance of the Place du Carrousel . . . and one of the four groups in front of the Grand Opera," and observed, "They are neither one thing nor the other."[12]

But it cannot be denied that the Beaux-Arts tradition affected Saint-Gaudens just as it had affected Richardson. It took Saint-Gaudens some time to get it out of his system, and there were occasional relapses into the idiom. The influence of the Class Jouffroy, to which belonged such famous French sculptors as Barrias and Falguière, generally speaking had a fateful influence on the development of American sculpture in the last quarter of the nineteenth century.

While Saint-Gaudens and Olin Warner—who did the bronze doors of the Library of Congress—were the only Americans who studied in the atelier Jouffroy during the sixties, under Falguière and then under Mercié—a classmate of Saint-Gaudens—it later became the studio most American sculptors attended. One of the accomplishments of the mature Saint-Gaudens was to keep American sculpture from entirely falling under that influence; but he paid tribute to the Beaux-Arts in his early works, such as "Hiawatha" and "Silence."[13]

They were done in Rome, where Saint-Gaudens resided after a trip to Switzerland in 1869 with Dammouse and his lifelong friend Albert Garnier. The outbreak of the Franco-Prussian War in 1870 kept him from returning to Paris, and he stayed in Italy until 1875, interrupted only by a brief visit to the United States in 1872. There was for a Saint-Gaudens nothing to learn from the Roman sculptors of his own time. Sculpture there had fallen to a level even lower than in Paris. Saint-Gaudens avoided the art of the American sculptor William W. Story, though he occasionally visited his studio, since it was the center for American artists and art lovers on their trips to Italy. Adams and his wife toured the Roman studios in 1873 and visited Story, as we have seen, but they do not mention their young countryman Saint-Gaudens.

Yet Saint-Gaudens managed to contact prominent traveling Americans without Story's help, for instance William M. Evarts, later senator, and Elihu Root, later secretary of state, though at first this meant such hackwork as copies of busts of Demosthenes and Cicero. A Mr. Gibbs commissioned "Hiawatha," of which only the subject is American—the rest is Beaux-Arts. It eventually landed at Hilton Park, Saratoga, New York, in the possession of Mrs. E. D. Morgan.

"Silence," commissioned by L. H. Willard for the principal stair-case of the Masonic Building, Twenty-third Street and Sixth Avenue, New York, is likewise as slick as any Pradier. Saint-Gaudens was anything but proud of it. "The less said about that statue the better," he wrote in his *Reminiscences.* Yet that early Roman work has some importance, for it may be looked upon as a forerunner to the Adams Memorial, though Saint-Gaudens himself does not mention any con-nection between the two. This assumed connection, however, lies not so much in what Saint-Gaudens did but in what he wanted to do and could not realize, which his letters revealed. He wrote on 26 August 1873 to Willard:

> It is not Egyptian . . . and is far more impressive than it could be in the Egyptian style. She has a fine drapery over the body that gives a pleasing character, and a heavy kind of veil that covers her head, drooping over the face so that it throws the face in shadow and gives a strong appearance of mystery. . . . the sub-ject being abstract, I think it better after all not to follow any ex-act style, for the reason that Silence is no more Egyptian than it is Greek or Roman or anything else. I think in that case "Le Style Libre" is the best.[14]

The reluctance to execute in any given style, the heavy veil throwing the face into shadow, the appearance of mystery, the very subject matter of an abstract nature are all characteristics of the Adams Mem-orial.

Three years later a letter to J. Q. A. Ward, the dean of American sculptors, revealed even more of the probably subconscious connec-tion between "Silence" and the Adams Memorial. Ward had praised the statue; Saint-Gaudens, however, thought "Silence" did not do him justice because of the "restrictions forced" upon him, and he contin-ued: "Had I had my own way completely I would have created an entirely different thing, with broad heavy drapery instead of its be-ing very fine. The left hand would have crossed the body sustaining the drapery and would have been entirely concealed."[15] Broad heavy drapery, with the entirely concealed left hand crossing the body and sustaining it, was realized in the Adams Monument.

The association with the older artists in the Adams circle gave Saint-Gaudens' career a decisive turn after his return to America in

1875. As noted above, his association with McKim and White in New York led to the acquaintance of Richardson and his participation in the decoration of the Boston Trinity Church as a painter. He felt especially indebted to La Farge:

> There is no doubt that my intimacy with La Farge has been a spur to higher endeavor, equal to, if not greater than any other I have received from outside sources. . . . I am not able, however, to mention with good taste all that I feel and would like to say about his influence. . . . Through La Farge, then, a period was finally placed to the bad conditions of my affairs.[16]

They also cooperated in the decoration of the interior of St. Thomas' Church in New York in the late seventies. In Paris Saint-Gaudens modeled a relief of the "Adoration of the Cross by Angels," to be placed in the chancel of the church, a work destroyed by fire in 1905. La Farge acted as adviser concerning the color scheme as well as the composition and style. Of importance in this connection is a letter from La Farge to Saint-Gaudens on the question of Protestant art: "There is no such thing as the Protestant in art. . . . Any mediaeval sculpture, or renaissance (not a late one), or painting of the early time (Italian) give the type that will be needed to be neither high nor low church."[17] The result, as shown in a wood engraving, was a fusion of Della Robbia with the line and sentiment of the Pre-Raphaelites; yet it is unmistakably Saint-Gaudens in its grace and loftiness, and the subtle treatment of the low relief.[18]

La Farge's encouragement of Saint-Gaudens to select the low relief as his special domain was even more important than his advice as to style and iconography. This took place in La Farge's studio where they were looking at plaster casts of Pisanello's superb medallions. Saint-Gaudens related: "When [I] expressed despair of ever attempting to do medallions after looking at these achievements, he said quietly and incisively, 'Why not? I don't see why you should not do as well.' This is no doubt the reason I have modeled so many medallions since, yet I fear I have fallen far short of what promise he saw in me."[19] In spite of the modesty expressed in these words, it was in the field of the low relief that Saint-Gaudens "considered himself a master," as his son Homer put it.[20] And certainly Saint-Gaudens was not only the first important American sculptor to turn to the art of the medallion and plaque, he also rivals the best work of his French contemporaries such as Chaplain and Ponscarme.

In Germany it was the sculptor Adolf von Hildebrandt, author of *Das Problem der Form* (1893), who turned to the medallion as an expression of idealistic form and thought, and was followed by numerous pupils. Greek and Roman coins as well as Renaissance medallions, especially those by Pisanello, were to all these artists an important source of inspiration. The revival of the medallion is one of the most important and longest lasting achievements of later idealism in sculpture. Its outstanding qualities are emphasis on form and line, and economy of design. After flourishing for a short period there followed a decline, brought about by the inroads made by realism, especially its overemphasis on details of costume and setting. Saint-Gaudens' smaller reliefs almost always avoided that danger—the secret of the lasting quality of this work. Although he made excellent likenesses, he subordinated the merely actual to design and loftiness of thought. It is *grace*, the quality he admired so much in the work of the Greeks, that characterizes his medallions.

The fame of Saint-Gaudens as a master of the medallion spread from Paris, where he first exhibited a large group of them at the Salon of 1879, together with the "Farragut." His portraits of the painter Jules Bastien-Lepage and the writer Robert Louis Stevenson are probably the masterpieces of Saint-Gaudens' work of this kind. In exchange Bastien-Lepage did Saint-Gaudens' portrait in oil, but it was unfortunately destroyed by fire in the latter's studio in 1904. They had become friends, and Saint-Gaudens was instrumental in the purchase of Bastien-Lepage's "Joan of Arc" for the Metropolitan Museum in New York. It was characteristic of Saint-Gaudens' taste in painting that he chose one of the pictures by the French painter— "the Bouguereau of Naturalism," as Degas called him—with a pseudo-idealistic theme, and not a scene from peasant life, such as the famous "Hay Harvest." That mistake in judgment indicated Saint-Gaudens' wavering between realism and idealism. Even Saint-Gaudens' important works, most of them in the full round, like the Farragut and Sherman memorials, show it. Only in the Adams Monument did Saint-Gaudens achieve an almost perfect unity.

The plan for the Farragut Monument, the first work to bring

Saint-Gaudens great public acclaim, goes back to his first years of intimacy with La Farge. The commission was obtained in 1877, but he
had familiarized himself with the admiral's features even before that,
having modeled a sketch of Farragut's head while still in Rome. The
Farragut Monument was exhibited, as already noted, in the Paris
Salon, and unveiled in 1881.

It was indeed a tremendous step forward in the evolution of the
American war memorial, since it was free from all theatrical heroism
in the realistic figure of the admiral in full uniform, standing on the
socle as though on the bridge of his flagship in the characteristic
sailor's stance. But the realism of the figure is surpassed by the symbolic low-relief on the socle depicting waves, a sword placed off center, two female figures of Loyalty and Courage, and two dolphins. In
its undular soft design the relief anticipates *Art Nouveau*, but its
stylized symbolism seems somewhat out of place along with the realistic statue.

The finely curved mass of stone socle, harmonizing with the undular quality of the relief, was designed by Stanford White. It is one
of the best contributions of the architect to the work of Saint-Gaudens with whom he usually cooperated. Other examples are the
Morgan, Randall, Ames, Linell, and Chapin monuments, the Chicago
Lincoln, and the Adams Memorial. Stanford White was one of Saint-
Gaudens most intimate friends. He stayed in his house in Paris in
1878, and together with McKim they made a trip down the Rhone
studying architecture and sculpture from Lyons to Avignon.

The inclination to anticipate *Art Nouveau* was probably due to
the influence of Burne-Jones' late Pre-Raphaelitism. Saint-Gaudens'
admiration for the art of Burne-Jones was acknowledged by his son
Homer Saint-Gaudens in his discussion of the draperies of the angels
in the Smith relief,[21] and it is also apparent in the angels of the St.
Thomas' Church relief, in "Amor Caritas," and in the Victory of the
Shaw Monument. Saint-Gaudens saw a Burne-Jones exhibition in
London and wrote about it to Miss Rose Nichols from Edinburgh in
1899: "The one thing that made a great impression on me was an exhibition of almost the entire life-work of Burne-Jones. He certainly
was a very big man, but his work contributed to the intense melancholy that seemed to seize me."[22] The noble Burne-Jonesian melan-

choly, however, was most appropriate in the Death-Victory relief figure of the Shaw Monument.

In an article in *Art et Decoration* Paul Leprieur compared the Victory to "the loveliest creations in this style by [George F.] Watts or Gustave Moreau."[23] It is interesting that Royal Cortissoz also ranked La Farge with these two masters. There is a certain spiritual and formal kinship among the later idealists in England, France, and America. The Death-Victory figure is one of the finest conceived by Saint-Gaudens, but here too the idealism of form and thought jars with the realism of Shaw and his Negro soldiers marching to their death. This discrepancy was felt by Saint-Gaudens' friend from the Beaux-Arts years, Bion. He wrote to Saint-Gaudens that the Victory was "as needless as 'Simplicity' would have been floating over Millet's 'Gleaners.' "[24] Saint-Gaudens defended himself by pointing to the fact that the "Greeks and Romans did it finely in their sculpture" and that failure and success depended on "the relation to the rest of the scheme." Compositionally Saint-Gaudens certainly blended reality and symbol, but it escaped him that what was a true symbol in the days of Greeks and Romans had degenerated into a pretty empty convention in his own time. The same can be said about the Victory of the Sherman Monument. Mrs. Adams visited the sculptor's studio in New York in the spring of 1883 and wrote:

> Tuesday early, went to Saint-Gaudens's studio. He's a friend of Miss Palmer; unhappily he was out and we had no time to get there again. His great bas-relief monument of Bob Shaw is very fine, they say—Anne Palmer has seen the cast or plan. It's to be inserted in the wall by the sidewalk in front of the State House and a seat under it; in low relief an infinite body of soldiers with bayonets pointing up, and in front, in much higher relief, Bob Shaw on horseback. Let us be grateful that William Story has not got this in hand; I dislike the man and all his works.[25]

It was Richardson who had been most influential in securing the commission of the Shaw Monument for Saint-Gaudens. The two men were very fond of each other. Saint-Gaudens' amusing description of Richardson's picturesque personality has been noted as a document of their friendship. The architect Daniel H. Burnham related in a letter to Homer Saint-Gaudens that Richardson asked Saint-Gaudens'

opinion about the sketches for the tower of the Allegheny County
Court House in Pittsburgh, and that "he had more confidence" in the
sculptor's judgment regarding mass and outline than in that of any
other man, since Saint-Gaudens "seemed to be able to pick out the
best instinctively."[26] It was probably Richardson who first brought
Saint-Gaudens and Adams together at the time of the building of
Trinity Church in Boston. The first mention of Saint-Gaudens in
Adams writings was, as we have seen, when he and La Farge, on their
way to Japan, "passed a delightful night with King, Saint-Gaudens,
etc.," in New York.

Besides the Adams Memorial, the *Education* mentions only the
Sherman Monument when it was at the Paris Exposition of 1899.
There is a cleverly hidden critical note in Adams' wording: "For a
symbol of power, Saint-Gaudens instinctively preferred the horse, as
was plain in his horse and Victory of the Sherman monument. Doubtless Sherman also felt it so."[27] This was written in recollection of a
trip to Amiens to study the cathedral and its statues with Saint-Gaudens.[28] Adams observed that the sculptor, like Ruskin, was unable
to see the Virgin, a woman, as a source of force, that "to St. Gaudens
she remained as before a channel of taste."[29] This applies not only to
the Sherman Victory but to the whole of Saint-Gaudens' work; its
existence was a result of taste and not of force, it was not carried and
nourished by the vital forces of the time. It is in that sense that Adams
spoke of "the futilities of St. Gaudens, Rodin and Besnard" at the
Paris Exposition of 1899.[30] Yet he paid tribute to the great success of
the work through repeated visits, as did other members of the circle.[31]
Henry James lauded it in an article in the *North American Review*
when the statue was finally placed in New York in 1906.[32]

We have gotten ahead of the chronological order as far as the
relations of Saint-Gaudens and Adams are concerned. We left them
in 1886 in New York, shortly before Adams and La Farge went to
Japan and spent some time together. It seems not improbable that
plans for the Adams Monument were made then and there. Adams
wrote to Dwight from Papete on 10 February 1891 that Saint-Gaudens occupied himself with the work for nearly five years, which
would place its beginning in 1886.[33] In any case, the trip to Japan and
Adams' contact with Buddhism and Kwannon were of great conse-

quence for the plans for the monument, or as James Truslow Adams said, "mood and thought for the Adams Memorial had come to Adams on his first trip with La Farge."[34] But it took three years before these moods and thoughts ripened into the definite plan for the monument. This must have taken place in 1889, but we have no knowledge of the exact date.

Adams had then finished his monumental *History of the United States during the Administrations of Jefferson and Madison*, and a chapter of his life's work was closed. His father's death in 1886 and his mother's in 1889 might also have had some connection with his decision to erect a tomb worthy of the one person whose death ended so tragically his married existence and the first period of his life. Adams had the historian's as well as the artist's awareness of life's rhythm, of turning points, of periods and accents. The commission given to Saint-Gaudens to create the memorial is such an accent.

Saint-Gaudens too had been very active since the return of Adams and La Farge from Japan in 1886. The Chicago Lincoln had been created (1887) and was followed, "on the scaffolding behind the Shaw," as Saint-Gaudens puts it in his *Reminiscences*, by the statue of Deacon Samuel Chapin, the so-called Puritan, likewise finished in 1887, to mention only the large commissions.

The circumstances of the commissioning of the Adams Monument have been unearthed through the painstaking researches of Harold D. Cater, who found among the Saint-Gaudens' papers in the Manuscript Division of the Library of Congress a press clipping from the *Evening Star* for Monday, 17 January 1910, which described an interview given by John La Farge to Gustav Kobbe. Cater wrote:

> In this interview John La Farge explained that he was present when Henry Adams gave the commission to Saint-Gaudens. After La Farge and Adams returned from Japan, the former helped Adams decide that the memorial should symbolize the Japanese Kwannon. La Farge is then quoted: "Mr. Adams described to him in a general way what he wanted, going, however, into no details, and really giving him no distinct clue, save the explanation that he wished the figure to symbolize 'the acceptance, intellectually of the inevitable.' Saint-Gaudens immediately became interested, and made a gesture indicating the pose

which Mr. Adams's words had suggested in his mind. 'No' said Mr. Adams 'the way that you're, that is a Penseroso.' Thereupon the sculptor made several other gestures until one of them struck Mr. Adams as corresponding with the idea. As good luck would have it, he would not wait for a woman model to be brought in and posed in accordance with the gesture indicated by the sculptor, so Saint-Gaudens grabbed the Italian boy who was mixing clay, put him into the pose, and draped a blanket over him. That very blanket, it may be stated here, is on the statue, and forms the drapery of the figure. 'Now that's done' said Mr. Adams 'the pose is settled. Go to La Farge about any original ideas of Kwannon. I don't want to see the statue till it's finished.' " All Mr. La Farge did was to read stories of Kwannon to Saint-Gaudens.[35]

The first mention of the project, then already in an advanced stage, in the Adams correspondence occurred about two years later. He wrote to Theodore F. Dwight during his second trip to the Orient with La Farge from Papeete, 25 January 1891: "The only matter much on my mind is Saint-Gaudens's bronze and Stanford White's construction. I earnestly hope to hear soon that this work at last is complete. It has caused me more anxiety than all my other affairs put together. If you can tell me this, you will tell me the best news you can send."[36] And on 10 February 1891:

On arriving here a week ago, I found a bundle of letters from you, all very satisfactory except in regard to Saint-Gaudens. Your previous letter had prepared me for that disappointment, so that it was less trying than it would otherwise have been. Apparently both Saint-Gaudens and White are afraid to write to me, and perhaps it is best they should not. I should either have to leave their letters unanswered, or express myself in a way that would do no good. White knows already my feelings on the subject, and I think Saint-Gaudens must suspect them, if no more. So I will continue my silence, as far as concerns them, and will wait to see where they are coming out. At times I begin to doubt whether Saint-Gaudens will ever let the work be finished. I half suspect that my refusal, to take the responsibility of formally approving it in the clay, frightened him. Had I cared less about it, I should have gone to see it, as he wished, and should have admired it as much as he liked, but I had many misgivings that I should not be wholly satisfied with his rendering of the idea; and that I might not be able to conceal my disappointment. So I devolved the duty on La Farge, and I know not what qualifications La Farge may have conveyed to Saint-Gaudens's mind. I knew well that I should only injure Saint-Gaudens's work without obtaining my own ideal by suggesting changes, for the artist is usually right in regarding changes, not his own, as blemishes. From the first I told Saint-Gaudens that he should be absolutely free from interference. The result is that after nearly five years I am not certain that his work will ever be delivered, although contract after contract, one more binding than another, has been signed without question or discussion on my part.

I tell you all this that you may be able to explain my situation in case of difficulty. I still trust that by the time this letter arrives, Saint-Gaudens will have delivered the bronze, and Norcross may be able to go on. If not, I suppose some explanation will be voluntarily given. I shall be very sorry indeed to have to demand one, but if May should arrive—a whole year after contract time—without producing the work, I shall have to call for some serious decision.[37]

This strong letter, which nearly accuses sculptor and architect of breach of contract, must have had the desired effect, for in the next letter to Dwight, 2 June 1891, Adams indicated he had received photographs of the completed work. Norcross must have been the contractor setting up the statue in Rock Creek Cemetery; Norcross Brothers was a firm of builders often employed by the Richardson office. The letter of 2 June said:

I will not make up my mind from the photographs, whether I am entirely satisfied with the work. I cannot be quite sure of my own feeling until I see it. At any rate the photographs make certain that I shall not *dis*-like it, which is a vast comfort to me, who have dreaded hating it. Of course I cannot hope that my own thoughts passing through another man's mind, and hands, will come out in a shape familiar to me; my only anxiety is to know that the execution is better than the ideal.[38]

Very similar ideas were expressed in a letter to his brother Charles from Sidney, Australia, 3 August 1891:

I find on arriving here your kind letter of May 3, on the subject of St. Gaudens' figure. It is natural that St. Gaudens should be nervous about the impression I might get of it, for I was myself so nervous about his success that I refused even to meet him from the moment he began the model, and persisted in the refusal till

I left. As my friends are determined that I shall be satisfied with the work, I am at least relieved of heavy anxiety on their account, though I can't help still looking forward with a little dread to my own first sight of it, not because I doubt that his artistic rendering of an idea must be better than my conception of the idea, but because the two could hardly be the same, and what is his in it might to me seem to mix badly with the image that had been in my mind. No doubt, time and familiarity with the work would set me right, but the first sense of a jar might be nasty.[39]

The newspaper clipping and the letters quoted establish three important factors in the genesis of the Adams Memorial: first, Adams had refused to see the model since he had settled the pose (1889); second, the great share and interest of La Farge in it; and third, Adams was to a great extent responsible for the conception of the idea.

Though Adams had granted the sculptor freedom from interference, Saint-Gaudens worked under difficult and delicate circumstances since he had to guard his own independence and artistic integrity by yielding apparently to the desires of others, especially to a mind as strong as that of Adams. It is regrettable that Augustus Saint-Gaudens himself was so reticent about the whole affair. His *Reminiscences* said only: "Following the 'Chapin' on the scaffolding was the figure in Rock Creek Cemetery which I modeled for Mr. Henry Adams."[40] The most idealistic work by Saint-Gaudens followed immediately after the most painfully realistic one!

Homer Saint-Gaudens felt strongly the need to elaborate on his father's very brief statement concerning the Adams Monument. He wrote that "at the date Mr. Adams gave Saint-Gaudens the commission he felt in sympathy with the religious attitudes of the East."[41] This, however, was not an entirely new interest in Adams' life. The idea of Nirvana had occupied him before he came in direct contact with the art and philosophy of Buddhism in Japan. It found then its most profound expression during Adams' trip to the South Seas and his stay in India, in his poem "Buddha and Brahma," written in Anuradjapura towards the end of the journey.[42] Some of the ideas expressed therein, for instance that of "the life behind the veil," must have been familiar to him before he put it on paper, since it contributed so largely to his conception of his wife's monument transmitted to Saint-Gaudens.

Augustus Saint-Gaudens himself intended to say more about the

Adams Monument, since his son found *Amplify* written on the margin of the manuscript of his *Reminiscences*, but it never came to that.[43] Fortunately, Homer came upon a faint ink sketch of the monument in his father's scrapbooks and around it the following notations: "Adams/Buddha/Mental repose/Calm reflection in contrast with the violence or force in nature."[44] The combining of the words *Adams* and *Buddha* with Adams' favorite concept, *force*, shows clearly that the suggestions came from Adams himself or were transmitted by La Farge. Homer Saint-Gaudens seems to have had this in mind when he wrote:

> Rather when [Adams] first discussed the matter, he explained that Mr. La Farge understood his ideas on this subject and that, accordingly, my father would do well, in his work, not to seek in any books for inspiration, but to talk to the painter and to have about him such objects as photographs of Michelangelo's frescoes in the Sistine chapel. . . . There posed sometimes a man sometimes a woman.[45]

This last sentence relates the Adams Monument to Michelangelo's "Sibyls."

Among three very rough early clay sketches reproduced in Homer Saint-Gaudens' book, there are two of seated and draped female figures, while the third one is a Socrates.[46] Thus Saint-Gaudens was at the beginning not only undecided as to the sex of his figure but also as to civilizations and religions. Although the figure of a Socrates would have been hardly appropriate, the sketch would suggest Saint-Gaudens made rather feeble attempts at counterproposals to his friend's Eastern inclinations, which were at first alien to him. It seems also significant, in view of Saint-Gaudens' Western predisposition, that the first pose for the Adams Monument was a *Penseroso*, according to the Kobbe report.

It is further interesting to note that in the rough sketches of the female figures were incorporated some of the improvements Saint-Gaudens was kept from applying to his early "Silence," "the broad heavy drapery" and "the left hand [crossing] the drapery." The drapery or veil drawn over the head, the closed eyes, even the classical cast of features, and finally the general feeling of mystery existed already, though in an immature way, in the "Silence," and seems to have come to the surface of consciousness again. It is necessary to establish the priority of these formal as well as spiritual conceptions of Saint-Gaudens, since one otherwise would be inclined to give too much credit to Adams' and La Farge's suggestions. The sculptor, however, in his great modesty and in his conviction of the superior mentality of his two friends, frankly acknowledged in his letters his dependence on their guidance, as excerpts from his letters to Adams show:

> Do you remember setting aside some photographs of Chinese statues, Buddha, etc. for me to take away from Washington? I forgot them. I should like to have them now. Is there any book *not long* that you think might assist me in grasping the situation? If so, please let me know so that I might get it. I propose soon to talk with La Farge on the subject, although I dread it a little. . . .
>
> If you catch me in, I will show you the result of Michelangelo, Buddha and Saint-Gaudens. I think what I will do, may not be quite as idiotic as if I had not had all these months to "chew the cud." . . .
>
> The question now with me is, rock or no rock; which when I have another sketch indicated, I will show La Farge. White holds that the rock requires a different treatment from the seat, and to prove it has made a stunning scheme. I'm half inclined to give in to him, but that also La Farge must pass on. . . .
>
> If the figure is cast in bronze in several pieces it can be set up in Washington about July first [1890]. This I consider inadvisable, as the statue can be cast in virtually one piece, which is seldom done in these days; for this however, twelve weeks are necessary. Should this be decided on and you be away when the figure is cast, I propose to bronze the plastercast and set it up at once in the place that the bronze will occupy in the monument in Washington, so that you can judge of the effect in metal. In any event, I should like to have you see the face of the figure in the clay. If it were not for that part of the work I would not trouble you. But the face is an instrument on which different strains can be played, and I may have struck a key in a direction quite different from your feeling in the matter. With a word from you I could strike another tone with as much interest and fervor as I have had in the present one. . . .
>
> My relations with you in this matter have been so unusually agreeable that you can appreciate how much I am troubled at the prospect of not having the bronze itself in place on July first.[47]

We have seen from his letters to Dwight and his brother Charles that Adams left for the South Seas without having seen the model or the face in the clay. He gave the reasons for his refusal to see anything of the work in a letter to the sculptor, the contents of which are summarized by Homer Saint-Gaudens, that "he would not look at it, since if he should not like it, he would carry the disappointment through his trip, whereas otherwise he would have only pleasure to anticipate."[48] Augustus Saint-Gaudens, prodded by Dwight, finally sent photographs of the completed bronze, which Adams acknowledged from Siwa, Fiji Islands, 23 June 1891:

> As far as the photographs go, they are satisfactory, but I trust much more the impression produced on John Hay, who writes me that he has been to Rock Creek, to see the figure. "The work is indescribably noble and imposing. It is to my mind Saint-Gaudens's master-piece. It is full of poetry and suggestion, infinite wisdom, a past without beginning and a future without end, a repose after limitless experience, a peace to which nothing matters—all are embodied in this austere and beautiful face and form."
>
> Certainly I could not have expressed my own wishes so exactly, and, if your work approaches Hay's description, you cannot fear criticism from me.[49]

Hay amplified the passage quoted by Adams (25 March 1891) in another letter to him (London, 4 June 1891) that Clarence King "thinks as I do, that it is the most important work yet done on our side—the best of Saint-Gaudens or anybody else."[50] The first letter by Saint-Gaudens to Adams after his return from the South Seas chiefly dealt with the setting:

> I meant that my first communication to you should be a word asking you to come and see the figure. However I have to give that up. You asked that, in whatever was placed back of the figure, the architecture should have nothing to say, and above all that it should not be classic. White and I have mulled over this a great deal, with the enclosed results. I do not object to the architecture or its classicism as indicated in Number One, whereas Number Two would, we both fear, be rather unpleasant. This matter must be settled immediately, and I cannot do that without asking you. I do not think the small classical cornice and base can affect the figure and, to my thinking, the monument would be better as a whole.
>
> If however the plain stone at the back of Number One, marked "front" is much preferable to you, we will carry it out.
>
> In about ten days you will hear from me, asking you to run

on. I've demolished the figure several times, and now it's all going at once.[51]

The last sentence evidently refers to previous changes in the figure,
and is obviously an attempt to apologize for the delay in the execution of the work. The date of this letter is not given; but the opening
sentence and especially the request, for Adams "to run on" to see the
completed bronze cast, make it clear that it was written after his return, which took place about the middle of February 1892 (letter to
Gaskell).[52]

Returning to White's design for the stone behind the figure,
Adams agreed to the small concession of the classical ornament. It is
an egg and dart pattern at the cornice and a ribboned laurel wreath
at the base. Though they affect one from a distance as purely textural
accents, the monument would probably have gained in simplicity
without these conventionalities. Adams fortunately succeeded in the
omission of any inscription on the stone. In his last will he stated
specifically that "no inscription, dates, letters or other attempt at
memorial" should ever be placed over his wife's and his joint grave.[53]
The work on the architectural setting and landscaping must definitely have stretched out into the spring of 1892, as the last letter
from Saint-Gaudens to Adams about the monument indicates:

> The monument is finished and all that remains to be done is the
> grading and the planting of some trees in the rear of the seat.
> White's work appears to me to be very fine, sober and strong. As
> to my work, you must judge for yourself. The rock on which the
> figure is seated, needs to be rubbed in order to get it darker. This
> will be done at once. I did not do it before setting up the work as
> I was uncertain as to the effect of the stone. That, however, is a
> small matter.[54]

The first approval of the work was given around the beginning of
March or even the end of February 1892, very shortly after Adams
had returned to Washington. He wrote to Dwight (10 March 1892):

> Hooper, Bigelow and I made a formal, and, so to speak, official
> examination of the Rock Creek work, and gave it final approval.
> Probably some day I may try to carry further the artist's wishes
> about planting, but just now we can wait. Many thanks for your
> devotion. Don't be too vindictive towards the clergyman. For
> my part, his attitude seems a form of appreciation.[55]

The last two sentences allude, as Ward Thoron explained in a foot-
note, to the attitude of Dr. Buck, "the very aged rector of the parish
which controlled the cemetery," who was "far from sympathetic or
admiring, or accommodating, and in consequence complained."
(We shall meet Dr. Buck as the voice of the clergy in the passage in
the *Education* dealing with the monument.) When spring came
Adams spent many hours with the monument, often riding to Rock
Creek Cemetery on horseback.[56] He wrote about these visits in his
Education:

> His first step, on returning to Washington, took him out to the
> cemetery known as Rock Creek, to see the bronze figure which
> St. Gaudens had made for him in his absence. Naturally every
> detail interested him; every line; every touch of the artist; every
> change of light and shade; every point of relation; every possible
> doubt of St. Gaudens's correctness of taste or feeling; so that, as
> the spring approached, he was apt to stop there often to see what
> the figure had to tell him that was new; but, in all, that it had to
> say, he never once thought of questioning what it meant. He
> supposed its meaning to be the one commonplace about it—the
> oldest idea known to human thought. He knew that if he asked
> an Asiatic its meaning, not a man, woman or child from Cairo to
> Kamtchatka would have needed more than a glance to reply.
> From the Egyptian Sphinx to the Kamakura Daibuts; from Pro-
> metheus to Christ, from Michael Angelo to Shelley, art had
> wrought on this eternal figure almost as though it had nothing
> else to say. The interest of the figure was not in its meaning, but in
> the response of the observer. As Adams sat there, numbers of
> people came, for the figure seemed to have become a tourist fash-
> ion, and all wanted to know its meaning. Most took it for a por-
> trait-statue, and the remnant were vacant-minded in the absence
> of a personal guide. None felt what would have been a nursery
> instinct to a Hindu baby or a Japanese jinricksha-runner. The
> only exceptions were the clergy, who taught a lesson even
> deeper. One after another brought companions there, and, ap-
> parently fascinated by their own reflection, broke out passion-
> ately against the expression they felt in the figure of despair, of
> atheism, of denial. Like the others, the priest saw only what he
> brought. Like all great artists, St. Gaudens held up the mirror
> and no more. The American layman had lost sight of ideals; the
> American priest had lost sight of faith. Both were more Ameri-
> can than the old, half-witted soldiers who denounced the wast-

ing, on a mere grave, of money which should have been given for drink.[57]

How the stupid remarks of the public must have hurt Adams in a matter so personal! How bitter was his verdict on the final failure of idealism and idealistic art in America and on the relation of art, artists and society! And he meant the whole of society, from the top, Washington "society" and President Theodore Roosevelt, to "half-witted soldiers." He wrote to Elizabeth Cameron from Washington on 19 April 1903:

> At dinner the other evening we were chaffing St. Gaudens because of his Rock Creek figure, which he has to tell the meaning of. As he never could use words at all, and least in explaining thoughts, he stumbles over it wearily. His wife, as usual, gets impatient, for she says it is now their favorite joke that whenever they go out to dinner here some one always drags St. Gaudens into a corner and says: "Do tell me what you meant in that figure?" As La Farge, in his introspective way remarked, he might answer that the figure was meant to express whatever was in the mind of the spectator; but this would be too fine. To a wearily historical mind like mine, it is curious that what would have been elementary to every other age of mankind, and which any beggar of Benares or Tokio would read at a glance, is a sealed mystery to the American mind. I sit there, and listen to the comments of the stream of visitors, I am astounded at the actually torpid perceptions of the average American; and the worst of all is the clerical preacher. He can see nothing but Despair. He shows what his own mind is full of; but the idea of Thought has been wholly effaced.[58]

One finds in this letter the material which gained its final formulation in the passage of the *Education*, written two years later and quoted above. Adams even lectured President Theodore Roosevelt in the matter of the figure: "But!!! . . . should you allude to my bronze figure, will you try to do St. Gaudens the justice to remark that his expression was a little higher than sex can give. As he meant it, he wanted to exclude sex and sink it in the idea of humanity. The figure is sexless."[59] Only once did Adams take the trouble to give to the nameless figure a name, in a letter to Saint-Gaudens' friend Richard W. Gilder, dated 14 October 1895:

I have written to Saint-Gaudens to use any drawings or photographs he likes, provided that no names of mine, or allusion to me or mine is attached. The whole meaning and feeling of the figure is in its universality and anonymity. My own name for it is "The Peace of God." La Farge would call it "Kwannon." Petrarch would say: "Siccome eterna vita è veder Dio," and a real artist would be very careful to give it no name that the public could turn into a limitation of its nature. With the understanding that there should be no such attempt at making it intelligible to the average mind, and no hint at ownership or personal relation, I hand it over to St.-Gaudens.[60]

The passage from one of Petrarch's sonnets, just quoted, "To succumb to eternal life and see God," occurs likewise in Adams' novel *Esther*, interestingly enough in conjunction with the term Nirvana, which became quite popular as a title for the Adams Monument. Since the lines in *Esther* were written before 1884, it is as though Adams with the poet's prophetic vision had seen ahead of the events to his wife's death and the atonement for it by the erection of a monument to love and death.

In the novel, Esther tried to paint the features of St. Cecilia for the St. John's murals, using Catherine Brooke as a model; Wharton was not satisfied with the quiet "earthly" expression of the head and made his own sketch for it. "He had narrowed the face, deepened its lines, made the eyes much stronger and darker . . . in order to give an expression of passion subsided and heaven attained. 'You have reached Nirvana,' said Esther . . . 'What is Nirvana?' asked Catherine [and Wharton answered:] 'Nirvana is what I mean by Paradise . . . It is eternal life, which, my poet says, consists in seeing God.' "[61] Mabel Hooper La Farge, using Adams' own words, spoke in her introduction to *Letters to a Niece* about "the peace of Nirvana"—"infinite and eternal peace—the peace of limitless consciousness unified with limitless will," and later continued:

The "life behind a veil" reveals itself in the monument in Rock Creek Cemetery. . . . Translated into Western thought, Henry Adams called it "The Peace of God." Sometimes he would call it "Kwannon," the compassionate Virgin of the East, merciful guardian of the human race. After the glory of the "Virgin of Chartres" had been revealed to him, however, the Divine Mother of the West blended in his mind, in the monument with the Virgin of the East.[62]

The reluctance of Adams to give a name to the figure was most strongly expressed in a letter to Homer Saint-Gaudens in reply to a request for his father's letters for publication in the *Reminiscences*:

> I will send you all I can find of your father's letters. . . . I have only one favor to ask of you in return. Do not allow the world to tag my figure with a name! Every magazine writer wants to label it as some American patent medicine for popular consumption, Grief, Despair, Pear's Soap, or Macy's Men's Suite Made to Measure. Your father meant it to ask a question, not to give an answer; and the man who answers will be damned to eternity like the man who answered the Sphinx. Undoubtedly a beneficient Deity, whether he exists or not, will some day commit our entire American—and European—society to eternal Hell-fire for *not* trying to answer your father's question; but this is no reason why we should undertake to act the part of Savior—much the contrary.[63]

Undoubtedly one of the reasons for Adams' almost pathological sensitiveness and secretiveness in the matter of the monument was his fear of disclosing to unconcerned strangers not only his philosophy of life and death but also his attitude towards the catastrophe of his wife's suicide. He hinted at that in the half-mocking manner so characteristic of him in a letter to Anna Cabot Mills Lodge: "I was lucky enough to get Saint-Gaudens to make a figure for me to express my notion that the most dignified thing for a worm to do, was to sit up and sit still. In my own judgement this is the last word of the song."[64]

The cult of Marian Adams, Kwannon, the Virgin, and of Death blend in the statue. When Adams himself was lying on his deathbed, "two blessed candles" were burning under Mabel Hooper La Farge's sketch of Saint-Gaudens' Adams Monument hanging in his bedroom.[65] The roads have come together from East and West, Past and Future, Love and Death, from Personal and Universal Grief, Personal and Universal Hope, to unite in the Adams Monument. The figure is a challenge to meditation, which several times found expression in poetry. A cycle of sonnets by Cecil Spring-Rice, the English diplomat friend of Adams, appeared under the title *The Saint-Gaudens Monument at Rock Creek Cemetery*. It was based on a Persian story.[66] Homer Saint-Gaudens reprinted a poem about the monument with the title "Nirvana" by Hildegarde Hawthorne along the theme of *Jenseits von Gut und Boese* (Nietzsche).[67]

We conclude the history of the Adams Monument—its conception, creation and its effects upon Adams and his contemporaries—with a conversation which took place in front of it between Augustus Saint-Gaudens, John Hay, and Mrs. Barrett Wendell, wife of the writer and Harvard English teacher, and was recorded in a letter from her to Homer Saint-Gaudens:

> I was in the Rock Creek Cemetery looking at the wonderful monument by Mr. Saint-Gaudens in memory of Mrs. Henry Adams when Mr. Saint-Gaudens and Mr. John Hay entered the little enclosure. I was deeply impressed and asked Mr. Saint-Gaudens what he called the figure. He hesitated and then said: "I call it the Mystery of the Hereafter." Then I said "It is not happiness?" "No" he said "it is beyond pain and joy." Mr. Hay turned to me and said "Thank you for asking. I have always wished to know."[68]

While there still reverberates in this conversation the rationalism and the optimism of the *pursuit of happiness* rampant in the nineteenth century and shared even by some of Adams' friends, the statue has come very much into its own in our more skeptical age as the most important and most profound American sculpture created around the turn of the century. What was once not understood and puzzling has become clear in the light of later developments. The Adams Monument is the first nearly modern work in American sculpture; it has a parallel only in Rodin's more abstract works.

Even such a conservative critic as Royal Cortissoz called it Saint-Gaudens' "one memorable effort in the sphere of the loftiest abstraction" in his book on Saint-Gaudens, and added: "Where Rodin would have made it speak of movement, . . . rugged and almost luridly epical, Saint-Gaudens has made the figure symbolical of rest itself."[69] When it is compared to Rodin's somewhat later "Thinker," to which it is related in theme (brooding meditation) and closed form, the difference again is between force (Rodin) and taste (Saint-Gaudens). But there are certain qualities in the Adams Monument by which it truly anticipates modern trends. It is designed not for rational understanding but for feeling and emotion. It is *symbol*, not allegory, and has therefore not one meaning but many. That is to say, it has no specific meaning at all. It is "poetry and suggestion," as John Hay put it, not prose and explanation. Indeed many strains could be played on it. Yet it is not quite as *sexless* as Adams wanted it to be. There is a certain sensuous appeal, that of the woman, even "behind a veil" of form, lofty thoughts, and abstraction.

Its abstract and truly modern qualities are in its stress on geometrical design and texture: a closed triangular form against the square of the monolith and the strong diagonal fold, running from left shoulder to right foot between the knees, which bisects the torso. It is interesting that Saint-Gaudens expressed the wish to change that; on a visit in 1903 he felt "the fold between the knees . . . makes too strong a line."[70] Purely abstract design considerations came second with him, not first! We have already criticized the unnecessary conventionalities of classical decorative carving at cornice and base, which Saint-Gaudens still thought of as improving the whole. But otherwise, the bareness of the rather high, smooth monolith of light red granite against the darker tone of the greenish bronze figure, and on the other hand, the harmony of the rough surface of the bronze figure with the crude natural piece of still darker rock, forming a seat for the figure, is a textural effect unique in American sculpture of that time and again paralleled only in the art of Rodin.

Saint-Gaudens worked out the color scheme with White and had the rock rubbed in order to get it darker after he had observed the effect of the whole in situ. Such careful consideration of color in sculpture and such color contrasts as the now malachite-green bronze of the figure standing out against the slightly mottled red of the stone are exceptional for the time, especially in a grave monument. While Richardson built the first *color church* in the United States, and La Farge was led to stained glass in his search for brilliant color, so Saint-Gaudens created in the Adams Monument the first colorful memorial in the history of American sculpture. In the class of tomb monuments in the nineteenth century, it is the great exception, an oasis of true feeling and true form, and not only in America. In totality it is the finest expression of the later idealistic style in this country.

Saint-Gaudens did another and much smaller work for Henry Adams, sometimes called the Adams Medallion. Though intended chiefly as a joke played by John Hay and Saint-Gaudens on their friend, it had its serious side and is related to the commissions Saint-Gaudens received for portraits in Adams' circle of statesmen friends, such as the relief of Attorney General Wayne McVeagh and his wife, and the bust of John Hay. They were among Sant-Gaudens' last works. The mood which prevailed then among the friends was the melancholy one of the old men of the world who, feeling their end is near, attempt to meet death with an attitude of gently sparkling irony.

Adams had tried before to get Saint-Gaudens a commission to do a relief of his Paris acquaintances Ralph Wormeley Curtis and his wife Lisetta.[71] But the McVeagh relief and the Hay bust were commissioned without Adams' having a share in it. He took a lively interest in them, however, and they brought the Saint-Gaudenses in close association with the circle gathering around his Washington breakfast table. Adams mentioned the McVeagh relief occasionally in his letters to Elizabeth Cameron, McVeagh's sister-in-law:

> The Saint-Gaudens's turned up at dinner last night. He is doing Wayne and Jinny [McVeagh] on a joint relief, and will be here a month. He expects much fun out of Wayne, but he can't get as much as I do [a reference to McVeagh's anti-Roosevelt policy]. Wayne's hatred for Theodore is a whole chapter of Saint Simon. Nothing fascinates me so much as to watch the stupid, blundering, bolting bull-calf of a Theodore, buck-jumping with frenzy under Wayne's stings, and unable to see the gadfly.[72]

And again: "The Saint-Gaudens's were here last night. He is beginning to find Wayne's high moral tone somewhat trying. Wayne's virtues are not exactly the artistic morality of the Renaissance."[73]

The McVeagh relief belongs to the group of Saint-Gaudens' popular double portraits, fine in design and their subtle very low relief, and excellent in characterization. The contrast of the foxy politician and the distinguished society matron with her lapdog is most entertaining. Less successful is the decorative fir tree frame, which gives to the whole a slightly stuffy note.

The Hay bust is a good likeness, especially in the marble version, and not much more. The details of moustache, goatee, necktie with pearl pin, rosette in the buttonhole, and pince-nez silk-cord are too obvious, and the expression lacks liveliness. Knowing that his face did not lend itself to sculpture, John Hay did not submit too gladly to "being busted." He wrote to Saint-Gaudens on 30 September 1903:

> I wonder if you could make anything of so philistine and insigni-ficant a head as mine. You succeed with all sorts and conditions of folks, but, to tell the truth, I do not recall any proposition you have ever tackled so unpromising as mine. I lack profile, size and every other requisite of sculpture, but I have been an unusual length of time in office and I fear that after I am dead, if not be-fore, some blacksmith will try to bust me. Turn it over a little in your mind.[74] [And later:] There are four copies of the work in different places, so that it is protected from loss unless the world blows up, in which event nobody would care except Henry Adams, who would shriek and yell in delight and derision as he sailed into the air.[75]

Adams mentioned it in his *Education*: "Saint-Gaudens came on to model his head, and Sargent painted his portrait, two steps essential to immortality which he bore with a certain degree of resignation."[76]

The bust of John Hay, which was after all a serious act of state, had its satyr-byplay in the Adams Medallion; Hay was the schemer and Saint-Gaudens his executant accomplice.[77] Homer Saint-Gau-dens related: "Adams's outward gruffness and inward gentleness had earned for him from Hay and father the title of 'Porcupine Poet-icus.' Hay and Saint-Gaudens made a bronze medallion showing Adams flying by means of wings feathered with porcupine quills."[78] An inscription runs around the edge: *Porcupinus·Angelicus·Henricus-Adamenso/Honi·Soit·Qui·Mal·Y·Pense/A. STG. Sculp.*; the date MCMIIII is between porcupine body and heraldic angel wings. In spite of its obviously caricature-like character, the allusion to Pisa-nello's animal representations is apparent. Besides the Adams Medal-lion, Saint-Gaudens' group of medallion caricatures includes one of himself with Stanford White and Charles McKim. He had a magnifi-cent talent for cartooning, surprising in so serious a man.

The letters exchanged on account of the Adams Medallion are no less amusing. Like the bronze itself they reveal the intimacy among the three old friends and the smiling sympathy for each other's pecu-liarities and foibles. Saint-Gaudens wrote to John Hay from Aspet, Windsor, Vermont, 19 August 1904: "A package has been sent you containing another which holds the bronze caricature of Adams. You said you would send it to him with diplomatic seals, etc. etc. Presently you will receive another for yourself."[78] Adams received the package in good spirits and thanked Saint-Gaudens for it:

> Your winged and pennated child arrived yesterday by the grace of God and his vicar the Secretary of State, or his satellites Adee and Vignaud. As this is the only way in which the Secretary will ever fulfill his promise of making me Cardinal and Pope I can see why he thinks to satisfy me by giving me medallic rank through you. Docile as I always am to suggestion, I agree that the medal is probably worth more than the hat. Work and make a lot more porcupusses. I'm sorry you can't give Hay wings too, he needs them more than I who live in holes. Adieu.[79]

Saint-Gaudens replied:

> It was good to hear of your automobile and the Salon, Rodin, Besnard and the Sixteen[th] Century glass. I recall some pretty fine stuff of that period in Brussels and in one or two of the "villes mortes" of Holland, Monnickendam and Marken. Run up there in your automobile, you will find it worthwhile. But what is the use of telling you anything you haven't seen or don't know about?
>
> I hope the medal makes you a little miserable. It was made for that purpose. . . . I succeeded in getting Hay here for a day and a half and his bust is finished and I am going to inflict two upon him.
>
> One he can give to you. Some day I hope to achieve a caricature of him, but I fear to approach it. Sometimes they are shameful. I never know how they tempt me.[80]

Three casts were made of the Adams Medallion, one for each of the three friends, Adams, Hay and Saint-Gaudens. Adams invited Margaret Chanler, his "dear Sainte Thomasine," to "come and you shall see Saint-Gaudens's portrait head of me as Porcupine."[81] The nickname *Porcupine* or *Porcupinus Poeticus* or *Porcupinus Angelicus* occurs several times in the Adams' correspondence. Adams called himself a "poor Porcupine" who can only see "the length of his tail" in a letter to Hay,[82] and Hay ended a letter to Saint-Gaudens from Europe where he had gone with Adams to take a cure:

> The Porcupinus Angelicus . . . has been kindness itself—the Porcupine has "passed in music out of sight" and the Angel has been perfected in him. As Sir Walter sings,

Oh; Adams in our hours of ease
Rather inclined to growl and tease,
When pain and anguish wring the brow
A ministering angel thou.[83]

In a letter to acknowledge a copy of Adams' privately printed
Chartres Saint-Gaudens wrote:

You dear old Porcupinus Poeticus:
You old Poeticus under a Bushelibus:

I thought I liked you fairly well, but I like you more for the
book you sent me the other day. Whether I like you more because
you have revealed to me the wonder of the twelfth century in a
way that never entered my head, or whether it is because of the
general guts and enthusiasm of the work, puzzles what courtesy
calls my brains. You know I never read, but last night I got as far
in your work as the Virgin, Eve and the Bees, and I cannot wait
to acknowledge it till I am through.

Thank you, dear Old Stick in the Mud,

Your brother in idiocy.[84]

Saint-Gaudens' last letter to "Dear Old Porcupine," written after the
recovery from a serious illness which, however, led to the sculptor's
death, contains no references to art but pays a nice little compliment
to the friend who had so often chaffed him for his inarticulateness
and his aversion to reading: "I am thinking why I did not do a lot of
things while I was younger than I am now—when I was as young as
you are for instance."[85]

Adams and other members of his circle were involved with some
of the projects of Saint-Gaudens' later years: the Chicago World's
Fair, the replanning of Washington, the Boston Public Library, and
the Phillips Brooks Memorial. They were all of national importance,
proof of the power wielded by the men of the Adams circle, which
actually pretty much controlled official American art around the
turn of the century.

We have already mentioned the Columbian Exposition at Chicago in 1893 and its pseudo-idealism, of which Adams was only too
aware. Yet, Saint-Gaudens delighted in it, and since he held the responsible position of adviser, he was not free of guilt in that style

débacle. His *Reminiscences* give an enthusiastic report of the exposition. On the invitation of the architect Daniel H. Burnham, Saint-
Gaudens accepted only the position of a general adviser for the whole
scheme. In that capacity he suggested the "Liberty" in the lagoon by
Daniel Chester French and the fountain opposite it, the work of his
former assistant Frederick W. MacMonnies. This fountain with its
rowing maidens was one of the most dreadful catastrophes to befall
American sculpture. Saint-Gaudens saw in it "the most beautiful conception of a fountain of modern times west of the Caspian Mountains."[86]

His own efforts for the exposition were confined to the figure of
Columbus in front of the Administration Building which, however,
was entirely modeled by his pupils, and to the medallion to be presented to the prize winners.[87] The Columbus Medallion involved the
most humiliating experience in Saint-Gaudens' otherwise so successful career. But the sculptor did not see that the same false sense of
values that reared the buildings and the fountains of the fair, which
he so greatly admired, was also responsible for the rejection of the
design of a nude Greek torchbearer on the reverse of the medallion!
It was, by the way, chaste Saint-Gaudens' only male nude. A false
morality rejected this true "bit of artistic idealism" (Homer Saint-
Gaudens) while it accepted the historicism of "Columbus setting foot
on American soil" on the obverse.[88]

Saint-Gaudens cooperated with Burnham and McKim again in
the plan drawn up by the Park Commission of Washington, D.C., for
the replanning of the capital. The great landscape architect Frederick
Law Olmsted was likewise a member of the commission. Nothing
came of the plan at that time, but it alarmed Adams, and he wrote to
Elizabeth Cameron:

> Today is the first of spring, a beautiful Washington Sunday and
> I've been out to my mansion at Rock Creek, and I have found it
> in good order for once, and ready for me to move in. I hardly
> know what still detains me; and the government seems to agree
> that I had better go, for the new plan of Burnham and Saint-
> Gaudens recommends turning Hay and me out of house and
> home into the cold. I am lucky to have a churchyard to shelter
> me, and out there I should have lots more visitors.[89]

Saint-Gaudens wrote about the ideas foremost in his mind for the re-planning of the city to President Theodore Roosevelt: "It would be deplorable in the extreme if [the new buildings] were not placed according to some comprehensive plan, binding all the Public Buildings with some idea of unity and harmony."[90]

The Boston Public Library by McKim, Mead and White, a "Temple of Later Idealism" as we called it above, became Saint-Gaudens' concern after the building had been erected and the question of decoration was discussed. In a letter to McKim he suggested a meeting with White and "that all the photographs of decorative work be got out—Masaccio, Carpaccio, Benozzo Gozzoli, Botticelli etc. to show and talk over." He also submitted a list of American mural painters for the job:

> Aside from La Farge, "qui va sans dire," and to whom undoubtedly the big room should be given, the following are the names that you should consider in this matter: Abbey, Bridgman, Cox, [Francis D.] Millet, Winslow Homer, who, Abbey tells me, has done some bully decorative things in Harper's office that we can go see together, and Howard Pyle. These are all strong men—every one of them.[91]

The inclusion of Winslow Homer is interesting. The main commission in the decoration of the library did not go to any American, however, but to Puvis de Chavannes, whom Saint-Gaudens too put before all others, even La Farge.

Saint-Gaudens himself was called upon to decorate the façade with two groups of sculpture. The idea went as far back as 1894, while the building was not yet completed. Saint-Gaudens suggested in a letter to Abbot: "On one pedestal Labor, represented by a man seated between two female figures—Science on one side and Art on the other—; on the other pedestal, a male figure of Law in the middle with female figures of Religion on one side and Force, or Power, on the other."[92] When Saint-Gaudens took up the plan later, the scheme was somewhat changed and death kept him from executing it. The early program for the work tells us something about his personal philosophy: labor between art and science; law between religion and force. But formally the whole was still dependent on the Beaux-Arts tradition and falls spiritually as well under the heading of devaluated symbols.

For the same Boston, whose hypercritical atmosphere Saint-Gaudens always feared, was executed his last project, the Phillips Brooks Memorial. It is strange that Trinity Church, which had acted as a focus for the formation of the circle, should cast its mighty shadow over this work, also Stanford White's last. In 1906 both chiefly occupied themselves with it. In the next year the sculptor was dead, the architect murdered, and the memorial was finished by others.

Here, as for the Boston library figures, the earliest plan goes far back, to 1893. But Saint-Gaudens did not take it up seriously before 1906, as the correspondence with Stanford White shows. The architect had this time an even larger share in the monument's setting than in the previous projects in which the two friends cooperated. They could not quite get together on the solution. Saint-Gaudens planned originally a covered monument, on the principle of the Scaglieri monuments in Verona.[93] But deeper anxieties beset the sculptor, as we learn from a letter to La Farge, who knew Phillips Brooks, minister of Trinity Church and Episcopalian Bishop of Massachusetts, intimately. Saint-Gaudens wrote: "I suppose I am getting well, as I am able to work seriously for the first time in a year on the 'Brooks.' Physically he is terribly difficult to represent, considering what he is in the minds of his admirers; and when beyond this there is the introduction of the Holy figure, it makes me feel abominably audacious."[94]

Saint-Gaudens had decided on the figure of Christ standing behind the preacher and gently touching him. It was the first time he attempted to model the figure of Christ, and it is characteristic of the degree he and his whole generation had "lost sight of ideals and faith" (Adams) that he did careful *research* for it in books. He read Renan's *Life of Christ*; he bought the French painter Tissot's illustrated iconographic book with the same title. He consulted Tissot by letter, "with regard to shape and size of garments, He wore." Finally he went, as Homer Saint-Gaudens related, to Henry Adams for recommendation of more reading matter on the subject of Christ.[95] Adams tersely suggested—the Bible. Thus Adams was, as in the years of Trinity Church, adviser and critic of his artist friends. The resultant "Head of Christ," the last piece Saint-Gaudens worked on with his own hand, is no *Beau-Dieu* of Amiens; at its best it is Thorvaldsen. The heartbeat of truly religious art was feeble at that time—idealism

tainted by materialism or reinforced by realism! It was—what paradox—research into ideals but it was not true idealism; it was *late*, that
is tired idealism. Saint-Gaudens' ideas on art and artists, as well as
most of his works, show that.

But inarticulate Saint-Gaudens, who according to Adams did
not care to talk art and hated theory, did not write books about it like
La Farge. His theoretical and historical pronouncements have to be
gleaned from letters and from what his students and his son recalled.
In determining Saint-Gaudens' place in the later idealistic movement
in America, we would rather label his art as idealized realism. He
knew that "art is not what a thing actually is but what it appears to
be" and that "you cannot reproduce things absolutely. So since you
must err, err only on the side of beauty."[96] That sounds almost like an
apology for idealism, makes it the second best choice, since *you cannot reproduce things absolutely.* But the idealistic belief in what is
called beauty in art may keep the artist from using what appears
beautiful in nature, as well as from using the ugly, the strong and the
characteristic.

In this respect Saint-Gaudens differed from Rodin who, in his
Conversations with Paul Gsell, defined the beautiful as being the
characteristic. According to Saint-Gaudens: "Art seemed to be the
concentration of the experience and sensations of life. . . . The imagination must be able to bring up the scenes, incidents that impress us
in life, condense them and the truer they are to nature the better.
The imagination may condemn that which has impressed us beautifully as well as the strong or characteristic or ugly."[97]

Saint-Gaudens shared with the later idealists the belief in *form*.
Homer Saint-Gaudens quoted a letter to him from the art critic William A. Coffin: "I have heard him more than once praise a painter's
work . . . for its attention to 'form.' But it was a peculiar form or style
which he meant by it and which he called 'strength with style' or
'strength with elegance.' "[98] This he found in the works of the Greeks
whose sculpture he put above all other. That is why he "urged his
pupils" to follow "the influence of the Greeks before that of Michelangelo."[99] The great Italian's art had too much force, so had the art
of Rodin, and Saint-Gaudens was on the side of *taste*, or *charm* as he
preferred to call it. He lectured to his students: "Charm may lie in

character, or in line, or in many things. But every man must have it to be successful . . . It is hard to know what gives it, perhaps the proper choice of things to accentuate or to suppress. Anything that is final or with no more to think about is uninteresting."[100]

The last passage explains why his works, especially his low reliefs, are somewhat sketchy in treatment, avoiding the high polished finish of the French medallists. We would today call this impressionistic, a quality which created a greater actuality and liveliness. In this respect Saint-Gaudens concurs with Rodin, except his impressionistic touch is gentle, that of the Frenchman strong. It sounds very Rodinish, but was obviously in self-defense when Saint-Gaudens once wrote to Gilder from Paris: "The finish or lack of finish has nothing to do in the classification of a work as good or bad—its character, regardless of that is the thing. For sculpture is only one of the means of expressing oneself, according to the temperament of the worker."[101]

A concession to the impressionistic-coloristic tendency of his time was also his insistence on the importance of "color and light in relief." To the pupil who made the background flat he would say: "Remember that your background is your atmosphere, and . . . part of the composition, and that the composition should extend from edge to edge of the frame."[102] This insistence on *background as atmosphere* in sculpture made him reject landscape or several planes in perspective. Ghiberti and his followers in the High Renaissance never appealed to him for that reason and Henry Adams' characterization of Saint-Gaudens as "a child of Benvenuto Cellini smothered in an American cradle" is not quite adequate.[103] The influence of Italian Renaissance art was generally less marked—with the exception of Pisanello—than the French Renaissance. Saint-Gaudens cherished French art most, in spite of his long stay in Rome.

In architecture Saint-Gaudens preferred the classical, often the pseudo-classical in the sense of the Beaux-Arts. His enthusiasm for Atwood's Art Building on the Chicago fair grounds, which he called the "best thing since the Parthenon," seems incomprehensible to us.[104] Though a friend of Richardson, his closest architect collaborators were McKim and White; his older architect associates were Hunt and Burnham.

In painting too, he was inclined toward the French, though he also owed something to the Pre-Raphaelites, especially to Burne-Jones, as we have seen. Pierre Puvis de Chavannes ranked first with him as a mural painter. Next to him as French muralists he listed Besnard, Raphael Collin, Luc-Oliver Merson, Maignan, Chartri, and Blanc.[105] Of the latter, only Besnard, whom Adams also appreciated, is remembered today. He knew personally Anders Zorn, who created a fine portrait etching of the sculptor in his characteristic impressionist style.

Saint-Gaudens knew Whistler through MacMonnies and associated with him in Paris at the time of the 1899 Exposition. The sculptor found in his work "a deep substratum of true feeling" where Adams saw chiefly vanity.[106] Saint-Gaudens created a memorial to Whistler to be erected at West Point, which the artist had attended. The inscription on the tablet, which Saint-Gaudens selected from Whistler's writings, is "The Story of the Beautiful is already completely hewn in the marbles of the Parthenon and broidered with the birds upon the fan of Hokusai."[107] The American muralists Saint-Gaudens admired were listed above. Of the easel painters with whom he associated, we might select Thomas W. Dewing, whose ethereal paintings he considered "the most delightful of their sort in the land."[108]

Of course Saint-Gaudens' chief interest was in sculpture. Among the work of his own pupils he ranked that of MacMonnies highest, though the only thing admirable about it seems to be his amazing technical skill. Other American sculptors he admired were Ward and French. Saint-Gaudens believed firmly in the future of American sculpture:

> The older I grow, the more and more I am convinced that as thorough and adequate training can be had here as abroad, that the work by the students here is equal to that produced by those in Europe. . . . Of course Europe, with its wealth and glory of art, must be seen and imbibed sooner or later. That goes without saying.[109]

European sculpture meant French sculpture. Saint-Gaudens wrote to a pupil: "The best modern sculpture is French—sculpture that we take our hats off to."[110] Saint-Gaudens enumerated the ten great sculptors of all ages in a letter to John W. Beatty:

Phidias—Praxiteles—Michelangelo—Donatello—Luca della Robbia—Jean Goujon—Houdon—Rude—David d'Angers—Paul Dubois, these are the names that occur to me at once. Of course, if we knew the names of the sculptors of the portal at Chartres or "le beau Christ d'Amiens" they would replace two of the more modern Frenchmen.[111]

The French names are conspicuous; one notices Rodin's is absent! Among the French Renaissance sculptors Goujon was especially dear to Saint-Gaudens. (The "Diana" made for the tower of New York's old Madison Square Garden, now in Philadelphia, is practically a Goujon.) There too he found *charme* or grace as in Greek sculpture.

In one of his few speeches he talked about the gratitude of the American sculptor for France. "Her hospitality has been without bounds, and her guidance most enlightening and inspiring under the masters of our day,—Barrias, Dubois, Falguière, Fremiet, Mercié, Rodin, as well as under the masters of the past, Jean Goujon, Germain Pillon, Houdon, David d'Angers, Rude, Barye—a glorious list."[112] Though Rodin appears in this list of French contemporaries, he is last. Two other famous names, not included in the lists, Homer Saint-Gaudens found on a slip of paper on his father's desk: Carpeaux and Meunier. Saint-Gaudens wrote that the Belgian Meunier was "one of the strong men of our times in a Millet-ish way, but minus the poetry."[113]

Among the French sculptors of his day Saint-Gaudens ranked Dubois first. In Dubois' works he found again the realization of his ideal, *strength with elegance*, especially in the equestrian statue of Jeanne d'Arc. Next to Dubois he placed Gérôme, sculptor and painter, the teacher of Thomas Eakins, and the typical Beaux-Arts representative, facile and empty. Not merely loyalty explains Saint-Gaudens' bias for the academic. His own "Amor Caritas," for which he received the Legion of Honor, blends quite well with the Beaux-Arts pieces of the Luxembourg Gallery in Paris, which purchased it. Rodin and Falguière, the rebels against the academicians, came in his esteem after Dubois and Gérôme.[114] Having been elected a member to the Société des Beaux-Arts, Saint-Gaudens associated with his French colleagues and wrote in his *Reminiscences*: "Among the other men of my acquaintance at that time there stand out most vividly

Paul Dubois and Auguste Rodin. Paul Dubois held a higher place in my esteem than any of the others, for his "Joan of Arc" is, to my thinking, one of the greatest statues in the world."[115]

Even when Saint-Gaudens paid tribute to Rodin, it was as though he had to convince himself to do it. When his "Sherman" and Rodin's "Eve" were shown at the Paris exposition he wrote: "Then the other day I called on Rodin, who it seems, felt hurt that I had not been to see him. There is no doubt, the doors he is doing are very fine, and I am deeply impressed."[116] The doors were the "Gates of Hell," of which the "Thinker" was originally a part. Saint-Gaudens had been, as his son wrote, an enthusiastic supporter of Rodin's early work, such as the "St. John the Baptist Preaching," and he also liked the "Age of Iron." But Rodin's "later eccentricities puzzled and bothered him." Homer Saint-Gaudens remembered his father's saying, as they looked at the plaster of Rodin's "Balzac," that it "gave him too much the effect of a guttering candle."[117] It is characteristic of Saint-Gaudens' taste that he lauded Rodin's early realistic phase and appreciated the master's late phase of literary symbolism as exemplified in the "Gates of Hell," but thought the abstract quality of the "Balzac" *eccentric*. His friend Adams would have used the word *decadent* instead. Like Adams and La Farge, Saint-Gaudens was blind to the values of modern twentieth century art which the "Balzac" announced.

Most characteristic of the attitude of Saint-Gaudens, as a representative of his generation, was his reaction to Tolstoi's *What is Art?* The book created a great stir when first published, since it defined art as expression, not as imitation, but limited its subject matter to the morally good. Saint-Gaudens wrote:

> He goes a great deal too far. . . . It has given me, however, a great admiration for Tolstoi's character, his sincerity and kindness of heart. But there are things in heaven and earth not dreamt of in his or anybody's philosophy, and the meaning of art is one of them.
>
> The prevailing thought in my life is that we are on a planet going no one knows where—probably to something higher (Darwinian evolution). But whatever it is, the passage is terribly sad and tragic, and to bear up against what seems at times the great doom that is over us, love and courage are the great things.[118]

There it is, that wavering of the nineteenth century artist between hope and despair, between Darwinian evolution towards progress and Adamsian doom, between rise and fall, which is in the final analysis responsible for the dichotomy of realism and idealism in the work of the artists in the *circle* of Henry Adams.

IV
The Virgin
and the Dynamo

11. Adams the Esthete

The quest for unity is the strongest link connecting Henry Adams and his artist friends, just precisely because that unity is largely lacking in their own work and their thoughts. Idealism and realism, progress and doom, religion and science, remain polarities with them, are thesis and antithesis, yet the synthesis of unity was rarely achieved by any of them. In this respect they are all figures from the second half of the nineteenth century, when thought and art suffered from that crack or fissure of dualism which runs through it full length. The deeper reason for it was that man had not yet assimilated his newly won power and pride of being apparent master of the forces of nature and keeper of the secrets of the universe, to his older and humbler beliefs of being God's creature, as well as to his growing doubts about the permanence of his new position as ruler of the universe. To those among the friends of the circle who survived for a decade and more into the twentieth century, the doubts became graver with the progress of the new era and enveloped them in doom and negation. Adams became their spokesman in this negative attitude towards the new century. In their relation to the art of the twentieth century, Post-Impressionism and Expressionism, as far as they lived long enough to see its beginnings, they were practically all negative or critical. They believed that art, in particular, reflected the general cultural situation. According to Adams, art had to be confused in order to express the confusion of the age. Though it might happen that some of them, especially Adams and La Farge, made an attempt to understand theoretically the new trend in painting and sculpture, their attitude towards the representatives of this art remained conservative. Witness Adams' and La Farge's aversion towards Gauguin, and Adams' and Saint-Gaudens' rather unsatisfactory relations with Rodin. The handy labels applied by them to the work of these trail blazers of modern art were *eccentric* and *decadent*.

Richardson was the one artist in the circle least affected by doubts about his own age and the future. He was not at all afflicted by its psychic accompaniment, melancholia, or as Adams liked to call it, *neurasthenia*, which created around the artists of later idealism an "aura of failure and frustration." On the contrary, the architect seemed to suffer from too much vigor and confidence in the industrial age and in the youth and destiny of his own country. His architecture, heavy and massive, seemed to symbolize the health of a young society with inexhaustible and still largely untapped resources. We must admit, however, that his architecture was sometimes an ornamental false front, hiding the great nineteenth century *crack* in back.

Yet, though Richardson was the one who died long before the turn of the century (1886), though he did not even reach the danger zone of the *fin de siècle*, and did not theorize and prophesy about the hopeless future, he was the one among the three artists of Adams' circle who in some of his buildings, especially his last ones, truly anticipated the style of the twentieth century and influenced modern art. It is true he did not build in the new materials of concrete and steel, but in his Marshall Field wholesale store in Chicago and in the Ames store in Boston, he laid the foundations of the American industrial style of the twentieth century. His art bridged the cleavage between the art of the nineteenth and twentieth centuries. La Farge and Saint-Gaudens remained behind. In their taste and sentiment they belonged actually to a preindustrial age.

And Adams? He had equally little confidence in the early expression of twentieth century machine art. His lines on the dynamo in the Hall of Machines at the Paris World's Fair of 1899-1900 do not mention the new type of architecture of which the hall was such a splendid early example.[1] He was also far from evaluating the dynamo or the automobile (he already owned one by 1904) as industrial design or even as art. They were to him merely a symbol of force, of horse-

power. Yet he experienced the dynamo esthetically, though not looking upon it as an object of art; that seems to be a contradiction we
must try to resolve.

The largely negative attitude of the members of the circle towards the cultural manifestations of their later life, particularly toward its art, which this résumé intends to establish, finds in Adams'
case its fuller explanation in his pessimistic philosophy of history. We
justify a brief investigation into that field, which is beyond the confines of a book on art and artists, by our belief that this philosophy
was primarily esthetically conditioned. At the beginning of the chapter on Adams' writings on art and artists, we offered as proof for this
the formulation of Adams' root metaphors, "The Virgin and the
Dynamo." As we went along we found many more illustrations for
the esthetic bias of Adams, the historian.

Works of art, chiefly from architecture and sculpture, were to the
historian Adams not only illustrations but even verification of his dynamic theory of rise and fall. From mother goddess idols and Egyptian pyramids to the architecture and sculpture of Delphi, the curve
rises, drops down somewhat to the Roman Forum, ascends to new
peaks in Mont-Saint-Michel and Chartres, to drop down again in a
rapid fall to Michelangelo's cupola of St. Peter's, finally reaching the
low in the eccentricities of twentieth century decadence. It is almost
amusing to see how the position of Hagia Sophia in Constantinople
caused him great embarrassment. As a theoretician of history he called
it with his characteristic self-mockery a *scandal*. The church's obvious strength and beauty must place it on the crest, while according
to his and his brother's degradation theory, it should be in the trough
of the curve. His correct esthetic judgment upset the pattern of his
historical theory, as he himself admitted.

But we use the term *esthetic* as applied to Adams in a wider
sense than is usually understood. The esthete Adams is to us not
merely the connoisseur of visual art or the professor of history with a
great liking for works of art. We employ the term in the sense of
Soeren Kierkegaard's philosophy of the *Either-Or* in which the na-
turalistic-esthetic type finds himself involved in a life and death struggle with the ethical-religious one.[2] To us Henry Adams is the esthetic
type; his brilliance, his sensitivity and love for the arts, his affinity

towards the female sex, but also his doubts, his melancholia, his feeling of failure, are all qualities of it. To Kierkegaard the esthetic type possessed sensuous geniality and he described the "aesthete's brilliance in words," which can be so well applied to Adams' mind:

> You see beneath you a multitude of knowledge, insight, studies, observations, which nevertheless have no true reality for you, but which you use and which you combine according to your mood or whim, and with which you decorate the palace in which you occasionally dwell as tastefully as possible for the luxury of the mind.[3]

The esthetic type so described remains always an amateur, because the amateur is in the position to evade choice, and the amateur is always an egotist. Kierkegaard expressed it: "If talent is not looked upon as a profession then talent is absolutely egotistical."[4] The egotistic attitude of the amateur, however, is "not evil but indifferent;"[5] Kierkegaard described the esthetic type "as not without conscience," but explains his conscience as "only like a higher kind of consciousness felt as restlessness, which does not accuse him but keeps him awake."[6] How well all this fits the esthete, amateur and egotist Henry Adams!

Adams' restlessness of conscience in his later years was to some degree the result of the moral-Puritan New England background of his childhood. The Puritan Adams continued to fight Adams the esthete. It was a vicious circle. Adams' increasing estheticism undermined the moralism of his youth, while the estheticism of his later years suffered from a bad conscience because of his earlier moralism, which he could not fully forget. Yvor Winters stated that in the later years Adams' "moral sense persisted strong as ever but running amuck for lack of guidance."[7] This lack of guidance, this loss of moral direction, we ascribe to Adams' esthetic involvement. Caught in this final dilemma, Adams, the esthetic egotist with the bad conscience, brought down the roof of the temple upon himself and his fellow men; his own negation forced him to see negation and final destruction everywhere.

We noticed how he looked for fellow sufferers, how he thought not only of himself but also of his friends as neurasthenics. Kierkegaard explained the reason for that too: the esthetic type suffers from melancholia. To the question, "What is melancholia?" Kierkegaard replied, "Hysteria of the spirit—Every aesthetic conception of life is despair."[8]

In the relation to the female, too, the esthetic type creates only final despair and tragedy, notwithstanding its initial seductive attraction. In one of the most famous sections of Kierkegaard's *Either-Or*, entitled "The Diary of a Seducer," Cordelia, the victim of such a "seduction by the spirit" of the mentally superior but morally inferior "aesthetic type," gives the following character portrait of the seducer:

> He was a wonderful instrument, always in motion. He had heights and depths like no other instrument, he was rich in feeling and mood; no thought was too great for him, none too desperate. He could sound like the storm of fall and he could whisper inaudibly.[9]

This description reminds one of the Reverend Hazard in *Esther*, largely a self-portrait of Adams. Written in his "heart's blood" as Adams himself put it,[10] this book deals with the failure of the esthetic type in his relation to the female. The novel is the story of a seduction through the spirit attempted by a self-centered, charming man of great esthetic sensitivity, and of the ethical struggle of a free soul, Esther, who chooses to destroy her happiness rather than to give up her spiritual independence. We are, however, reluctant to draw too close a parallel between fiction and life, between Hazard and Adams. We respect the deep grief, the proud silence, even the harsh gruffness with which Adams in his writings guarded the secret of the greatest personal tragedy of his life.

It seems, though, that it remained the ever bleeding wound from which his heart's blood continued to flow, and that it was the most personal cause from which stemmed to a great extent the feeling of failure and frustration entertained by Adams increasingly during the second period of his life. It was also the cause for his esthetic cult of the Virgin. There was a connection between Marian Adams' death and the worship of the Virgin, or as Robert E. Spiller expressed it, "Esther was now enshrined in Chartres."[11]

Many incidents given in this book support the contention that Adams was an "aesthetic type"; he was not primarily interested in truth for its own sake as an ethical demand, but often only when he found the search for truth *amusing* or even *fun*, in other words, esthetically attractive. Adams played with ideas, and for that reason often contradicted his own theories. As noted above, "not thought-content, but thought-structure or thought-form interested him first of all." Thus, he could write in his *Education*: "The pen works for itself, and acts like a hand, modeling the plastic material over and over again to the form that suits it best."[12]

As a historian, Adams was primarily led by the esthetically felt necessity for sequences assuming relationships, and second, only by the truthfulness of such arrangements. Among his contemporaries it was La Farge who felt that the historian Adams was an artist when he wrote, "Adams's historic sense amounts to poetry." Among contemporary critics, Robert E. Spiller concisely expressed the very same thought: "Henry Adams was at heart an artist first, an historian second."[13] Spiller most emphatically stressed the fact that Adams was first of all an artist, that "only in the aesthetic expression of his position did he reach any degree of finality." To Adams, Spiller continued, "his major works the 'Chartres' and the 'Education' focussed a unified, albeit an imperfect whole. . . . The two books in concept are one, a planned work of the imagination rather than an historical, autobiographical or scientific record or argument." Spiller proceeds then to show the *symbolic parallelism* in the tripartite structure of the two books.

It is certain that Adams, as the architect of this structure which the two books have in common, was aware of it. He used the terms *architecture, sculpture* and *line* in his essay "The Rule of Phase Applied to History" as the only values which scientific writing teaches.[14] Yet the real *fun*, according to the same letter, was *narratives* which teach "color and follow the laws of music and painting." Therefore, in another letter, he explained the *failure* of his *Education* to be the mixture of *narrative* and *didactic* (scientific) purpose and style, "which cannot be successfully done." Yet he consoled himself by saying that "the charm of the effort is not in winning the game but in playing it." In order to safeguard as much as possible the form of his writings, Adams had to add a purely didactic part at the end of both *Chartres* and his *Education*. "The last three chapters of each make one didactic work in disguise," he wrote in a letter to Wendell.[15]

Seen in this *formally-structural* way, the unifying relationship of the terms *Virgin* and *dynamo*—so shockingly different in character—consists in their function of being hinges.

From the very beginning it was clear to Adams that these two root metaphors of his philosophy of history, "The Virgin and the Dynamo," have in common only the "attraction on his own mind"; or he called them, "two kingdoms of force which had nothing in common but attraction," and it was purposely left ambiguous whether by *attraction* he meant their magnetism for mankind as a whole, or merely for the individual Henry Adams.[16] It is the use of the word *force* which leads to a semantic deception. Both terms, the *Virgin* and the *dynamo*, were chosen because they were to Adams symbols of force. Force is the *tertium comparationis*. The Virgin was to Adams the procreative force in nature, a symbol of fertility, the greatest mystery of creation; the dynamo was the symbol of mechanical force which, according to his theory, leads to chaos and destruction. It is not our purpose to consider here the reasons for such a dualism of natural and mechanical forces, the one representing unity and God, the other complexity, multiplicity, and Satan. Adams' awe before the dynamo's silent power reminds one of William Morris' fear of the machine; Morris too saw only evil in it. But it is certainly true that the Virgin, as an ideal metaphorical force of faith, is on a level of meaning entirely different from the physical measurable force of the dynamo, which can be made in units of horsepower. It is a playing with the word *force*! Besides their deceptive semantic unity in the word *force*, the Virgin and the dynamo have only the attraction of force in common—yet only for the esthetic type Adams! They were unified only in Adams' individual visual experiences. In his books they were used as dialectic terms. The Virgin was applied to the past, the Middle Ages, according to Adams the world of faith and unity, the dynamo became the symbol of Adams' present, to him the world of science and multiplicity.

This contrasting use of the terms, though satisfactory to the esthete Adams as a means of organizing history since the Middle Ages, bothered the moralist Adams in his quest for unity. Therefore, he did not cease in his attempts to reconcile faith and science, for which the Virgin and the dynamo were symbols.

It is typical of the dilemma increasing in the nineteenth century, that it thought of faith and science as irreconcilable, and at the same time, suffering from the assumed irreconcilability, desired to overcome it. One way out of this impasse was to prove by scientific experiment or method the very things one believed in by faith. Adams did that in his *Degradation of the Democratic Dogma*, and suffered shipwreck. In the "Letter to the American Teachers of History," an essay in this book, later selected and edited by his brother Brooks, Adams turned to a cynical kind of pragmatism to sell unity to his colleagues. He was so afraid to reveal unity as an article of his own faith that he called it "a natural instinct of man" (using the then so popular scientific term), "innate and intuitive, surviving the idea of God or Universe."[17] He degraded unity to a mere convenience, exhorting his colleagues, "The convenience of unity is beyond question, where a vast majority of minds, educated or not, are invited to live in a complex of anarchical energies, with only the privilege of acting as chief anarchists."[18] Nevertheless, one is convinced that in spite of his often confessed lack of faith, Adams knew all the time the belief in unity is faith, or as he called it, *vision* or *doctrine*, but these are words mistrusted by an enlightened scientific mind in the nineteenth century.[19]

Because of his lack of faith and his toying with truth, Adams has been called "a modern nihilist and hence a hedonist or nothing" by Yvor Winters.[20] Similarly Paul Elmer More accused Adams of "sentimental nihilism, a compensation, genuine if inadequate for a lost religion."[21] But had Adams lost his religion completely at the end of his life? Of course we do not understand by religion any specific creed but religiosity. The "Prayer to the Virgin"—found after his death in a wallet containing personal papers—seems to prove the opposite, and his lifelong struggle for unity—a search after faith—seems likewise to contradict Adams' avowed irreligiosity. Yet in the development of his personality, Adams hardly ever achieved Kierkegaard's "equilibrium between the aesthetic and the ethical." There seemed to be a proclivity towards the esthetic in spite of the persistence of the ethical, of which the "Prayer to the Virgin" was merely a temporary outburst.

Being an esthetic type, Adams was also, like most people belonging to this category, a visual one. The visual type is gifted with *seeing* relations between objects, which the ordinary observer would classify as belonging to entirely different spheres and therefore as beyond the possibility of association. This ability *to see* connections where others see none, might be especially evoked when the observation of two seemingly contrasting objects follows close upon each other. That happened in Adams' case with the dynamo and the Virgin. His meeting with the dynamo and his standing before the Virgin followed immediately one after the other.

Adams left the St. Louis World's Fair with its impressive display of mechanical force in the early summer of 1904 and stood only some weeks later before the statue of the Virgin in the church of Coutances in Normandy. The closeness of the two observations in time helped certainly to bring forth the spark of association which sprang from the dynamo to the Virgin, revealing their connection to Adams as though in a sudden illuminating flash. The very strong initial experience of the Virgin of Coutances became fused with the later meeting with the Virgin of Chartres, who in his books *Mont-Saint-Michel and Chartres* and *Education* almost replaced the Virgin of Coutances. Conversely the dynamo at the St. Louis World's Fair, with which Adams became acquainted after his visit to the Hall of Machines at the Paris World's Fair, lost out in importance to the Parisian "silent giants" when written about in his *Education*. This change of locale was possibly undertaken because of the greater fame of Chartres and Paris.

The writing of Adams which deals with the Virgin and the dynamo in closest confrontation is the poem "Prayer to the Virgin of Chartres." It was written between *Chartres* and *Education*,[22] which as we have seen pivot around these two *root-metaphors*. Since Adams' discovery of the Virgin was dealt with extensively in the chapter on *Chartres*, it is only necessary here to follow Adams in his description of meeting the dynamo:

> To Adams the dynamo became a symbol of infinity. As he grew accustomed to the great gallery of machines, he began to feel the forty-foot dynamo as a moral force, much as the early Christians felt the Cross. The planet itself seemed less impressive in its old fashioned, deliberate, annual or daily revolution, than this huge

wheel, revolving within arm's length at some vertiginous speed, and barely murmuring—scarcely humming an audible warning to stand a hair's breadth farther for respect of power—while it would not wake the baby lying close against the frame. Before the end, one began to pray to it; inherited instinct taught the natural expression of man before silent and infinite force. Among the thousand symbols of ultimate energy, the dynamo was not so human as some, but it was the most expressive.[23]

What a deliberate transfer of qualities and imagery from the Virgin to the dynamo! Adams spoke of the dynamo as the *symbol of infinity*, as a *moral force*, at the frame of which the baby may lie sleeping like the Christ Child at the feet of the Madonna, and confessed finally the instinct to pray to it as to the statue of the Virgin.

How sensuous Adams' language is in expressing an *attraction* similar to that felt in a church before a statue of the Madonna. His mind played with the dynamo's nearly silent yet dangerous forces as the Christ Child plays with the dove, lovingly and innocently. At last he prayed to the machine, or at least pretended to bend his knee before it. Indeed, in his "Prayer to the Virgin of Chartres," not only the Virgin but also the dynamo is worshiped, the latter addressed as a god:

> Yet we have Gods,
> For even our strong nerve
> Falters before the energy we own.

But of the two, the Virgin, *the great mother*, is the more human, and is a woman. Adams' esthetic sympathies definitely preferred her to the machine. The unity he could find neither in the religion of his Puritan ancestors nor in western and eastern philosophy nor in science, he seems finally to have discovered in the Virgin of the Middle Ages. The path to Her was tortuous and long. It led from the superstitious fear of the boy in Boston, taught to look upon the cult of the Virgin as *idolatry*,[24] and instructed that even in its sublimations sex was sin, to the scientific attitude of the mature man who coolly identified Her with the fecund mother-goddesses of the East, and finally to the worship of the skeptical old sage who wrote prayers to Her and tucked them away in a wallet.

Because of Her, who had become his final symbol of unity, he saw unity in the Middle Ages which definitely did not possess it, not even relatively, any more than other periods, even when one concentrates on the era of the Crusades, as Adams did. To demonstrate the lack of unity in this period of the Middle Ages is like crashing into open gates; Winters has done so with specific application to Adams' assumptions. He pointed to the chasm between Nominalism and Realism, to the contrast between the culture of the ruling class and the stone age character of the peasant civilization which remained pagan, to the chaotic character of the feudal system. Even the unity of the medieval church, insofar as it had been achieved, was "due less to the spirit of the age than to the mind of Thomas Aquinas."[25]

That explains why Adams admired St. Thomas more than any other medieval thinker. He said that he at least "linked together the joints of his machine," and that in his system, "Thought alone was Form. Mind and unity flourished and perished together."[26] Herbert L. Creek summed up in "The Mediaevalism of Henry Adams": "In his mediaeval studies he was engaged in the romantic quest, his blue flower being the simple faith that reared the great cathedrals, and his dream-woman, Mary herself."[27]

While Adams overestimated the unity of the Middle Ages, he underestimated that of the machine age, which he called chaotic, multiple, and divided. It is, however, a fact that the modern world, as the result of industrialization, transportation, spreading of western languages and customs, showed more unity, at least in its appearance in Adams' lifetime, than the Middle Ages. This process has gone on ever since, but the attitude of the champions of One World in our day is no less an article of faith and desire than Adams' romantic longing for the Middle Ages and the Virgin. Unity is never a complete reality, since it is an ideal. In the last analysis the desire for unity cannot exist without multiplicity and vice versa; they depend upon each other mutually. That is true for the realms of man, nature, art, and beyond them, for the universe. We shall never cease to long for unity, though everything manifests multiplicity, man assuming only the existence of unity. And this desire is as burning today as it was in the Middle Ages.

Adams' amazingly acute awareness of our present stage, which he called the "phase of the ether," seems to contradict not only his theory of increasing multiplicity but also that of the final degradation or doom of mankind. But the final fall too was Adams' personal faith, and his longing for destruction was no less the product of his most personal experiences, failures, and frustrations, than his longing for unity through the aid of the Woman, the Mother, the Virgin. The vision of the thinker and seer is here clouded by the spiteful desire of an egotistic, death-tired man, who enjoyed "the crumblings of worlds as fun."[28]

Adams' vision of the "phase of the ether" is indeed phenomenal for an amateur in the sciences. In his *Education* he spoke of the coming of that supersensual phase as "a far vaster universe where all the old roads run about in every direction" towards "a larger synthesis to unify the anarchy again." In such words Adams stated the philosophy, the physics, the sociology, the esthetics of the *Open Form.* "Evolution becoming change of form broken by freaks of force," Adams called it.[29] His "roads running about in every direction" might be compared to Arthur Koestler's *network* which replaced "the fatalistic trap of physical determinism," into which Adams in spite of his vision had fallen almost by an act of will.[30] What Adams called *freaks of force* is absorbed by what modern scientists call the "Heisenberg principle of indeterminacy," according to which "laws are nothing more than statistics of probability." Ray F. Nichols, in his article "The Dynamic Interpretation of History," which deals specifically with Adams' theory of history in relation to the exact sciences, makes that point: "Today the atmosphere of scientific thought is entirely different from the physical determinism dominant in the nineteenth century . . . units are not acting according to fixed laws but seem to exercise free will."[31]

Even the liberation of energy in the atom and Einstein's discovery of the transformation of mass into energy and vice versa, were foreseen by Adams. He could not, of course, have had it from Einstein, whose vogue came later, but from Ernst Mach, "who admitted but two processes in nature—change of place and interconversion of forms. Matter was Motion—Motion was Matter—the thing moved."[32] This anticipation of Einstein's theory was also noted by Robert A. Hume, who wrote that "Adams was in a sense 'ahead of his time' in arriving at an intellectual attitude of uncertainty and uneasiness that might be inferred in recent decades from, for example, Einsteinian relativity."[33]

Adams was certainly aware of the interrelationship of unity and multiplicity when he said that "the scientific synthesis commonly called Unity *was* the scientific analysis commonly called Multiplicity. The two things were the same, all forms being shifting phases of motion."[34] But the belief that "kinetic atoms lead only to motion never to direction or progress," seemed to him identical with admittance of chaos, and chaos was to him the same as the *final fall*.[35]

In spite of his prophetic glimpse at a *larger synthesis* which would unify chaos again, Adams could not free himself entirely from the nineteenth century belief in direction linked to determinism; he could not even relinquish completely its optimistic variety, the Spencerian belief in progress. Adams could never disentangle himself from that blatant contradiction between his theory of degeneration and the Spencerian creed of progress, even when he had lost faith in American optimism and the "evolution from lower to higher."

Ray F. Nichols has shown that two dynamic theories co-existed in the nineteenth century which conflicted with each other, the one optimistic, the other pessimistic: "The first of these was the law of evolution or indefinite progress; the other the law of entropy or ultimate degradation."[36] After having been an adherent of the theory of evolution in his younger years, Adams embraced that of degradation in his old age, attempting to prove it through the scientific laws of thermo-dynamics, phases and squares. As a true son of the nineteenth century, he felt it necessary to prove scientifically what he emotionally believed in.

It is not necessary here to critically consider the details of the entropy theory as set forth by Adams in his *Degradation of the Democratic Dogma*, since Nichols did it so well in the article cited above. He refuted Adams' theory with the latest theories in science and concluded that "there is a tendency in the universe to overcome entropy; the running down of the second law is balanced by a corresponding running up; the law is but one aspect of a twofold synthesis." And he said later that "such a new formulation will be neither a law of progress foretold by the Spencerians, nor will it be that law of degradation which impressed Adams. It will be the law or laws of adaptation . . . based on the secret of the human potential."[37]

We have often stressed Adams' pessimistic outlook on the future of mankind, the result of his own life, his character and his tragic experiences. It is therefore no wonder that the great vogue for his writings came in a period of pessimism after the end of World War I, the outbreak of which he so accurately predicted. He appealed then to the disillusioned younger generation, which had discarded the flat optimism of the Spencerian progress creed. He functioned as a kind of American Spengler. Horace M. Kallen drew a parallel between Adams' and Spengler's *Untergang* predictions: "Thus Spengler, drawing from neo-vitalistic biological analogies a philosophical fantasy, non-Hegelian, yet a Hegelism, regarded the course of history as depressed in mood as those Henry Adams draws from pre-Einsteinian physics."[38]

Now, in the era of the atom bomb after World War II, Adams has proven again a prophet. He wrote in his *Education*: "The next great influx of new forces seemed near at hand and its style of education promised to be violently coercive."[39] Thus he conceded that there exist coercive factors which could eventually act as a countermeasure to total destruction.

As noted above, the entropy theory, in which Adams wrapped his belief in the *final fall*, has been scientifically challenged. Furthermore, determinism does not seem inevitable to a generation which "had learned to think in contradictions," to use Adams' own words.[40] He said of this new generation, "the child born in 1900 would, then, be born into a new world, which would not be a unity but a multiple."[41] "Evidently the new American would need to think in contradictions. . . . The new universe would know no law that could not be proved by its anti-law."[42]

Adams said of his friend La Farge that "he contradicted even his own contradictions." In a higher degree that was true of Adams himself. His initial belief in the increasing chaotic multiplicity of our age was contradicted by the vision of the "larger synthesis of the multiverse." His prophecy of doom, as expounded in *Degradation of the Democratic Dogma*, was contradicted in certain passages in the last chapter of his *Education,* where he did not shut so definitely the door on doomed mankind, but still gave it a last chance. He wrote: "The movement from unity to multiplicity, between 1200 and 1900, was unbroken in sequence, and rapid in acceleration. Prolonged one generation longer, it would fail to react—but it would need to jump."[43]

Thus, it is then still a matter of choice and will, and not of deterministic fate, for mankind to survive or not. Affirming this positive view, the title of the last chapter of his *Education* is "Nunc Age" (act now), evidently an appeal to action addressed to his fellow men to save themselves in time. This is the same as the rajah's advice to his son, a disciple of Buddha, in Adams' poem "Buddha and Brahma" (1891): "Think not! Strike."[44] And he gave himself a chance to overcome danger and doom through action and faith in the following verses from the "Prayer to the Dynamo":

> Mysterious Power! Gentle Friend!
> Despotic Master! Tireless Force!
> You and we are near the End.
> Either You or We must bend
> To bear the martyrs' Cross.
>
> We know not whether You are kind,
> Or cruel in your fiercer mood;
> But be you Matter, be you Mind,
> We think we know that you are blind,
> And we alone are good.
>
> What are we then? the lords of space?
> The master-mind whose tasks you do?
> Jockey who rides you in the race?
> Or are we atoms whirled apace,
> Shaped and controlled by you?
>
> Seize, then, the Atom! rack his joints,
> Tear out of him his secret spring!
> Grind him to nothing!—though he points
> To us, and his life-blood anoints
> Me—the dead Atom—king!

And turning again to the Virgin:

So while we slowly rack and torture death
And wait for what the final void will show,
Waiting I feel the energy of faith
Not in the future science, but in You![45]

References, Abbreviations,
and Short Titles Used in the Notes

AA   James T. Adams, "At Mr. Adams's," *New Republic* 15 (25 May 1918): 106-8.

Adams   James T. Adams, *Henry Adams*, NY, A. & C. Boni, 1933.

ALJ   John La Farge, *An Artist's Letters from Japan*, NY, Century Co., 1897.

AS-G   Royal Cortissoz, *Augustus Saint-Gaudens*, Boston, Houghton Mifflin Co., 1907.

Baym   Max I. Baym, *The French Education of Henry Adams*, NY, Columbia Univ. Press, 1951.

Boas   George Boas, ed., *Courbet and the Naturalistic Movement*, Baltimore, Johns Hopkins Press, 1938.

Brooks   Van Wyck Brooks, *New England Indian Summer, 1865-1915*, NY, E. P. Dutton & Co., 1940.

Bud.   Henry Adams, "Buddha and Brahma," *Yale Review* 5 (Oct. 1915): 82-89.

Cat.   Max I. Baym, "The 1858 Catalogue of Henry Adams's Library," *Colophon* 3 (Autumn 1938): 483-89.

Cater   *Henry Adams and his Friends, a Collection of his Unpublished Letters* (intro. by Harold D. Cater), Boston, Houghton Mifflin Co., 1947.

Char.   Henry Adams, *Mont-Saint-Michel and Chartres* (intro. by Ralph A. Cram), Boston, Houghton Mifflin Co., 1933.

Clark   Kenneth Clark, *Ruskin Today*, Lon., John Murray, 1964.

col.   college(s).

coll.   collection(s).

COP   John La Farge, *Considerations on Painting*, NY, Macmillan & Co., 1895.

Creek   Herbert L. Creek, "The Mediaevalism of Henry Adams," *South Atlantic Quarterly* 24 (Jan. 1925): 86-97.

Degr.   Henry Adams, *Degradation of the Democratic Dogma* (intro. by Brooks Adams), NY, Macmillan Co., 1920.

Educ.   *The Education of Henry Adams, an Autobiography*, Boston, Houghton Mifflin Co., 1924.

EIA   Frank J. Mather, "John La Farge—an Appreciation," *Estimates in Art* 1, NY, Charles Scribner's Sons, 1916: 241-65.

E-O   Soeren A. Kierkegaard, *Entweder-Oder*, Dresden, 1909.

Esth.   Henry Adams, *Esther* (a novel by "Francis Snow Compton," with intro. by Robert E. Spiller), NY, Scholars' Facsimiles & Reprints, 1938.

Exh.   *Exhibition of the Work of John La Farge*, NY, Metropolitan Museum of Art, 23 Mar.–26 Apr. 1936.

Foc.   Henri Focillon, "John La Farge," *American Magazine of Art* 29 (May 1936): 311-19.

GM   John La Farge, *Great Masters*, NY, McClure, Phillips & Co., 1903.

HAH   Worthington C. Ford, "Henry Adams, Historian," *Nation* 106 (8 June 1918): 674-75.

Hay   William R. Thayer, *The Life and Letters of John Hay*, Boston, Houghton Mifflin Co., 1915, 2 vol.

HHR   Henry-R. Hitchcock, *The Architecture of H. H. Richardson and his Times*, NY, Museum of Modern Art, 1936.

Hist.   Henry Adams, *The Formative Years, a History of the United States During the Administrations of Jefferson and Madison* (condensed & ed. Herbert Agar), Boston, Houghton Mifflin Co., 1947, 2 vol.

HLA   John La Farge, *The Higher Life in Art*, NY, McClure Co., 1908.

Hom.   Abigail A. Homans, *Education by Uncles*, Boston, Houghton Mifflin Co., 1966.

Hume   Robert A. Hume, *Runaway Star, an Appreciation of Henry Adams*, Ithaca, Cornell Univ. Press, 1951.

Hunt   *W. M. Hunt's Talks on Art*, first ser., Boston, H. O. Houghton & Co., 1875.

James   Henry James, *Notes of a Son and Brother*, NY, Charles Scribner's Sons, 1914.

JLF   Royal Cortissoz, *John La Farge, a Memoir and a Study*, Boston, Houghton Mifflin Co., 1911.

Kallen   Horace M. Kallen, *Art and Freedom*, NY, Duell, Sloan & Pearce, 1942, 2 vol.

L   Worthington C. Ford, ed., *Letters of Henry Adams (1858-1918)*, Boston, Houghton Mifflin Co., 1930-38, 2 vol.

Lee   Katharine C. Lee, "John La Farge, Drawings and Watercolors," Toledo Museum of Art *Museum News* 11 (1968): 3-22.

Lev.   Jacob C. Levenson, *The Mind and Art of Henry Adams*, Boston, Houghton Mifflin Co., 1957.

LJH   *Letters of John Hay and Extracts from Diary*, Washington, D. C., 1908, 3 vol.

LMA   Ward Thoron, ed., *The Letters of Mrs. Henry Adams, 1865-1883*, Boston, Little, Brown & Co., 1936.

LN   Henry Adams, *Letters to a Niece and Prayer to the Virgin of Chartres* (with "A Niece's Memories" by Mabel La Farge), Boston, Houghton Mifflin Co., 1920.

Lodge   Henry Adams, *The Life of George Cabot Lodge*, Boston, Houghton Mifflin Co., 1911.

Lon.   London, England.

Lotus   Vern Wagner, "The Lotus of Henry Adams," *New England Quarterly* 27 (Mar. 1954): 75-94.

Nich.   Ray F. Nichols, "The Dynamic Interpretation of History," *New England Quarterly* 8 (June 1935): 163-78.

NY   New York, N. Y.

Rem.   Homer Saint-Gaudens, ed., *The Reminiscences of Augustus Saint-Gaudens*, NY, Century Co., 1913, 2 vol.

Rich.   Edgar P. Richardson, *The Way of Western Art, 1776-1914*, Cambridge, Harvard Univ. Press, 1939.

RSS   John La Farge, *Reminiscences of the South Seas*, Garden City, N. Y., Doubleday, Page & Co., 1912.

Sam. 1   Ernest Samuels, *The Young Henry Adams*, Cambridge, Harvard Univ. Press, 1948.

Sam. 2   Ernest Samuels, *Henry Adams, The Middle Years*, Cambridge, Harvard Univ. Press, 1958.

Sam. 3   Ernest Samuels, *Henry Adams, the Major Phase*, Cambridge, Harvard Univ. Press, 1964.

Sim.   Katharine Simonds, "The Tragedy of Mrs. Henry Adams," *New England Quarterly* 9 (Dec. 1936): 564-82

Soby   James T. Soby and Dorothy C. Miller, *Romantic Painting in America*, NY, Museum of Modern Art, 1943.

Spiller   Robert E. Spiller, "Henry Adams, Man of Letters," *Saturday Review of Literature* 30 (22 Feb. 1947): 11-12, 33-34.

Stev.   Elizabeth Stevenson, *Henry Adams, a Biography*, NY, Macmillan Co., 1955.

Tahiti Henry Adams, *Memoirs of Arii Taimai e Marama of Eimeo, Teriirere or Tooarai, Terrinui of Tahiti Tauraatua i Amo*, Paris, 1901; repr. as *Tahiti* (ed. with intro. by Robert E. Spiller), NY, Scholars' Facsimiles & reprints, 1947.

univ.   university.

Waern   Cecilia Waern, *John La Farge, Artist and Writer*, NY, Macmillan & Co., 1896.

Wagner   Vern Wagner, *The Suspension of Henry Adams, a Study of Manner and Matter*, Detroit, Wayne State Univ. Press, 1969.

WDC   Washington, D. C.

Win.   Yvor Winters, "Henry Adams; or, The Creation of Confusion," *The Anatomy of Nonsense*, Norfolk, Conn., New Directions, 1943.

YC   Arthur Koestler, *The Yogi and the Commissar, and Other Essays*, NY, Macmillan Co., 1945.

Chapter 1
1. L2: 558.
2. *Educ.*: 315.
3. L2: 619-20. Bret Harte, short story writer and humorist of the Gold Rush era, was a friend of King.
4. Rich.: 141.
5. Rich.: 142.
6. Quoted, *Adams*: 100.
7. L2: 414, Paris, 18 Nov. 1903.
8. Albert Schinz, "Naturalism in Literature," in Boas: 13.
9. Quoted, Jonathan Mayne, tr. & ed., *The Mirror of Art, Critical Studies by Charles Baudelaire*, Garden City, N. Y., 1956: 205.
10. Guy de Maupassant, "Preface to *Pierre et Jean*," in Boas: 84.
11. Clark: 154.
12. Clark: xix.
13. Clark: 132.
14. Quoted, Clark: 142.
15. Quoted, Clark: 131.
16. "Ariadne Florentina," quoted, Clark: 154.
17. Soby, "Preface."
18. Charles Sawyer, "Naturalism in America," in Boas: 117-18.
19. Brooks: 161.
20. L2: 392, 10 Aug. 1902, to Brooks Adams.

Chapter 2
1. L1: 160, 21 May 1869.

2. Cater: xxii.
3. Cater: 772, Nov. 1915.
4. L2: 490, WDC, 17 Feb. 1908.
5. Stev.: 364-65.
6. L1: 2, 3 Nov. 1858.
7. L1: 5, id.
8. *Educ.*: 81.
9. L1: 17, Berlin, 9 Feb. 1859.
10. Cater: 4-5, id., 28 Jan. 1859. Franz Kugler founded and organized the Berlin museums. His *Handbuch der Geschichte der Malerei* was first publ. in 2 vol., 1837; an English tr. appeared as *Manual of the History of Painting from the Time of Constantine the Great to the Present Day*. A tr. ed. Edmund Head of part on German, Flemish and Dutch schools was first publ. in 1846; Adams must have used this part.
11. L1: 44, 46, Nuernberg, 3, 4 July 1859.
12. *Educ.*: 81.
13. LN: 24; also L2: 608, 615, 617; see further Cater: xcviii-ix. Adams hired 2 specialists to search archives of the Bibliothèque Nationale and the Arsenal, Paris, and left a ms. with notes on 12th and 13th cent. music.
14. LJH1: 213.
15. L2: 335-37, Nuernberg, 3 Aug. 1901.
16. L2: 499-500, Paris, 16 June 1908.

17. This interest in Hegel's philosophy, rampant on the Harvard campus when Adams was a student there, is shown in a letter from Henry James to Eliot Cabot (James: 287).
18. See Sam. 1: 22.
19. *Educ.*: 62.
20. Publ. in Cat.
21. *Educ.*: 75.
22. *Educ.*: 81.
23. Kallen 1: 523.
24. As teacher of history at Harvard, Adams "stressed the legal aspect of the Middle Ages, the early German, Norman and Anglo-Saxon institutions, along with domestic life and architecture" (Brooks: 265). His course, beginning with primitive man, continued through the Salic Franks to the Norman English. "At once he put his classes on Hallam's 'Middle Ages' and Duruy's 'Histoire du Moyen Age' " (HAH). A complete survey of Adams' offerings at Harvard is given by Samuels (Sam. 1: 339-41); he conducted classes on German, French, and English Middle Ages, and during his last 3 years at Harvard, advanced ones on the history of America, 1789-1840.
25. Samuel E. Morison, *The Development of Harvard University since the Inauguration of President Eliot —1869-1928*, Cambridge, Mass., 1930: 154-57.
26. *Educ.*: 306.
27. L1: 203-4, Harvard Col., 27 Mar. 1871.
28. L2: 332, wdc, 4 May 1901.
29. Sam. 1: 239.
30. LMA: 55-56.
31. *Educ.*: 406.
32. Lodge.
33. *Educ.*: 449.
34. *Educ.*: 406.
35. *Educ.*: 451.
36. Win.
37. L2: 535, wdc, 17 Feb. 1910.
38. "A Letter to American Teachers of History" (*Degr.*: 148) contains a passing reference to Hegel, and a longer one to Schopenhauer's identification of will in man with energy in nature in his *Die Welt als Wille und Vorstellung.*
39. *Educ.*: 489.
40. Adams had asked his brother Brooks to send him a book on the "Economical Theory of History in the works of Marx, Engels and the socialist authorities" (Cater: 484, Paris, 21 Oct. 1899); he commented, "Of course I've read Marx, at least Capital, but I've not read Engels." Brooks sent Bernstein's just publ. book with a ch. entitled "Der Marxismus und die Hegelsche Dialektik."
41. L2: 248.
42. The librarian of the Boston Athenaeum, which was given part of Henry Adams' library, wrote (letter, 31 Oct. 1945), "An examination of whole books by or about Hegel—not including books with chapters only—has yielded no gifts by Henry Adams."
43. *Educ.*: 226.
44. *Educ.*: 232.
45. *Educ.*: 225.

Chapter 3
1. AA: 106.
2. *Cater*: liv and n. 121.
3. *Cater*: lxiii-iv.
4. Cambridge, Mass., 1966: 45.
5. *Educ.*: 215.
6. *Educ.*: 214.
7. L1: 352, wdc, 10 June 1883.
8. *Educ.*: 214.
9. *Educ.*: 213.
10. L1: 203, Harvard Col., 27 Mar. 1871.
11. *A History of American Letters*, Boston, 1936: 320.
12. *Educ.*: 387.

13. Ruskin, however, was not unaware of the "Norman." His lines about the tower of the cathedral at Coutances (*Lectures on Architecture and Painting, Delivered at Edinburgh in Nov. 1853*, NY, 1868: 42) are inspired by admiration, but a bias for Italian Gothic is quite marked in all his writings.
14. L2: 468, WDC, 23 April 1906.
15. L1: 2, Berlin, 3 Nov. 1858.
16. L1: 40, Dresden, 15-17 May 1859.
17. L1: 55, id., 23 Nov. 1859.
18. Win.: 46-47.
19. *Educ.*: 213.
20. *Educ.*: 220.
21. According to F. Lugt (*Les Marques de Collections*, Amsterdam, 1921: 35), Westcombe, friend of Horace Walpole and patron of Handel, died 1752; his coll. was auctioned in London, 22 Dec. 1857. Lugt indicates his drawings seem to have been generally of fine quality.
22. Oscar Fischel (*Raphael Zeichnungen*, Berlin, 1924, pt. 5, no. 241) reproduces drawing in the British Museum but makes no reference to the one formerly in Adams' possession; investigations in Boston as to its present whereabouts led to no results.
23. L1: 141, Lon., 30 Mar. 1868.
24. L1: 125, id., 26 Mar. 1867.
25. *Vente* XI: 247, no. 1348.
26. *Educ.*: 215.
27. L1: 247, Lon. 1873.
28 LMA (to her father Dr. Hooper).
29. LMA: 20-23, Antwerp, 7 Aug. 1872.
30. The description fits a drawing formerly in Walter Gay coll., Paris, illus. K. T. Parker (*The Drawings of Antoine Watteau*, Lon., 1931, no. 80).
31. LMA: 111-12, Oxford, 1 June 1873.
32. LMA: 21, Lon., 7 Aug. 1872.

33. Edward W. Hooper, treasurer of Harvard, was not only "one of the first Americans to appreciate and collect Blake," but also "a lover of good books and fine bindings and had a penchant for Chinese objets d'art" (Cater: lxii).
34. LMA: 112, Oxford, 1 June 1873. The Adams Blake is now in Boston; it was in the Butts coll. sold at Sotheby's, 29 Apr. 1862, then Palgrave and Adams; Mrs. Robert Homans gave it to the Museum of Fine Arts in 1927. Lit.: Gilchrist, *Life of William Blake*, Lon., 1863, 2: 202, no. 13; 1880, 2: 208, no. 15; A. G. B. Russell, *Cat. of Loan Exhib. of Works by W. Blake*, Lon., Nat Gall. of Brit. Art, 1913, no. 17; *Cat.*, Burlington F. A. Club Blake Centenary Exhib., 1927, no. 11.
35. LMA: 161, Picadilly, 27 July 1879.
36. LMA: 111, Oxford, 1 June 1873.
37. LMA: 156, Lon., 13 July 1879.
38. LMA: 321, WDC, 15 Jan. 1882.
39. LMA: 231, Wormley's, 9 Nov. 1880.
40. LMA: 237, WDC, 24 Nov. 1880.
41. LMA: 243, id., 12 Dec. 1880.
42. LMA: 321, id., 15 Jan. 1882.
43. Cater: xlvii.
44. Information was most generously given by Miss Agnes Mongan of the Fogg Art Museum.
45. The Adamses visited a great many coll. of the landed aristocracy in England. Mrs. Adams noted paintings by Reynolds in coll. of Sir Richard Wallace in Hertford House, Sir Watkin Wynn at Wynnstay, and Sir Robert Cunliffe at Acton Park, Wrexham, where she also saw a portrait by Gainsborough; Van Dycks were noted in coll. of Sir Philip Sidney at Penshurst (LMA: 120, 138-39, 145).
46. L2: 288, Paris, 31 May 1900; 314, WDC, 8 Feb. 1901.

47. Cater: 362, wDC, 18 Feb. 1896.
48. Cater: 485, Paris, 18 Nov. 1899.
49. Cater: 584 and n. 2, id., 13 June 1906.
50. Cater: 578, 9 Feb. 1906.
51. L2: 521, Paris, 1 Aug. 1909.
52. L2: 479 and n. 3, id., 23 May 1907.
53. LMA: 149, 29 June 1879; 161, Lon., 27 July 1879: "I think my Zoffany will fill your little soul."
54. LMA: 341, 31 Jan. 1882.
55. LMA: 348, 12 Feb. 1882.
56. LMA: 348, 14 Feb. 1882.
57. LMA: 351, 19 Feb. 1882.
58. LMA: 368, 26 Mar. 1882.
59. LMA: 245-46, 19 Dec. 1880.
60. LMA: 193, Madrid, 26 Oct. 1879.
61. LMA: 340, wDC, 31 Jan. 1882.
62. LMA: 111, Oxford, 1 June 1873.
63. LMA: 203, Granada, 9 Nov. 1879.
64. LMA: 399, wDC, 19 Nov. 1882.
65. LJH3: 280.
66. Cater: xciii.
67. Cater: xciv.
68. Cater: 750, wDC, 1 Dec. 1912, to Brooks Adams.
69. L1: 143, Florence, 5 Mar. 1868.
70. L2: 520, Paris, 5 July 1909.
71. L2: 165, Athens, 10 Apr. 1898.
72. L2: 177, Belgrade, 5 May 1898.
73. L2: 348-49, St. Petersburg, 1 Sept. 1901, and n. 2, which refers to its listing in *Murray's Handbook for Travellers in Russia*, 4th ed.: 120.
74. L1: 242, Rome, 28 Mar. 1873.
75. LMA: 111, Oxford, 1 June 1873.
76. L2: 152, Cairo, 6 Mar. 1898.
77. LJH2: 132.
78. LJH3: 26.
79. LJH2: 199, 9 Oct. 1890.
80. Miss Steinbach of the Frick Art Reference Library, NY, suggests the picture might be identical with a "Madonna in Adoration," attributed to "School of Botticelli" by Richard Offner. John La Farge and August F. Jacacci (*Noteworthy Paintings in American Private Collections*, 1907: 3) cite the Hay "Botticelli," but connect it incorrectly with a similar one listed in Crowe and Cavalcaselle (*History of Painting in North Italy*, Lon., 1864, 2: 425). The Frick Art Reference Library records that its size is 38 x 22 in. and that it was once in the Baron Zezza coll., Florence. It was purchased by Hay in Florence in 1890 through Larkin G. Meade; present location unknown.
81. *Esth.*
82. *Esth.*: 21.
83. *Esth.*: 51.
84. *Esth.*: 63.
85. Collecting of East Asiatic art, especially Japanese, had been started by the Adamses prior to the writing of *Esth.* Mrs. Adams wrote (LMA: 99, Paris, 21 Apr.), "We buy a pretty thing now and then; some Japan bronzes the other day (14th century or even earlier)." Again from Paris, six years later (LMA: 183, 28 Sept. 1879): "Tell Bill Bigelow we went to 'Bing' and were much interested in Japanese things. I succumbed to a small piece of Japanese silver, a matchbox, which I wear as a pendant from my chatelaine. Tiffany's are good, but this is better."
86. See *Cat. of the Art and Literary Property Collected by the Late Clarence King*, NY, American Art Assoc., 1903. King was a member of the Society for the Advancement of Truth in Art, nicknamed the American Pre-Raphaelites, and a contributor to their magazine, *The New Path*, 1863-65. He was a host to the American landscapist Albert Bierstadt in the Sierra Nevadas. Early influenced by the writings of Ruskin, he came to know Ruskin in England and ac-

quired watercolors by Turner from
Ruskin's private coll. He also came
in personal contact with Israels,
Mesdag, Doré, and Fortuny, and
owned works by them as well as
by Millet and Gérôme. (See David
H. Dickason, "Clarence King, Scientist and Art Amateur," *Art in
America* 32 (1944): 41 ff.) La
Farge's coll. too contained chiefly
Oriental art, largely acquired on
his trip to Japan with Adams. It
was auctioned in NY by the American Art Assoc. in 1908 (*Cat. of
Rare Oriental Art Objects, Japanese Paintings, Prints and Screens,
Textiles and Curios Collected by
John La Farge*). Henry Adams
wrote about this auction to Ann
Cabot Mills Lodge, wDC, 13 Feb.
1908 (Cater: 613): "La Farge is
today throwing all his Jap and
Chinese stuff into the street—a
vente La Farge. What a moral for
me! Why go to China! Why buy
things! Why nothing!"
87. *Educ.* 60.
88. Brooks: 358.
89. *Educ.*: 309; see also 224. Adams'
article on Lyell was a critical review of a new ed. of *Principles of
Geology* (1866); Adams recommended Lyell's *Antiquity of Man*
(1863) to his brother Charles
Francis, then in the Union Army
(L1: 95).
90. *Educ.*: 225. Adams studied Paleontology in England in 1867, as
he wrote to Charles M. Gaskell
(L1: 127), "I have got me Owen's
Palaeontology."
91. L2: 458, Paris, 19 Aug. 1905, to
Charles M. Gaskell.
92. L2: 574, 23 Sept. 1911, 15 Oct.
1911, n. 1, to Elizabeth Cameron;
600, South Lincoln, Mass., 27 July
1912, to Cecil Spring-Rice.
93. Cater: 718, Paris, 9 Aug. 1911.

94. Cater: 728, 19 Feb. 1912.
95. Cater: 739, 29 July 1912.
96. L2: 574, wDC, 8 Oct. 1911.

Chapter 4
1. L2: 134-35, Paris, 25 Oct. 1897,
to Charles M. Gaskell.
2. *Educ.*: 89.
3. *Educ.*: 91.
4. *Educ.*: 90.
5. L1: 119.
6. *Educ.*: 90.
7. L2: 227, Girgenti, 23 Apr. 1899,
to Elizabeth Cameron.
8. LN: 97-98, wDC, 25 Mar. 1897.
9. LN: 100-1, Lon., 2 May 1897.
10. Cater: 403-4, Lon., 21 Apr. 1897.
11. Nicky Mariano, *Forty Years with
Berenson*, NY, 1966.
12. L2: 87, Paris, 25 Sept. 1895, to
Elizabeth Cameron.
13. L2: 81, id., 12, Sept. 1895, to id.
14. L2: 84, Tours, 18 Sept. 1895, to id.
15. L2: 345, 348, St. Petersburg, 1
Sept. 1901, to id.
16. L2: 351, Trondhjem, Nor., 10
Sept. 1901, to id.
17. L2: 113, Paris, 3 Aug. 1896, to
id.
18. L2: 78, id., 29 Aug. 1895, to id.
19. L2: 346, St. Petersburg, 1 Sept.
1901, to id.
20. L2: 349, id.
21. L1: 315, Madrid, 24 Oct. 1879, to
Charles M. Gaskell.
22. L1: 317, Gibraltar, 21 Nov. 1879,
to id.
23. *Educ.*: 355.
24. L2: 58, 12 Dec. 1894, to Elizabeth
Cameron.
25. L2: 64, Cuautla, Mex., 8 Jan.
1895, to Sir Robert Cunliffe.
26. Cater: 312, 4 Mar. 1894.
27. These photos and those of Philae
are in archives, Massachusetts Historical Society, Boston (illus.,
LMA: 64, 104). Mrs. Adams too
was very much interested in pho-

tography but thought her husband's achievements superior to hers; she said (LMA: 452), he "is really owing to Richardson" in this art.

28. L1: 240, Cairo, 4 Mar. 1873, to Charles M. Gaskell.
29. LN: 102, 20 Feb. 1898.
30. *Educ.*: 360.
31. L2: 153, Cairo, 6 Mar. 1898, to Elizabeth Cameron.
32. L2: 170, 23 Apr. 1898.
33. L2: 164, Athens, 10 Apr. 1898, to Elizabeth Cameron.
34. L2: 170, id., 23 Apr. 1898, to Charles M. Gaskell.
35. Cater: 479, Paris, 10 Sept. 1899, to Brooks Adams.
36. L2: 170-71, Athens, 23 Apr. 1898, to Charles M. Gaskell.
37. L2: 169, id., 20 Apr. 1898, to Elizabeth Cameron.
38. L2: 229, Girgenti, 23 Apr. 1899, to id.
39. L2: 228, id.
40. L2: 166-67, Athens, 20 Apr. 1898, to id.
41. L2: 171, Athens, 23 Apr. 1898, to Charles M. Gaskell.
42. Cater: 506-7.
43. L2: 108-9, Venice, 15 July 1896, to Elizabeth Cameron.
44. L2: 172, Constantinople, 29 Apr. 1898, to id.
45. L2: 340, Moscow, 21 Aug. 1901, to id.
46. L2: 228, Girgenti, 23 Apr. 1899, to id.
47. Brooks: 358; see also Katherine B. Hathaway, *The Little Locksmith*, NY, 1942: 19-21.
48. Brooks: 359.
49. Cater: 66, Beverly Farms, 24 May 1875.
50. Cater: 773, 26 Dec. 1915.
51. L1: 365, San Francisco, 11 June 1886, to John Hay.
52. L1: 372, Nikko, 24 July 1886, to id.

53. Adams: 165.
54. "Reminiscences" in JLF: 163-64.
55. L1: 368, Yokohama, 9 July 1886, to John Hay.
56. L1: 372, Nikko, 27 July 1886, to id.
57. L1: 366-67, Yokohama, 9 July 1886, to id.
58. L1: 374, Nikko, 13 Aug. 1886, to Elizabeth Cameron.
59. L1: 374-75, id., 22 Aug. 1886, to John Hay.
60. Cater: 170, 31 Aug. 1886.
61. Cater: 171-72, Kioto, 16 Sept. 1886.
62. L1: 379, id., 9 Sept. 1886, to John Hay.
63. Cater: 174.
64. L1: 369, Yokohama, 9 July 1886.
65. L1: 380, Kioto, 9 Sept. 1886, to John Hay.
66. L1: 372, Nikko, 24 July 1886, to id.
67. L1: 378, Kioto, 9 Sept. 1886, to id.
68. L1: 371-72, Nikko, 24 July 1886, to id.
69. LN: 9.
70. *Educ.*: 316.
71. Gauguin sailed for Tahiti in Apr. 1891, and arrived there 8 June; Adams and La Farge left Tahiti 5 June.
72. L1: 430, Samoa, 21 Oct. 1890, to Ann Cabot Mills Lodge.
73. LN: 10.
74. L1: 422, Apia, 9 Oct. 1890, to Elizabeth Cameron.
75 L1: 424-25, 16 Oct.; 448, 5 Dec. 1890, both to id.
76. L1: 492.
77. LN: 33, Samoa, 19 Jan. 1891.
78. Cater: 195-96, 20 Aug. 1890.
79. LN: 32, Honolulu, 10 Sept. 1890.
80. L1: 407, id., 2 Sept. 1890.
81. LN: 33, Samoa, 19 Jan. 1891.
82. L1: 414, 24 Sept. 1890, to Elizabeth Cameron.
83. LN: 49-50, Tahiti, 6 Apr. 1891.
84. L1: 477, Tautira, 29 Mar. 1891.

85. Cater: 245, 6 May 1891.
86. L2: 40, 1 Mar. 1894, to Elizabeth Cameron.
87. Cater: 296, wdc, 6 Dec. 1893.
88. Cater: 324-25.
89. L1: 518, 26 Aug. 1891, to Elizabeth Cameron.
90. L1: 523-24, 8 Sept. 1891, to id.
91. L1: 525-26, 8 Sept. 1891, to id.
92. LN: 61-62, Red Sea, 30 Sept. 1891.
93. L1: 520, 1 Sept. 1891, to Elizabeth Cameron.

Chapter 5
1. L2: 79, Paris, 1 Sept. 1895.
2. Cater: 346-48, id., 7 Sept. 1895.
3. L2: 78, id., 29 Aug. 1895.
4. LN: 79-82, id., 1 Sept. 1895.
5. *Educ.*: 354-55.
6. *Educ.*: 74.
7. *Educ.*: 83.
8. *Educ.*: 87.
9. *Educ.*: 81.
10. L1: 32, Dresden, 22 Apr. 1859, to Charles F. Adams.
11. L1: 46, Nuernberg, 3 July 1859, to id.
12. L1: 46, id., 4 July 1859, to id.
13. L2: 335, id., 3 Aug. 1901, to Elizabeth Cameron.
14. LMA: 26, Geneva, 23 Aug. 1872.
15. LMA: 34, Nuernberg, 5 Sept. 1872.
16. LMA: 27, Geneva, 23 Aug. 1872.
17. L2: 334, 26 July 1901.
18. *Educ.*: 207.
19. LMA: 17-18, Wenlock, 26 July 1872; cf. photo. fac. 18.
20. L2: 482-83, Paris, 19 Sept. 1907.
21. L2: 581, wdc, 16 Feb. 1912.
22. Sam. 1: 209.
23. Creek.
24. *Educ.*: 369.
25. L2: 240, Paris, 18 Sept. 1899, to Elizabeth Cameron.
26. L2: 246, id., 23 Oct. 1899, to id.
27. L2: 243, Paris, 9 Oct. 1899, to Charles M. Gaskell.
28. L2: 260, wdc, 1 Feb. 1900.
29. L2: 291, Paris, 28 June 1900, to John Hay: "I read only St. Thomas Aquinas."
30. L2: 295, id., 27 July 1900, to Charles M. Gaskell.
31. L2: 396, wdc, 8 Feb. 1903.
32. L2: 403, n. 1.
33. L2: 422, n. 1.
34. L2: 423, wdc, 7 Feb. 1904: "Baltimore was burned, with my Chartres manuscript and money to print it."
35. L2: 426, id., 24 Feb. 1904, to Elizabeth Cameron.
36. L2: 441, Paris, 29 Aug. 1904, to John Hay.
37. L2: 498, id., 2 June 1908, to Elizabeth Cameron.
38. L2: 444, wdc, 20 Dec. 1904.
39. L2: 450, Paris, 13 May 1905, to Elizabeth Cameron.
40. L2: 458-59, id., 19 Aug. 1905.
41. L2: 478, id., 15 May 1907.
42. L2: 542, id., 19 May 1910.
43. L2: 564, wdc, 7 Mar. 1911, to Charles M. Gaskell.
44. L2: 544, Paris, 5 July 1910.
45. L2: 561, wdc, 7 Feb. 1911, to Elizabeth Cameron.
46. L2: 563, id., 27 Feb. 1911.
47. L2: 577.
48. L2: 580, wdc, 2 Feb. 1912.
49. L2: 619, id., 24 Nov. 1913, "Chartres is now my complaint. Cram has brought out his new edition with a flaming preface."
50. L2: 621, wdc, 19 Feb. 1914, to Charles M. Gaskell: "By the way, the Society of Architects has stolen my volume about Mont-Saint-Michel."
51. L2: 623, id., 13 Mar. 1914, to id.: "Don't say I let 'em publish Chartres. I kicked so as to be a credit to my years. But what could I do? One can't made a fool of oneself to that point. Let the architects do that."

52. L2: 621, id., 19 Feb. 1914, to id.
53. L2: 624, id., 15 Mar. 1914, to Elizabeth Cameron.
54. Brooks: 488; L2: 608, wDC, 25 Nov. 1912, to id.
55. Helen Gardner, *Art Through the Ages*, NY, 1936: 133.
56. LN: 75, wDC, 6 Oct. 1894.
57. *Esth.*: 104.
58. L2: 546, Paris, 6 Aug. 1910.
59. *Char.*: 4.
60. L2: 491, wDC, 21 Feb. 1908.
61. Hans Sedlmayr, *Die Entstehung der Kathedrale*, Zurich, 1950: 531.
62. *Char.*: 1.
63. *Char.*: 2.
64. L2: 591, wDC, 8 Apr. 1912.
65. *Char.*: 60.
66. *Char.*: 106.
67. *Char.*: 130.
68. *Char.*: 153.
69. *Char.*: 78.
70. Hume: 73, 188.
71. *Char.*: 3.
72. LN: 125.
73. *Char.*: 4-5.
74. *Char.*: 6-7.
75. *Char.*: 7.
76. Lev.: 288.
77. L2: 240, Paris, 18 Sept. 1899.
78. *Char.*: 8.
79. *Char.*: 9.
80. L2: 80.
81. *Char.*: 51.
82. *Char.*: 8.
83. *Char.*: 10.
84. *Char.*: 9.
85. *Char.*: 10.
86. *Char.*: 12.
87. *Char.*: 21.
88. *Char.*: 32.
89. *Char.*: 33.
90. Win.: 47.
91. *Char.*: 33.
92. *Char.*: 34.
93. *Char.*: 317-18.
94. *Char.*: 36.
95. *Char.*: 44.
96. *Char.*: 45.
97. *Char.*: 48.
98. *Char.*: 46.
99. *Char.*: 51.
100. *Char.*: 50.
101. *Char.*: 47.
102. *Char.*: 48.
103. *Char.*: 54.
104. *Char.*: 55.
105. *Char.*: 69.
106. *Char.*: 73.
107. *Char.*: 74.
108. *Char.*: 75.
109. *Char.*: 81.
110. *Char.*: 77.
111. *Char.*: 82-83.
112. *Char.*: 87.
113. *Char.*: 98.
114. *Char.*: 88.
115. *Char.*: 88.
116. *Char.*: 90.
117. *Char.*: 93.
118. *Die Romantische Schule*, Hamburg, 1833.
119. *Char.*: 97.
120. *Char.*: 98.
121. *Char.*: 107.
122. *Char.*: 113.
123. *Char.*: 127.
124. *Char.*: 122.
125. *Char.*: 128.
126. *Char.*: 141.

Chapter 6

1. Cater: 464.
2. Cater: 476, to Mabel H. La Farge.
3. LN: 18.
4. LN: 90-91, wDC, 12 Jan. 1897.
5. LN: 94-96, id., 28 Jan. 1897.
6. *Char.*: 138.
7. *Educ.*: 331.
8. L2: 116, Homburg, 24 Aug. 1896, to Charles M. Gaskell.
9. L2: 533, wDC, 30 Jan. 1910, to Brooks Adams.
10. *Esth.*: 60.
11. LMA: 385, wDC, 14 May 1882.

12. LMA: 440, id., 15 Apr. 1883.
13. *Hist.* 1: 77.
14. *Hist.* 2: 1016-17.
15. *Hist.* 1: 65.
16. LMA: 384-85, wdc, 14 May 1882.
17. *Educ.*: 10-11.
18. L1: 161, wdc, 20 June 1869, to Charles M. Gaskell.
19. L1: 163.
20. L1: 209, Harvard Col., 22 May 1871, to Charles M. Gaskell.
21. Hom. 12-14.
22. *Hist.* 1: 11.
23. *Hist.* 1: 57.
24. *Educ.*: 213.
25. L1: 132-33.
26. *Esth.*: 50.
27. LMA: 181, Paris, 21 Sept. 1879.
28. *Educ.*: 93.
29. L1: 117-18, Rome, 23 Apr. 1865, to Charles M. Gaskell.
30. LMA: 94-95, Paris, 20 Apr. 1873.
31. LMA: 95, id.
32. LMA: 112.
33. LMA: 96, Paris, 20 Apr. 1873.
34. L1: 242, Rome, 28 Mar. 1873, to Charles M. Gaskell.
35. LMA: 107, Lon., 14 May 1873.
36. LMA: 208, Ceuta, 19 Nov. 1879.
37. L2: 414, Paris, 18 Nov. 1903.
38. Cater: 404-5.
39. Cater: 632, wdc, 19 Dec. 1908, to Mabel Hooper.
40. L2: 398, n. 3, id., 8 Mar. 1903, to Elizabeth Cameron.
41. L2: 398-99, id., 15 Feb. 1903, to id.
42. LMA: 438, id., 15 Apr. 1883.
43. L2: 567, Paris, 12 May 1911, to Royal Cortissoz.
44. *Educ.*: 371, 386.
45. LMA: 22-23, Antwerp, 7 Aug. 1872.
46. LMA: 141, Lon., 15 June 1879.
47. LMA: 159, id., 27 July 1879.
48. LMA: 416, wdc, 14 Jan. 1883.
49. L2: 521, Paris, 1 Aug. 1909, to Elizabeth Cameron.

50. L2: 349, St. Petersburg, 1 Sept. 1901, to id.
51. L2: 351, Trondhjem, 10 Sept. 1901, to id.
52. LMA: 141, Lon., 15 June 1879.
53. LMA: 22, Antwerp, 7 Aug. 1872.
54 LMA: 116, Oxford, 1 June 1873.
55. LMA: 139, 8 June 1879.
56. *Educ.*: 220.
57. *Educ.*: 214.
58. L2: 234, Paris, 14 Aug. 1899, to Elizabeth Cameron.
59. Cater: 259, id., 21 Dec. 1891.
60. Cater: 706, id., 29 Dec. 1910.
61. *Educ.*: 391.
62. Cater: 491-92.
63. L2: 568, Paris, 13 June 1911, to Charles M. Gaskell.
64. L2: 497, id., 14 May 1908, to Elizabeth Cameron.
65. Blanche portrayed Henry James (L2: 469); Helleu did a pastel of Elizabeth Cameron's daughter Martha (L2: 230).
66. Cater: 652, Paris, 12 Apr. 1909; see n. 1.
67. Cater: 657-58, id., 28 June 1909.
68. L2: 78, id., 29 Aug. 1895.
69. L2: 87-88, id., 27 Aug. 1895, to Elizabeth Cameron.
70. L2: 230, id., 31 May 1899.
71. L2: 232, id., June 1899.
72. L2: 409, id., 15 Sept. 1903.
73. *Vincent van Gogh*, Lon., 1912: 74.
74. LMA: 177, Paris, 14 Sept. 1879.
75. LMA: 188, id., 12 Oct. 1879.
76. LMA: 183, id., 28 Sept. 1879.
77. LMA: 182-83, id.
78. LMA: 186, id., 5 Oct. 1879.
79. JLF: 244-45.

Chapter 7

1. J. T. Soby called La Farge "a professional of beauty with an amateur's eclecticism of taste" (Soby). Even the more conservative F. J. Mather saw in La Farge an "eclectic" and in his art "discursive

eclecticism" (EIA: 244). La Farge became a member of the National Academy of Design in 1869 and was active in "building up an American School of Art, constantly figuring in the world of exhibitions and general organization, training assistants and transmitting his knowledge through lectures and writings" (JLF: 127). Augustus Saint-Gaudens was a founder of the Society of American Artists, which seceded from the N.A.D. in 1877.

2. L2: 559, WDC, 26 Jan. 1911, to Royal Cortissoz.

3. The house stood at 1603 H. Street, facing south on Lafayette Square, directly across from the White House. After World War I it was torn down and the Hay-Adams Hotel was erected on the site: a tablet has been installed there by the WDC Chapter, D.A.R., to commemorate Hay and Adams. The interior woodwork of the hall of the Hay part of the house is still in existence, put in storage by Hay's daughter Mrs. James W. Wadsworth (HHR: 271).

4. La Farge did two stained glass panels for Hay's dining room, "Peacock and Peonies" and "Peonies in the Wind," which came into the possession of Hay's son-in-law J. W. Wadsworth (see L2: 26 and n.). Adams wrote to Hay from WDC (Cater: 294, 18 Oct. 1893): "I have looked into your house to see your windows, which are exquisite. Perhaps after all, I will accept your offer, and move into your house, just to live with the windows. Better than windows anywhere."

5. Cater: lxxvi.

6. *Hay* 2: 63.

7. HHR, JLF, *Rem.*

Chapter 8

1. *Educ.*: 55.

2. *Educ.*: 64.

3. *Educ.*: 213-14.

4. Richardson failed the entrance exams in 1859, but passed them in 1860.

5. L1: 110, to Henry Lee Higginson

6. HHR: 42.

7. Almost twenty years later Adams called him "Hal Richardson" (L1: 335, WDC, 30 Apr. 1882, to J. Hay).

8. L1: 471, Papeete, 23 Feb. 1891, to Elizabeth Cameron.

9. L1: 490, Hitiaa, Tahiti, 4 June 1891, to id.

10. L1: 481, Papara, 8 Apr. 1891, to id.

11. LMA: 310, WDC, 11 Dec. 1881.

12. LMA: 377, WDC, 30 Apr. 1882.

13. LMA: 379, WDC, 7 May 1882.

14. RSS1: 380.

15. RSS1: 328.

16. HHR: 22.

17. HHR: 87.

18. HHR: 184, n.4.

19. The only German work Hitchcock mentioned as probably in his possession by 1870 was Huebsch's *Altchristliche Kirchen*, French tr. of 1866 (HHR:101). What Richardson might have known through photos of German Romanesque buildings is unknown.

20. HHR: 101 and n.

21. HHR: 43.

22. JLF: 153.

23. The other French architects for whom Richardson worked were Jules-Louis André, his Beaux-Arts professor, and Jacob I. Hittorf, architect of the Gare du Nord, Paris.

24. HHR: 45.

25. JLF: 152.

26. Waern.

27. *Educ.*: 369.

28. Cater: lxiii.

29. Sam. 1: 217.
30. HHR: 142, Homer Saint-Gaudens said the work at Trinity preceded the King Monument and quoted a letter from his aunt Mrs. Oliver Emerson that Saint-Gaudens painted in Trinity Church not only "Angels" but also the seated figure of St. James and had some part in that of St. Paul (*Rem.* 1: 164-65).
31. Adams "shared in the discussions of church-arrangement and decoration" (Brooks: 356).
32. L1: 365, San Francisco, 11 June 1888, to John Hay.
33. Waern: 33-36.
34. JLF: 155-56.
35. See HHR, plate 38; the perspective for Trinity Church, Buffalo, 1872 (plate 39), is still more dependent on Brattle Street Church.
36. JLF: 153-54.
37. HHR: 139.
38. Waern: 33-36; JLF: 156-58.
39. *Esth.*: xvii-viii.
40. *Esth.*: 1, 4.
41. *Esth.*: 73.
42. *Esth.*: 75.
43. Waern: 29; cf. study, illus.: 31.
44. *Esth.*: 74.
45. *Esth.*: 3.
46. HHR: 142.
47. *Esth.*: 93.
48. HHR: 249.
49. HHR: 245-47.
50. HHR: 245.
51. HHR: 187.
52. HHR: 268.
53. ALJ: 100, 105.
54. HHR: 270-72.
55. Sam. 2: 219.
56. HHR: 270; plates 121-23.
57. HHR: 268.
58. Mabel La Farge said, "The Uncle and Aunt had built the new house in Washington together, but he was alone to move into it" (LN: 8-9); see also Sim. Among the factors contributing to Mrs. Adams' suicide was "the new house" which "with all its attendent anxieties caused" her "great concern" (Cater: li).
59. *Educ.*: 318.
60. *Hay* 2: 67.
61. L1: 361.
62. LMA: 442.
63. Cater: 143, 146-47.
64. L1: 363.
65. Cater: 152.
66. Cater: 152, Beverly Farms, 28 Aug. 1885.
67. Cater: 153.
68. L1: 363-64.
69. Cater: 154.
70. Cater: 155.
71. Cater: 156.
72. L1: 364.
73. Cater: 159.
74. HHR, plate 123.
75. Brooks: 354.
76. Cater: cxv, n. 138.
77. AA.
78. *Persons and Places*, NY, 1944: 234.
79. Cater: lxiii-iv; see also HHR, plates 121-22.
80. Hom.: 43.
81. L2: 240, Paris, 18 Sept. 1899, to Elizabeth Cameron.
82. HHR: 298.
83. Cater: 385, Paris, 8 Sept. 1896, to Mabel La Farge.
84. HHR: 299.
85. Cater: 291-92, wDC, 18 Oct. 1893.
86. *Educ.*: 340.
87. *Educ.*: 340-41.

Chapter 9

1. Focillon acknowledged that by stating, "He is a writer by instinct and breeding, a great art critic" (Foc).
2. *Educ.*: 367-70.
3. Compare snapshot of Henry Adams, 1890-91 (L2: frontis-

piece) with photo of John La Farge, 1902 (JLF: 206).

4. *The American Artist and his Times*, NY, 1941: 153.

5. *Esth.*: 22-23; see also JLF, frontispiece.

6. Foc.: 311.

7. JLF: 50.

8. JLF: 70.

9. JLF: 67.

10. JLF: 68.

11. JLF: 69.

12. JLF: 72.

13. JLF: 81-82.

14 JLF: 85.

15. HLA: 9-12.

16. Illus., Foc.: 312.

17. Focillon also pointed to the connection between the art of Chassériau and La Farge as a "fugitive apparition of those resemblances which unify the members of a spiritual family" (Foc.: 316).

18. JLF: 91.

19. JLF: 93.

20. JLF: 96.

21. HLA: 8.

22. HLA: 20.

23. HLA: 7.

24. HLA: 28.

25. HLA: 29.

26. HLA: 29-30.

27. HLA: 69.

28. HLA: 70.

29. HLA: 78.

30. HLA: 88.

31. HLA: 90-91.

32. HLA: 89.

33. HLA: 91.

34. HLA: 128.

35. HLA: 137-39.

36. HLA: 178.

37. HLA: 43-44.

38. Waern: 13.

39. ALJ: 143.

40. JLF: 89.

41. JLF: 97.

42. Waern: 28.

43. JLF: 186-87.

44. JLF: 259.

45. JLF: 98.

46. Waern: 12-13.

47. JLF: 109.

48. JLF: 137.

49. JLF: 138.

50. Plate fac. JLF: 56.

51. JLF: 243.

52. James J. Jarves has been cited as another early American collector of Japanese prints: "He was the donor of one of Ruskin's Hokusais; and what La Farge, Millet and Whistler owe to Japanese painting, they owe because of Jarves" (Kallen 1: 522).

53. Soby: 30.

54. JLF: 122-23.

55. JLF: 104.

56. ALJ: 129.

57. GM: viii.

58. JLF: 110.

59. JLF: 111.

60. Hunt: 49.

61. Brooks: 161-63.

62. JLF: 111-12.

63. JLF: 88.

64. Illus., Waern: 25; other studies belonging to the same group were sometime in coll. of Mrs. John L. Gardner, Boston, and Sir William van Horne, Montreal.

65. JLF: 114.

66. JLF: 129-31.

67. JLF: 118.

68. James: 106-7.

69. James: 69.

70. James: 84-85.

71. James: 88.

72. James: 90.

73. James: 91.

74. James: 98-99.

75. Cater: lxiii.

76. L1: 365, 11 June 1886.

77. L1: 382, wdc, 12 Dec. 1880.

78. L1: 368-69, Yokohama, 9 July 1886.
79. L1: 381, Kioto, 9, 15 Sept. 1886.
80. ALJ: 25.
81. ALJ: 126.
82. ALJ: 127.
83. ALJ: 241.
84. ALJ: 87.
85. L1: 404, NY, 16 Aug. 1890.
86. Watercolors illus., RSS: 48, 52, 338, 354, 452, 460.
87. L1: 434, Iva in Savai, 26 Oct. 1890, to Elizabeth Cameron.
88. L1: 473-74, Pateete, 23 Feb. 1891, to id.
89. "Fiji Festival" by La Farge appeared in *Century Magazine* 67 (1902): 518, before the book was publ.
90. L2: 139, Paris, 31 Dec. 1897, to Elizabeth Cameron.
91. RSS: 479.
92. RSS: 94.
93. Cater: 401.
94. According to F. J. Mather, "Henry James called the Church of the Ascension one of the most appealing of personal monuments" (EIA: 264).
95. EIA: 246.
96. JLF: 163-66.
97. ALJ: 170.
98. JLF: 166.
99. JLF: 164.
100. JLF: 173.
101. EIA: 249.
102. Cater: 555, 30 Nov. 1904.
103. Cater: 576-77, wdc, 10 Dec. 1905.
104. JLF: 176.
105. JLF: 181. Confucius also appears in the Baltimore Court House murals.
106. L2: 332-33, wdc, 4 May 1901.
107. *Educ.*: 371-72.
108. Foc.: 313.
109. JLF: 87-88.
110. JLF: 193-94.
111. JLF: 184.
112. JLF: 37-38. Wilhelm von Bode, director of the Berlin museum, planned an exhibit of La Farge's glass.
113. Publ. by the Century Club in honor of Clarence King; quoted, JLF: 198.
114. *Educ.*: 369.
115. Cater: lxi.
116. L2: 327.
117. L2: 555.
118. COP: lectures given in 1893 at the Metropolitan Museum.
119. *Educ.*: 317.
120. Quoted by Homer Saint-Gaudens, *The American Artist and his Times*, NY, 1941: 154.
121. EIA: 256.
122. See Kallen's sympathetic criticism of Jarves' writings (521-23). Jarves was equally important as art collector and art critic; he brought Charles Eliot Norton and Ruskin together.
123. EIA2: 60.
124. COP: 6.
125. COP: 17.
126. COP: 41.
127. COP. 129, n. 1.
128. COP: 212.
129. COP: 213.
130. COP: 240.
131. COP: 24.
132. COP: 40-41.
133. COP: 24.
134. COP: 74.
135. COP: 75.
136. COP: 87.
137. COP: 38.
138. COP: 36.
139. COP: 126.
140. COP: 168.
141. COP: 249.
142. *Educ.*: 369.
143. L2: 558-60, wdc, 26 Jan. 1911.

144. L2: 567-68, Paris, 12 May 1911.
145. L2: 571-72, *id.*, 20 Sept. 1911.

Chapter 10
1. *Educ.*: 328.
2. L2: 233, n., Paris, 13 July 1899, to Elizabeth Cameron.
3. Cater: 469, id., 18 July 1899.
4. *Educ.*: 385-86.
5. L2: 138, n., Paris, 10 Dec. 1897, to Elizabeth Cameron.
6. Cater: 423, id., 3 Dec. 1897.
7. L2: 327, 22 Apr. 1901, to Elizabeth Cameron.
8. L2: 433, wdc, 27 Apr. 1904 to Charles M. Gaskell.
9. *Educ.*: 387.
10. *Rem.* 1: 39.
11. *Rem.* 1: 63.
12. *Rem.* 1: 77.
13. *Rem.* 1: 116, illus.
14. *Rem.* 1: 140-41, 26 Aug. 1873.
15. *Rem.* 1: 142-43, 5 July 1876.
16. *Rem.* 1: 161-62.
17. *Rem.* 1: 191, 13 Aug. 1877.
18. *Rem.* 1: 197; illus. fac. 196.
19. *Rem.* 1: 162.
20. *Rem.* 1: 215.
21. *Rem.* 1: 354-55.
22. *Rem.* 1: 126, Edinburgh, 7 Jan. 1899.
23. Quoted, *Rem.* 2: 187-88.
24. *Rem.* 1: 344.
25. LMA: 438.
26. *Rem.* 1: 327.
27. *Educ.*: 388.
28. L2: 245, Paris, 23 Oct. 1899, to Elizabeth Cameron.
29. *Educ.*: 387.
30. *Educ.*: 391.
31. L2: 230, Paris, 31 May 1899, to John Hay; 232, id., June 1899, to Gaskell.
32. Quoted, *Rem.* 2: 296. Henry's brother William James delivered the address at unveiling of the Shaw Monument (*Rem.* 2: 79).
33. LMA: 456.

34. *Adams*: 165.
35. Cater: cxviii, n. 212.
36. LMA: 455.
37. LMA: 455-56.
38. Cater: 247.
39. L1: 509.
40. *Rem.* 1: 354.
41. *Rem.* 1: 356.
42. Bud.
43. *Rem.* 1: 356.
44. *Rem.* 1: 362.
45. *Rem.* 1: 356-57.
46. *Rem.* 1: fac. 359.
47. *Rem.* 1: 359-61. Dates of letters not given; the first must have been written in early 1890. In this year Saint-Gaudens visited Adams in WDC to discuss the monument. A separate head of the figure exists in Cornish, N. H. (see *Cat. of a Memorial Exhib. of the Works of Augustus Saint-Gaudens*, Pittsburgh, Carnegie Institute, 1909, no. 52); a cast of the whole figure, made with Henry Adams' permission, is in the Metropolitan Museum, NY (see ibid., no. 53).
48. *Rem.* 1: 365.
49. *Rem.* 1: 365 (not in L).
50. LJH: 222.
51. *Rem.* 1: 360-61.
52. L2: 6, wdc, 26 Feb. 1892.
53. *Adams*: 209.
54. *Rem.* 1: 361.
55. LMA: 457.
56. L2: 6, wdc, 5 June 1892, to Elizabeth Cameron.
57. *Educ.*: 329.
58. L2: 406-7.
59. L2: 513, wdc, 16 Dec. 1908.
60. *Rem.* 1: 363-64 (not in L).
61. *Esth.*: 79.
62. LN: 9, 14.
63. Cater: 609-10, wdc, 24 Jan. 1908.
64. Cater: 712-13, id., 24 May 1911.
65. Cater: 779. Letter to Eileen Tone, Henry Adams' secretary the last 5 years of his life, from Mabel La

Farge, 1603 H Street, wdc, 29 Mar. 1918.

66. Written 1893: publ. in *Atlantic Monthly* (Nov. 1917): 607 f., and in Stephen Gwynn, *The Letters and Friendships of Sir Cecil Arthur Spring-Rice*, Boston, 1929, 1: 450.
67. *Rem.* 1: 362-63.
68. *Rem.* 1: 362.
69. AS-G: 33-34.
70. *Rem.* 1: 362.
71. L2: 245, Paris, 23 Oct. 1899, to Elizabeth Cameron.
72. L2: 382-83, 1 Apr. 1902.
73. L2: 386, 20 Apr. 1902.
74. LJH3: 278.
75. *Rem.* 2: 337, 30 Aug. 1904.
76. *Educ.*: 465.
77. Illus., *Rem.* 1: 156.
78. *Rem.* 2: 334.
79. *Rem.* 2: 338, Paris, 3 Sept. 1904.
80. *Rem.* 2: 339, Aspet, 15 Sept. 1904.
81. Cater: 554, wdc, 21 Nov. 1904.
82. L2: 441, Paris, 8 Sept. 1904.
83. *Rem.* 2: 340, 12 Apr. 1905.
84. *Rem.* 2: 343-44, 6 Apr. 1905.
85. *Rem.* 2: 344, 24 Apr. 1906.
86. *Rem.* 2: 72-74.
87. Illus., *Rem.* 2: 45.
88. *Rem.* 2: 44.
89. L2: 367, 18 Jan. 1902.
90. *Rem.* 2: 272, 15 Aug. 1903.
91. *Rem.* 2: 53-54.
92. *Rem.* 2: 305, 21 May 1894.
93. *Rem.* 2: 314-17.
94. *Rem.* 2: 318, probably 1906.
95. *Rem.* 2: 323-24.
96. *Rem.* 2: 25-26.
97. *Rem.* 2: 16.
98. *Rem.* 2: 50-51.
99. *Rem.* 2: 18.
100. *Rem.* 2: 25.
101. *Rem.* 1: 278, 21 Feb. 1881.
102. *Rem.* 2: 23.
103. *Educ.*: 387.
104. *Rem.* 2: 66.

105. *Rem.* 2: 53.
106. *Rem.* 2: 180.
107. Freely adapted from *The Gentle Art of Making Enemies* 1: 288-83.
108. *Rem.* 1: 282-83.
109. *Rem.* 2: 39, 17 Dec. 1905.
110. *Rem.* 2: 29, to Charles Keck.
111. *Rem.* 2: 18, 10 July 1905.
112. *Rem.* 2: 49.
113. *Rem.* 2: 51.
114. *Rem.* 2: 50.
115. *Rem.* 2: 183.
116. *Rem.* 2: 194, 12 Apr. 1899.
117. *Rem.* 2: 50.
118. *Rem.* 2: 204-5.

Chapter 11

1. S. Giedion, *Space, Time, and Architecture*, Cambridge, Mass., 1941: 205-6. The Hall of Machines was built 10 years before Adams' visit for the 1889 World's Fair.
2. E-O: My tr. given.
3. E-O: 549.
4. E-O: 659.
5. E-O: 520.
6. E-O: 267.
7. Win. 5, 57.
8. E-O: 537.
9. E-O: 268.
10. L1: 377.
11. *Esth.*: xix.
12. *Educ.*: 389.
13. Spiller: 11 ff.
14. Cater: 642-43, wdc, 8 Mar. 1909, to George Cabot Lodge.
15. Cater: 645-46, id., 12 Mar. 1909, to Barret Wendell.
16. *Educ.*: 383.
17. *Degr.*: 212.
18. *Degr.*: 241.
19. Both terms are used in his discussion of "unity" (*Educ.*: 398, 400).
20. Win.: 62.
21. *A New England Group and Others*, NY, 1921; 139-40.

22. LN: 26-27.
23. *Educ.*: 380.
24. *Educ.*: 383.
25. Win.: 62.
26. *Educ.*: 429.
27. Creek: 87.
28. L2: 627, Paris, 13 Aug. 1914, to Charles M. Gaskell after outbreak of World War I.
29. *Educ.*: 400 f.
30. YC: 11-13.
31. Nich.: 169.
32. *Educ.*: 453.
33. Hume: 209.
34. *Educ.*: 431.

35. *Educ.*: 377.
36. Nich.: 165.
37. Nich.: 177.
38. Kallen 2: 841-42.
39. *Educ.*: 498.
40. *Educ.*: 497-98.
41. *Educ.*: 457.
42. *Educ.*: 497-98.
43. *Educ.*: 498.
44. Compare analysis in Lotus.
45. "Prayer to the Dynamo," 2nd pt. of "Prayer to the Virgin of Chartres" in LN: 128-34; quoted here in part only.

Bibliography of Ernst Scheyer*

In German

Dissertations

"Volkseinkommen und Individualeinkommen im Werdegang der theoretischen Nationalökonomie." Dissertation (Doctor rerum politicarum), Univ. of Freiburg 1922 (distributed in typescript).

Chinoiserien in den Seidengeweben des 17. und 18. Jahrhunderts. Dissertation (Ph.D.), Univ. of Cologne 1926. Oldenburg, G. Stalling, 1928.

Books

Zwei Hundert Jahre Breslauer Stadt-Theater. Breslau, W. G. Korn, 1930.

Eine alte Gemäldesammlung im Hause W. G. Korn, Breslau und ihre Geschichte. Breslau, W. G. Korn, 1930.

Die Kölner Bortenweberei des Mittelalters. Augsburg, Benno Filser, 1932.

Die Kunstakademie Breslau und Oskar Moll. Würzburg, Holzner, 1961.

Schlesische Malerei der Biedermeierzeit. Frankfurt, Weidlich, 1965.

Breslau, So wie es war. Düsseldorf, Droste, 1969.

Contributions to Books and Yearbooks

"Gespenster und Grotesken im Japanischen Holzschnitt," *Jahrbuch der Asiatischen Kunst* 2. Leipzig 1925.

"Paul Dobers," *Künstler Schlesiens* 3. Breslau 1929.

"August Kopisch," *Schlesische Lebensbilder* 4. Breslau 1931.

"Aus Carl Fohrs künstlerischer Hinterlassenschaft," *Neue Heidelberger Jahrbücher.* 1932.

"Eine Pariser Alabastergruppe um 1400," *Jahrbuch des Schlesischen Museums für Kunstgewerbe und Altertümer* 10. Breslau 1933.

"Die Textilien," *Die Kunstdenkmäler der Stadt Breslau*, 3 v. Breslau, W. G. Korn, 1930-34.

---

* Items in this bibliography are not included in the index.

"Breslau als Theaterstadt," *Breslau, Hauptstadt Schlesiens,* ed. Herbert Hupka. München, Gräfe und Unzer, 1955.

"Eichendorff und die Bildende Kunst," *Aurora, Eichendorff Almanach* 16. Neumarkt 1956.

"Christoph Nathe," *Aurora, Eichendorff Almanach* 18. Würzburg 1958.

"Biedermeier in der Literatur und Kunstgeschichte," *Aurora, Eichendorff Almanach* 20. Würzburg 1960.

"Geistiges Leben in der Emigration," *Jahrbuch der Schlesischen Friedrich Wilhelms Universität zu Breslau* 5. Würzburg 1960.

"Franz Theodor Kugler. Der musische Geheimrat," *Aurora, Eichendorff Almanach* 22. Würzburg 1962.

"Das Problem de modernen amerikanischen Kunst," *Die Insel, Hamburger Künstlerclub Almanach* 1960.

"Joseph Raabe als Porträtist," *Bewahren und Gestalten* (Festschrift für Günther Grundmann). Hamburg 1962.

"Der Beitrag des Judentums zur modernen Kunst," *Ernte der Synagoga.* Frankfurt, Ner-Tamid, 1962.

"Gerhart Hauptmann und die bildende Kunst," *Die Insel, Hamburger Künstlerclub Almanach* (1961/62) 1962.

"Bildung in Breslau," *Leben in Schlesien,* ed. Herbert Hupka. München, Graefe und Unzer, 1962.

"Der Symbolgehalt in der Ornamentik der prähistorischen Kunst Nordamerikas," *Symbolon, Jahrbuch für Symbolforschung* 3. Basel 1962.

"Julius Hübner (1806-1882) vom Biedermeier zur Akademie," *Aurora, Eichendorff Almanach* 23. Regensburg 1963.

"Carl Friedrich Lessing und die deutsche Landschaft," *Aurora, Eichendorff Almanach* 25. Regensburg 1965.

"Leutze und Lessing. Amerika und Düsseldorf." *Aurora, Eichendorff Almanach* 26. Regensburg, 1966.

"Julius Hübner und das schlesische Biedermeier-Portrait," *Der Frühe Realismus in Deutschland 1800–1850,* ed. Konrad Kaiser. Nürnberg 1967.

"Zu Briefen von und an August Kopisch. Aus seiner Kunstakademie Zeit 1814-1824," *Aurora, Eichendorff Almanach* 27. Regensburg 1967.

"Otto Mueller 1874-1930," *Grosse Deutsche aus Schlesien,* ed. Herbert Hupka. München, Gräfe und Unzer, 1969.

Museum Guidebook

Führer und Katalog zur Sammlung alter Musikinstrumente, with Peter Epstein. Breslau, Schlesisches Museum für Kunstgewerbe und Altertümer, 1932.

Catalogs

Hans Wildermann—Ein Werkverzeichnis, with Carl Niessen. Regensburg, Gustav Bosse, 1933.

"Die holländischen Zeichnungen der weiland Sammlung F. Koenigs, Haarlem." Amsterdam 1935 (distributed in typescript).

"Sammlung Georg Tillmann, Amsterdam, Hausmaler Fayencen, Wiener und Meissner Porzellan," 4 v. Amsterdam 1935 (distributed in typescript).

Articles in Periodicals and Newspapers

"Die Neuordnung des Kölner Kunstgewerbe Museums," *Belvedere* 10. Wien 1926.

"Zur Ausstellung asiatischer Kunst in Köln," *Belvedere* 11. Wien 1927.

"Geschichte des Kölner Kunstlebens," *Der Sammler* 17. Berlin 1927.

"Textilklasse Margarethe Seel an den Kölner Werkschulen," *Stickereien und Spitzen* 28. Darmstadt 1928.

"Die Kölner Museen," *Frankfurter Zeitung*, 12 May 1929.

"Neue Werke von George Minne," *Der Cicerone* 21. Leipzig 1929.

"Breslauer Handwerkskultur," *Jahresbericht der Schlesischen Gesellschaft für Vaterländische Kultur* 102. Breslau 1929.

"Armand G. Zausig," *Schlesische Monatschefte* 6. 1929.

"Lebende Museen," *Der Sammler* 19. Berlin 1929.

"Schlesisches Biedermeier," "Um das Neisser Haus," *Schlesische Monatschefte* 7. 1930.

"Aus der Geschichte der Warmbrunner Architektur," *Der Wanderer im Riesengebirge* 50. 1930.

"Die Kirchliche Stickerei des Mittelalters," *Die Christliche Kunst* 26. München 1930.

"Eine alte Breslauer Gemäldesammlung im Festsaal des Hauses Wilhelm Gottlieb Korn," *Schlesische Zeitung*, 20 Sept. 1930.

"Von alten Breslauer Sammlungen und Kunstausstellungen," *Schlesische Zeitung*, 26 Nov. 1930.

"Karneval im alten Breslau," "Ein Breslauer Innungshaus," "Adolf Dressler und seine Schule," "Anfänge der Photographie in Schlesien," *Schlesische Monatshefte* 8. 1931.

"Sprungbrett Breslau?" *Frankfurter Zeitung*, 21 Feb. 1931.

"Carl Hermann, Ein Oberschlesischer Nazarener," "Schlesiens Land—Schlesiens Städte," "Gustaf Adolph Boenischs kunstgeschichtliche Bedeutung," *Der Oberschlesier* 13. 1931.

"Das Schlesische Gesicht zur Biedermeier Zeit," *Die Bergstadt* 19. 1931.

"Maler Hermann's Schlösser—Reise in das Riesengebirge," *Wanderer im Riesengebirge* 51. 1931.

"Fahrend Volk (Nach Materialien aus dem Breslauer Stadtarchiv)," *Schlesische Zeitung*, 15 Feb. 1931.

"Leonhard Posch, Der Meister des preussischen Eisenkunstgusses," *Schlesische Zeitung*, 9 July 1931.

"Das Breslauer Stadtbild des vorigen Jahrhunderts in der Kunst," *Schlesische Zeitung*, 25 July 1931.

"Professor Erwin Hintze" (with Karl Masner), *Schlesische Zeitung*, 2 Aug. 1931.

"Gerhart Hauptmann der Plastiker," *Neue Rundschau* 53. Berlin 1932.

"Das Breslauer Festspiel 1913 von Gerhart Hauptmann," *Die Literatur* 25. Nov. 1932.

"Gerhart Hauptmann und Schlesien," *Der Oberschlesier* 14. 1932.

"Gerhart Hauptmann als Bildhauer," "Gerhart Hauptmann und die bildende Kunst," *Schlesische Monatshefte* 9. 1932.

"A. E. Schaeffer, Ein Freund J. v. Eichendorffs," *Eichendorff Almanach* 2. 1932.

"Aus Schinkels Reisebemerkungen einer Reise durch Schlesien 1832," *Der Oberschlesier* 14. 1932.

"Schinkel in Schlesien," "Ein Narrenfest im alten Breslau," *Schlesische Monatshefte* 9. 1932.

"Breslauer Hausmusik vor 150 Jahren (Aus den Papieren der Breslauer Musikalischen Gesellschaft "Schwägerei," 1781-1842)," *Schlesische Zeitung*, 6 Apr. 1932.

"Der Maler Ignaz Strobel," *Ostdeutsche Monatshefte* 13. Danzig 1933.

"Der holländische Malerei in der Gegenwart," "Max Liebermanns künstlerische Entwicklung," "Julius Meier-Graefe zum Gedächtnis," *Die Sammlung* 2. Amsterdam, Querido, 1935.

"Joseph Raabe, Der Maler Goethes," *Germanic Review* 23, New York 1947.

"Amerikanische Malerei," *Der Ruf* 2. München, 1 July 1947.

"Kunsterziehung in Amerika," *Schule und Gegenwart* 2. München, Dec. 1950.

"Johann Christian Claussen Dahl als Landschaftszeichner," *Die Kunst* 50. München, Apr. 1952.

"Musik, Ein Materialbild von Rolf Nesch," *Die Kunst* 50. München, May 1952.

"Zur Breslauer Gerhart Hauptmann Ausstellung, 1932," *Schlesien* 1. Würzburg 1956.

"Was kann Eichendorff dem Deutsch-Amerikanertum sein?" *Schlesien* 2. Würzburg 1957.

"Professor Franz Landsberger, 75 Jahre," *Schlesien* 3. Würzburg 1958.

"Das schlesische Bürgerporträt, 1800-1850," *Schlesien* 4. Würzburg 1959.

"Paul Dobers zum Gedächtnis," *Schlesien* 5. Würzburg 1960.

"Schlesische Kultur in amerikanischer Sicht," "Gerhart Hauptmann und die bildende Kunst," *Schlesien* 7. Würzburg 1962.

"Ludwig Meidner. Zu seinem 80. Geburtstag," *Schlesien* 9. Regensburg 1964.

"Eugen Spiro. Ein Brief zum neunzigsten Geburtstag," *Schlesien* 10. Regensburg 1965.

"Fürstenstein und Salzbrunn—Menschen und Bauten. Zu August von Kloeber's Skizzen aus dem Jahre 1837," *Schlesien* 11. Regensburg 1966.

"Ein lang vermisstes Portrait Eichendorffs wieder aufgetaucht," *Der Schlesier*, 12 Oct. 1967.

"Breslauer Sammler und Sammlungen. Von der Renaissance zur Neuzeit," *Schlesien* 14. Regensburg 1969.

Book Reviews

William Cohn, *Buddha in der bildenden Kunst des Ostens* (*Jahrbuch der Asiatischen Kunst* 2. 1925).

Karl With, *Bildwerke Ost- und Südasiens aus der Sammlung Yi Yüan* (*Jahrbuch der Asiatischen Kunst* 2. 1925).

Gustav Hartlaub, *Meisterwerke des japanischen Farbenholzschnitts* (*Artibus Asiae* 2. 1927).

Adolf Hackmack, *Der chinesische Teppich* (*Artibus Asiae* 2. 1927).

Yone Noguchi, *Korin* (*Artibus Asiae* 2. 1927).

L. Paffendorf, *Südbelgische Kriegerfriedhöfe* (*Kölner Tageblatt*, 7 Nov. 1927).

Emil Waldmann, *Die Kunst des Realismus und des Impressionismus im 19. Jahrhundert* (*Kölner Tageblatt*, 21 Dec. 1927).

Coriolan Petranu, *Die Kunstdenkmäler der siebenbürger Rumänen* (*Artibus Asiae* 3. 1928).

Joseph Strzygowski, *Der Norden in der bildenden Kunst Westeuropas* (*Artibus Asiae* 3. 1928).

Adolf Feulner, *Kunstgeschichte des Möbels* (*Kölner Tageblatt*, 14 Feb. 1928).

Adolf Beenken, *Bildhauer des 14. Jahrhunderts* (*Kölner Tageblatt*, 16 Apr. 1928).

Oscar und Cäcilie Graf, *Japanisches Gespensterbuch* (*Der Cicerone* 20. 1928).

Yone Noguchi, *Hiroshige; Hokusai; Utamaro* (*Artibus Asiae* 3. 1929).

Herbert Kühn, *Kunst und Kultur der Vorzeit Europas* (*Der Cicerone* 21. 1929).

Albert Renger-Patzsch and W. Burmeister, *Norddeutsche Backsteindome* (*Schlesische Monatshefte* 7. 1930).

August Grisebach, *Die alte Deutsche Stadt in ihrer Stammeseigenart* (*Schlesische Monatschefte* 7. 1930).

Günther Grundmann, *Das Riesengebirge in der Malerei der Romantik* (*Die Bergstadt* 14. 1931/32) (*Schlesische Zeitung*, 25 Feb. 1935).

Lydia Baruchsen, *Die schlesische Mariensäule* (*Zeitschrift für Bildende Kunst*. Aug. and Sept. 1931).

Erwin Hintze, *Führer durch das Schlossmuseum Breslau* (*Schlesische Monatshefte* 8. 1931).

Franz Landsberger, *Die Kunst der Goethe-Zeit* (*Schlesische Zeitung*, 16 Dec. 1931).

Günther Grundmann, *Schlesische Architekten im Dienste der Herrschaft Schaffgotsch* (*Schlesische Monatshefte* 8. 1931).

Moeller van den Bruck, *Der Preussische Stil* (*Schlesische Monatshefte* 8. 1931).

Rudolf Stein, *Das Breslauer Bürgerhaus* (*Schlesische Monatshefte* 8. 1931).

Erich Meyer, *Michael Klahr d. Ä.* (*Schlesische Monatshefte* 8. 1931).

Erich Hintze, *Süddeutsche Zinngiesser* (*Schlesische Monatshefte* 9. 1932).

Friedrich Schinkel, *Polen, Preussen und Deutschland* (*Schlesische Monatshefte* 10. 1933).

Günther Grundmann, *Das Riesengebirge in der Malerei der Romantik* (*Aurora, Eichendorf Almanach*. 1959).

Wolfgang v. Websky, *Monographie, Einführung von Herbert Frh. v. Buttlar* (*Schlesien* 12. Regensburg 1967).

Reviews of Exhibits

"Kölner Kunstausstellungen, Kunstgewerbemuseum," *Kölner Tageblatt*, 20 Aug. 1926.

"Zur Ausstellung alter Tapeten, Lichthof des Kunstgewerbemuseums in Köln," *Kölner Tageblatt*, 29 June 1926.

"Aus dem Kölner Kunstgewerbemuseum," *Kölner Tageblatt*, 15 Dec. 1926.

"Das unbekannte Italien—Graphische Arbeiten von Theo Blum. Ausstellung im Kölner Kunstgewerbemuseum," *Kölner Tageblatt*, 21 Mar. 1927.

"Photographie als Kunst, Zur Ausstellung von Photographien im Lichthof des Kölner Kunstgewerbe Museums," *Kölner Tageblatt*, 20 Apr. 1927.

"Köln durchs Objektiv, Ausstellung des Preisbilderwettbewerbs im Kunstgewerbe Museum," *Kölner Tageblatt*, 9 Sept. 1927.

"Zur Ausstellung Mittelalterlicher Kunst in Kölner Privatbesitz," *Kölner Tageblatt*, 12 Oct. 1927.

"Die Schule Reimann-Berlin, Ausstellung im Kunstgewerbemuseum Köln," *Kölner Tageblatt*, 7 Dec. 1927.

"Ausstellung von Entwürfen für kirchliche und profane Möbel von dem Kölner Jesuiten-Frater Wilhelm Hinselmann, 1724-1792," *Kölner Tageblatt*, 4 Feb. 1928.

"Die Kölner Borte Ende des 13.–Anfang des 16. Jahrhunderts, Zur Ausstellung im Lichthof des Kölner Kunstgewerbe-Museums," *Kölner Tageblatt*, 11 Mar. 1928.

"Ausstellung von Neuerwerbungen der Bibliothek des Kunstgewerbe-Museums," *Kölner Tageblatt*, 7 July 1928.

"Die Leibl Ausstellung im Wallraf-Richartz Museum, Köln," *Der Cicerone* 21. Leipzig 1929.

"Breslauer Ausstellungen," *Schlesische Zeitung*, 7 Jan. 1931.

"Chinesische Kunst im Breslauer Museum," *Schlesische Monatschefte* 8. 1931.

"China Ausstellung des Breslauer Kunstgewerbemuseums," *Schlesische Zeitung*, 28 Jan. 1931.

"China Ausstellung in Breslau," *Weltkunst* 5. 15 Feb. 1931.

"Der Schweizer Maler Otto Meyer in der Breslauer Kunstakademie," *Schlesische Zeitung*, 11 Mar. 1931.

"Graphik alter Meister im Museum der Bildenden Künste (Breslau)," *Schlesische Zeitung*, 20 Mar. 1931.

"Preussische Geschichte auf Berliner Porzellan. Ausstellung im Schlossmuseum, Breslau," *Schlesische Zeitung,* Mar. 1931.

"Schlesisches in Neuerwerbungen der Breslauer Städtischen Sammlungen," *Schlesische Zeitung,* 5 May 1931.

"Berliner Kunstfrühling–Künstler unter sich," *Schlesische Zeitung,* 10 June 1931.

"Berliner Kunstfrühling–Museums Insel," *Schlesische Zeitung,* 16 June 1931.

"Berliner Bauausstellung," *Schlesische Zeitung,* 20 June 1931.

"Neuerwerbungen des Schlesischen Museums der Bildenden Künste," *Schlesische Zeitung,* 5 Aug. 1931.

"Vom Guckkasten zum Stereoskop. Ausstellung der Sammlung v. Schweinichen-Pawelwitz im Kunstgewerbemuseum Breslau," *Schlesische Zeitung,* 10 Sept. 1931.

"KPM, altes und neues. Zur Ausstellung der Staatlichen Porzellan Manufaktur Berlin im Breslauer Schlossmuseum," *Schlesische Zeitung,* Mar. 1932.

"Schlesien auf der Karte. Zur Kupferstich Ausstellung "Altbreslau und Schlesien" bei Wertheim," *Schlesische Zeitung,* 15 Mar. 1932.

Neuerwerbungen des Museums Vereins für das Schlesische Museum der Bildenden Künste," *Schlesische Zeitung,* 11 May 1932.

"Die Rembrandt Ausstellung in Amsterdam," *Pantheon.* Sept. 1935.

"Otto Mueller," *Kunstblätter der Galerie Nierendorf* 4/5. Berlin, 1964.

In French (translated)

Review of Exhibits

"L'Exposition de Cologne. Eté 1929," *Cahiers d'Art* 4. 1929.

"Les Musées Allemandes et les Expositions de 1920-1930," *Mouseion* 15. Paris 1931.

In Dutch

Catalogs (compiled and partly prefaced)

Tentoonstelling van Moderne Kunst. Amsterdam, J. Goudstikker, Oct. 1933.

Charley Toorop, Schilderijen en Teekeningen. Wolf Demeter, Plastiek en Teekeningen. Amsterdam, J. Goudstikker, Nov. 1933.

Tentoonstelling van Moderne Kunst. Amsterdam, J. Goudstikker, Dec. 1933.

Tentoonstelling Japansche Schilderijen uit onzen tijd. Amsterdam, J. Goudstikker, Jan.–Feb. 1934.

Tentoonstelling Victor Tischler. Amsterdam, J. Goudstikker, Feb.–Mar. 1934.

Tentoonstelling Moissy Kogan/Ottokar Coubine. Amsterdam, J. Goudstikker, Mar.–Apr. 1934.

Patrick Bakker Nagelaten Werken. Amsterdam, J. Goudstikker, Apr. 1934.

Articles in Periodicals and Newspapers

"William Morris' Strijd om den Stijl," *De Telegraaf*, 24 Mar. 1934.

"Humanisme in de Hollandsche Schilderkunst van Heden." *Maandblad voor Beeldende Kunst* 12. Amsterdam 1935.

In English

Books

Lyonel Feininger: Caricature and Fantasy. Detroit, Wayne State Univ. Press, 1964.

The New German Dance and the Visual Arts. Mary Wigman—Oscar Schlemmer. New York, Dance Perspectives, 1970.

The Circle of Henry Adams: Art and Artists. Detroit, Wayne State Univ. Press, 1970.

Contributions to Books

Comments on plates in William J. Bossenbrook et al., *Foundations of Civilization; Development of Civilization*. Boston, D. C. Heath, 1939/40.

"Chinoiserie," "Japonism" in *Encyclopedia of the Arts*, ed. Dagobert D. Runes. New York, Philosophical Library, 1946.

"Rolf Nesch, Prints into Assemblage," *Prints/Multiples*. Seattle, Seattle Art Museum, 1969.

Guidebooks

Drawings and Miniatures. Detroit, Detroit Institute of Arts, 1936.

Baroque Painting. Detroit, Detroit Institute of Arts, 1937.

Catalogs

"Collection of Mr. and Mrs. Ralph Harman Booth." 1950 (distributed in typescript).

Contemporary Prints, Drawings and Watercolors from the Netherlands and Germany. Collection of Ernst and Evelyne Scheyer. Detroit, Detroit Institute of Arts, 1962.

"Albert Bloch—an American Blauer Reiter," *Albert Bloch (1882-1961). An exhibit of Watercolors, Drawings and Drypoints*. Lawrence, Univ. of Kansas Museum of Art, 1963.

"The Early Feininger," *Lyonel Feininger: The Formative Years*, ed. Robert D. Kinsman. Detroit, Detroit Institute of Arts, 1964.

"The First Alfred Kubin Show in Detroit," *Alfred Kubin*. Detroit, Detroit Graphic Arts Society, 1965.

Betty Jacob, Sculpture. Detroit, Garelick's Gallery, 1965.

"Introduction," *Bernard Schultze. A Variety of Works*. Detroit, London Arts, 1967.

"Introduction," *German Expressionist Prints, Drawings, and Watercolors: Die Brücke,* ed. Ellen Sharp. Detroit, Detroit Institute of Arts, 1966.

Catalog notes, *The Graphic Art of Rolf Nesch,* ed. Ellen Sharp. Detroit, Detroit Institute of Arts, 1969.

Articles in Periodicals

"Drawings by Correggio," *Detroit Institute of Arts Bulletin* 15. 1935.

"Some Paintings by Tiepolo," "Allessandro Magnasco," "Drawings by Cesare da Sesto," *Detroit Institute of Arts Bulletin* 16. 1936/37.

"Allessandro Magnasco," *Apollo* 18. Aug. 1938.

"Portrait of the Brothers Van Ostade," *Art Quarterly* 2. 1939.

"Drawings of the French Revolution and the Empire," *Art Quarterly* 4. 1942.

"Frédéric Bazille and the Beginnings of French Impressionism," *Art Quarterly* 5. 1942.

"East Asiatic Art and French Impressionism," *Art Quarterly* 6. 1943.

"Dali and We; We and Dali," *Wayne Panorama* 3. Feb. 1943.

"German Expressionism," *Baltimore Museum of Art News* 11. Nov. 1947.

"La Sultane Lisant—Two Drawings by François Boucher," *Art Quarterly* 11. 1948.

"Goethe and the Visual Arts," *Art Quarterly* 12. 1949.

"Expressionism in Holland," *Maandblad voor Beeldende Kunst* 26. Amsterdam 1950.

"Henry Adams as a Collector of Art," *Art Quarterly* 15. 1952.

"Henry Adams and Henry Hobson Richardson," *Journal of the Society of Architectural Historians* 12. 1953.

"Henry Adams' Mont-Saint-Michel and Chartres," *Journal of the Society of Architectural Historians* 13. 1954.

"The Adams Memorial by Augustus Saint-Gaudens." *Art Quarterly* 19. 1956.

"Art in Michigan," *Papers of the Michigan Academy of Science, Arts and Letters* 43. 1958 (1957 Meeting).

"Modern Art as Expression of the Space Age," *Inside Wayne* 19, 23 Apr. 1958.

"Art History and Liberal Education, *Wayne State Univ. Graduate Comment* 3. Oct. 1959.

"Baroque Painting in Germany and Austria," *Art Journal* 20. Fall 1960.

"A Drawing attributed to Giovanni Antonio Pellegrini," *Pantheon* 18. 1960.

"Impressions of Israel," *Wayne State Univ. Graduate Comment* 5. May 1962.

"The Aesthete Henry Adams," *Criticism* 4. Fall 1962.

"In Memorian Adèle Coulin Weibel, 1880-1963," *Art Quarterly* 26. 1963.

"The Wedding Dance by Pieter Bruegel the Elder in the Detroit Institute of Arts," *Art Quarterly* 28. 1965.

"Molzahn, Muche, and the Weimar Bauhaus," *Art Journal* 28. Spring 1969.

Book Reviews

Algemeene Kunstgeschiedenis, Deel VI, 1951 (*Artibus Asiae* 17. 1952).

"Dagobert Frey Festschrift," *Zeitschrift für Ostforschung* 2 (*Art Quarterly* 17. 1954).

Will Grohmann, Zwischen den beiden Kriegen 3 (*Art Quarterly* 17. 1954).

Werner Haftmann, *Malerei im Zwanzigsten Jahrhundert* (*Art Quarterly* 18. 1955).

Alfred Hentzen, *Rolf Nesch, Graphik, Materialbilder, Plastik* (*Criticism* 4. Summer 1962).

Folke Nordstrom, *Goya, Saturn and Melancholy* (*Art Quarterly* 26. 1963).

Wolfgang Kayser, *The Grotesque in Art and Literature* (*Art Quarterly* 26. 1963).

S. Giedion, *The Eternal Present: A Contribution on Constancy and Change* (*Criticism* 6. Spring 1964).

Franklin D. Scott, *Wertmüller—Artist and Immigrant Farmer* (*Art Quarterly* 27. 1964).

Jean Selz, *Sculpture, Origins and Evolution* (*Art Quarterly* 27. 1964).

Francis Haskell, *Patrons and Painters, a Study in the Relations between Italian Art and Society in the Age of the Baroque* (*Art Quarterly* 27. 1964).

Hans Richter, *Dada: Art and Anti Art* (*Art Quarterly* 28. 1965).

Sammlung Sprengel, Kunstverein Hannover (*Art Quarterly* 28. 1965).

Thomas Grochowiak, *Ludwig Meidner* (*Art Quarterly* 30. 1967).

UNESCO, *Catalogue of Colour Reproductions of Paintings, 1860-1965* (*Art Quarterly* 29. 1966).

Alan Gowans, *The Restless Arts, a History of Painters and Paintings 1760-1960* (*Art Quarterly* 29. 1966).

Lucas Heinrich Wüthrich, *Das Druckgraphische Werk von Matthaeus Merian* 1 (*Art Quarterly* 29. 1966).

Fritz Grossmann, *The Paintings of Bruegel* (*Art Quarterly* 30. 1967).

Alfred Werner, *Ernst Barlach* (*Art Quarterly* 31. 1968).

Translation (German into English)

Carola Giedion-Welcker, "Max Ernst: Irony—Myth—Structure," *Criticism* 6. Spring 1964.

Index of Persons and Places

In general mere mention of places of origin or addressees of correspondence and of subjects or owners of works of art are not indexed. Many listings are *passim*. Short title abbreviations (pp. 269-71) are placed in parentheses with their authors, editors, and subjects, as applicable.

Ernst Scheyer is Professor of History of Art, Wayne State University. He was educated in Germany and earned his Ph.D. degree at Cologne University (1926). In 1964 his book *Lyonel Feininger: Caricature and Fantasy* was published by Wayne State University Press. *The Circle of Henry Adams: Art and Artists* honors his seventieth birthday.

Other books by Dr. Scheyer have been published in Germany and he has written many articles and essays for scholarly European and American art history periodicals, guide books, and catalogs. A list of his writings on the visual arts is given in this book. Among other honors, he is Honorary Research Fellow, The Detroit Institute of Arts.

Charles H. Elam edited the manuscript. This book was designed by Richard Kinney. The type face used is Mergenthaler's Caledonia, designed by W. A. Dwiggins for Mergenthaler in 1937. The display type used is Bookman. This book is printed on Bradford Book, bound with Columbia Mills Riverside Linen cloth over binder's boards. Manufactured in the United States of America.